AF540660

Industrial Organisation and Management

INDUSTRIAL ORGANISATION AND MANAGEMENT

DR. SHARAD KUMAR
Reader in Commerce
Regional Institute of Education
Bhopal

Discovery Publishing House
New Delhi - 110002 (India)

First Published - 1997

Reprinted-2011

ISBN 81-7141-382-X

Published by :

Discovery Publishing House
4831/24, Ansari Road, Darya Ganj,
New Delhi - 110 002 (INDIA)
Phone : 327 9245
Fax. : 91-11-3253475

Laser Typeset by :

Debug Computer Services
Delhi.

Mehra Offset Press
Delhi

Contents

Preface

Industrialisation plays a very important role in the socio-economic development of the country. It not only brings prosperity in the society but also accelerates the various sectors of the economy. During the last decade the growth of industry has been very impressive, though not without problems and constraints. Management is a process through which managers combine the physical, capital and human resources to achieve the predetermined objectives.

The present volume depicts a vivid picture of various aspects of industrial management. Besides the above the book deals with the industrial policy reforms which were enunciated in July 1991.

The book is designed to fulfil the needs of the graduate and post graduate students of Indian universities in commerce, Economics and Management.

I am thankful to all my friends and colleagues who have enriched my knowledge through discussions and have helped me in completing this book.

Sharad Kumar

Part 1

The Industrial Structure

1

Evolution of Commerce and Industry

Commerce is concerned with the exchange of goods and services; with all that is involved in the transactions of goods at any state in their progress from raw materials to finished goods in the hands of consumers. It provides a link between the manufacturers and the consumers. It covers not only the functioning of buying, selling and handling goods but also many other ancillary services which must be provided to finance, insure, store and transport goods in the course of these exchanges.

The growth and development of commerce is closely connected with civilisation. It has expanded with the development of society. But commerce developed fast only when division of labour was introduced in man's economic life. Once it started growing, it extended its tentacles throughout the length and breadth of the world leading to its present day complex organisation. To study the growth of commerce we shall discuss the various stages through which the economic life of man has gone through.

The Hunting Stage

In the early ages of human history man lived as a hunter. He depended on the nature for his food. He used to hunt animals and use their meat as food and skin as clothes. He moved from place to place and had no settled place for residence. He made weapons from sticks and stones on his own. There was no trade and exchange. All the requirements were produced and consumed by them only. It was a stage of self sufficiency.

The Pastoral Stage

With the passing of time man began to live at fixed places and instead of killing animals they started rearing them for domestic purposes. Fishing became an important occupation. They settled by side of lakes, rivers and near other sources of water, because grass and water could be found plenty at such places. At this stage also hunting remained an important activity though it was supplemented by domestication of animals.

Agricultural Stage

When people settled on the banks of rivers, lakes and sea coasts, they began to grow corn for their domestic consumption and they produced more than they needed. They had surplus food which they exchanged for other goods. It was at this stage, commerce made its beginning. Thus the base for trade was laid down. People settled at fixed places, engaged themselves in agriculture and reared animals for domestic purposes. They built houses and started possessing property. This led to the growth of concept of private property and the concept of family.

Barter System

The exchange of goods for goods is known as barter. Under the barter system, trade increased to a certain extent, but it was localized. Exchange could take place only when two persons having some common needs could be found. Transactions were few due to this difficulty. To remove this the system of fairs started. This helped in the exchange of goods to a considerable extent. Fairs were held periodically and people assembled there to exchange goods like food stuffs, cattle, tools, handicrafts and other such goods. Hence we can say that commerce started with this crude form of trade.

Introduction of Money

The limitations and inconveniences of Barter System led to the evolution of money. It was unsuitable for the expansion of trade and it was difficult to find a common measure of value. Many commodities such as cattle, skins furs and feathers, iron and copper, etc. were used as a medium of exchange but they differed according to place. Ultimately coined money was introduced by the Greeks. Gold and silver were used for coining metallic currency which began to be used for exchange purposes. Barter System was replaced by money economy which gave an

impetus to trade and commerce. It became possible to collect and pay taxes, rents, wages, etc.

The evolution of money gave fillip to the trade and commerce. During the reign of Alexander the Great, trade developed between the East and the West. During the period of Roman Empire trade flourished between a number of countries and the goods traded were things like carpets, wine, handicrafts goods etc. Slowly money developed markets on the national level. The opening of new areas, improvements in the various sectors of the economy, innovations and development of modern techniques of production, and commercial dealings increased which have led to the modern system of exchange.

With the application of newer techniques, mass production of goods has been made possible, and with the development in the different sectors of the economy, such as transport and communications, banking and insurance, storage and ware-housing, the quantum of trade has increased manifold. The goods produced, not only cater to the needs of the domestic market, but are also exported all over the world. Some people were engaged in production of agricultural goods which are raw materials to the production process while some are engaged in the manufacture of goods. Some people are engaged in trade while others are engaged in performing marketing functions. The specialisation in various fields has helped greatly in the development of commerce.

With the technological and scientific advancement in practically all the sectors of the economy, goods are now sold in different parts of the world. The country produces only those goods in which it has some advantage over others. In the international trade a few currencies have been accepted as a medium of exchange which have opened new areas and facilitated the growth of trade and commerce on a large scale.

Evolution of Industry

With the introduction of money, trade and commerce expanded appreciably and it embraced the entire economic life of man. People met at fixed places at fixed time periodically to exchange goods. This gave rise to periodical markets and fairs. The division of labour which was confirmed to a single family, extended to the village and towns as a whole. The development can be studied under the following heads :

Help or Hire System : As the time passed, the production of goods started picking up and it was beyond the capabilities of the family to look after. Thus, the family started taking the help of other workmen. They were given raw materials which they processed into finished products at the residence of the family which provided them employment. They were paid in kind for the services they provided.

Handicraft System : This system refers to that form of industry which is based on mannual labour. This system developed due to increasing needs of the hired labour. Small families felt the need of hired labour to get their work done. Bigger families had their surplus members to work for others on hire. Thus there came into existance a new class of people called *Artisans*. These artisans produced goods for their village. They used simple tools and worked with their members of the family only. Divisions of labour between the persons engaged in agriculture and artisans engaged in producing hand tools required by the farmers became a permanent feature of the economic life of the village.

The Guild System : In the village or the town economy working population organised themselves into guilds. These Guilds were of two types - The Merchant Guild and the Craft Guild. People carrying on the business of purchasing and selling of goods comprised themselves into *merchant guilds* and those artisans who were engaged themselves in the time of occupation associated themselves into *craft guilds*. Both the types of guild associations were organised to protect the interests of the members and to help mutually. They were mainly formed in villages or towns and their membership was compulsory. The merchant guilds regulated the trade in the towns. The members were allowed to carry on transaction freely. They enforced fair trading at customary prices, fixation of prices was resorted to the interest of the customers was also protected. Every merchant guild made regulations regarding the quality of goods offered for sale, regulations of weights and measures and regulated trade with other towns. The members assisted the distressed, helped the orphans and widows and financed the disabled persons.

There were several craft guilds in a town. Their basic aim was to maintain the group interests and give equal opportunities for its members so that they could maintain their standard of living. The guild also made attempts to avoid competitions among the members. These guilds made considerable effort in the development of industry. They regulated the production and technique, quality of goods produced by an individual craftsman and fixed the selling price. These prices were required to be reasonable both to the craftsman and the buyer. They were classified into three categories : (i) Master-craftsmen, (ii) Apprentices, (iii) Journey-men.

A *master craftsman* was an artisan who had his own workshop, where he manufactured goods with the help of his family members and other fellow workers. The *apprentice* was a person who learned any one of the crafts under the supervision and guidance of master craftsman for about seven years without any payment of wages. After completing the period of apprenticeship, these apprentices became *journeymen*, and they worked for wages for the master craftsmen. After collecting some amount of capital these journeymen could start their own workshop and become master craftsmen and attain the membership of the guild association to their craft.

Domestic System : Domestic system of industrial organisation developed after the fall of the guild associations. This system is also known as putting out system. It is only under this system that a link between the producer of goods and consumers started playing an important role as an agency of commerce. With the increase in population, development of trade, expansion of markets and the increase in capital gave rise to a new class of people known as middlemen. In the initial stages the craftsman supplied the raw materials, manufactured the required goods either himself or with the help of journeymen and supplied them to persons concerned. But with the inventions of newer techniques of production, increasing costs of tools, etc. made it difficult for the poor craftsman to buy new tools. This led the craftsmen to work on contract for the new class of entrepreneurs known as middlemen. These middlemen gave their attention only to purchases and sales. They were neither craftsmen nor they spent their time in the supervision of manufacture. They bought the goods at a lower price and sold at a higher price and the difference constituted their profits. Ultimately, the artisans lost their independence and the intermediaries started playing an important role.

With the growth of middlemen in the transaction business capitalism grew slowly. Craftsmen became wage earners because the production was controlled by these middlemen. Goods were produced not for domestic consumption but for sale to earn profits.

Industrial Revolution : Industrial Revolution is a word used to describe a number of changes which took place in England between 1760 and 1850. It brought about far reaching changes in the economic life of people.

Numerous inventions took place during that period which changed the entire system of production and distribution. The use of machines involved a change in the methods of industrial organisation and brought about a change from a domestic system to the factory system of production involving large scale and complex division of labour. The discovery of steam, as an important source of power, helped to increase the production many a times. The use of machines necessitated large amount of capital which led to concentration of economic power and growth of large enterprises.

Consequences of Industrial Revolution

Economic : With the introduction of power driven machinery, mass production became possible. Large scale industries started coming up and the production on large scale reduced the cost and a number of commodities were produced by machines which were within the reach of the common man. The division of labour was introduced in industries which helped in specialisation. The rise of new industries brought a radical transformation of trade and commerce. New industrial areas and towns came into prominence. Most of the industries were located in the vicinity of coal and iron fields. Industrial Revolution gave rise to factory system which led to the decline of handicraft and domestic system of production. The members of the family went out in the morning and came late in the night. There were no rules and regulations for the welfare of the workers.

Industrial Revolution gave a boost to the expansion of trade and commerce. The developed means of transport and communication led to the expansion of markets. The revolution forced governments to change their economic policies. Many governments adopted a policy of Laissez-faire., i.e. freedom to carry any kind of business. As the result of this policy, economic power concentrated in the hands of a few people and gave rise to a class of capitalists. But side by side the standards of living of the people increased. Luxurious goods were available at cheaper rates. People started enjoying better and more comfortable life.

Social : Industrial Revolution had adverse social effects. There was a shift of population from the far-flung areas to those places where these factories were located. Labourers were exploited by their Masters. They had to work for long hours with low wages. The working conditions of the factories were very bad as there were no lighting, heating or sanitary facilities in the factories. These factors badly effected the health and efficiency of workers. The employers who were interested in maximising their profits employed female child labour at very low wages which led to infant mortality and short life for those who survived the rigours of childhood. These conditions led to unrest among the workers and gave birth to Trade Unions. Workers got united for better conditions. With the passage of time the governments of various countries framed laws protecting the interest of the workers and improving their conditions. Today we have numerous laws which grant a number of benefits to the workers.

Political : The people started migrating to the cities. Cities provided more educational opportunities. Education spread among the masses and it created political awakenings. It also gave birth to the doctrines of socialism and democracy. In many countries workers got united and also captured the political power.

Factory System : Industrial Revolution brought about tremendous changes in the method of production and distribution. The rise of the factory system is one of the important outcomes of this revolution. Domestic system was replaced by factory system of production. There was an increased use of the machinery. Development of quicker, cheaper and safer modes of transport facilitated the movement of goods and created markets all over the world. Hundreds of workers were employed by these factories and the goods were produced on a large scale to be consumed all over the world. The division of labour was introduced which led to specialisation in production and standardisation of goods was possible.

But in the 20th century there has been tremendous technological advancements. Today more of automisation is found in the factories. Numerous industries have latest devices which help them in producing standard and quality goods. Computers have changed the entire production scene in the world. The use of Atomic energy, Solar Energy and other sources of energy have further revolutionised the industrial field.

2

Entrepreneurship Development

The basic objective of developing countries especially like India, is to achieve a balanced and sustained rate of economic and industrial development. The Government is striving hard to create conditions in which the resources available can be used for productive purposes for rapid growth in various sectors of the economy. This necessitates in structural adjustments and changes in the socio-economic fabric so that economic development can go on smoothly without any hindrances. In order to achieve the above, there is a need to bring co-ordination among all the sectors of the economy and at the same time greater involvement of people is required at all levels.

While 'enterprise' is a specific feature of an entrepreneur, entrepreneur plays the main role in any economic activity. He is the most important factor in bringing about socio-economic change.

Concept of Entrepreneur

The term 'entrepreneur' has been derived from the French language. In the 16th Century, it was applied to persons engaged in military expeditions. Later in the 17th Century, its scope was extended to cover civil engineering activities such as construction and fortification.[1] It was only in the beginning of the 18th Century that the word was used to refer economic activities. Since then the term entrepreneur is used in various ways and different senses. We discuss below the various dimensions of entrepreneur.

(a) *Risk-Bearing Function*

Richard Canfillon, an Irishman living in France was the first to use the term 'entrepreneur' to refer to economic activities. He defined an entrepreneur as, "the agent who buys means of production at certain prices in order to combine them into a product that he is going to sell at prices that are uncertain at the moment at which he commits himself to his costs".[2] He illustrated by taking a case of a farmer, who pays out contractual incomes that are 'certain' to the landlords and labourers and sells at prices that are 'uncertain'. Therefore, the stress is laid on the element of risk involved.

F.H. Knight developed the theory that the entrepreneurs are a specialised group of people who bear risks and deal with uncertainty. According to him, entrepreneur is the economic functionary who undertakes such responsibility which by its very nature cannot be insured nor salaried. He also guarantees specified sums to others in return for assignments made to them. He has drawn distinction between risk and uncertainty. A risk can be reduced through the insurance principle whereas uncertainty is the risk which cannot be calculated.

(b) *Organisational Function*

J.B. Say developed the concept of entrepreneur a little further. He emphasized on the function of co-ordination, organisation and supervision. According to him, "Entrepreneur is the economic agent who unites all means of production, the labour force of the one and the capital or land of the others and who funds in the value of the products which results from their employment, the reconstitution of the entire capital that he utilizes and the value of the wages, the interest and the rent which he pays as well as profit belonging to himself".[3] Say clarified the concept by distinguishing the role of the capitalist as financier and the entrepreneur as the organiser.

David Ricardo treated the industrial manufacturer and the agricultural farmer synonymously as entrepreneurs. In his words, "the farmer and the manufacturer can no more live without profit than the labour without wages."[4]

John Stuart Mill used the word entrepreneur in the sense of an organiser who is paid for his "non-manual type of work." Marshal also stressed the significance of organisation among the sources of a special class of undertakers, undertaking risks, bringing risks, bringing together capital and labour required for the work, arranging an engineering the general plan and superintending minor details.[5]

(c) *Innovation Function*

Schumpeter has put the human agent at the centre of the process of economic development and given a very important role to the entrepreneur in his theory of economic development. According to him, "The entrepreneur in an advanced economy is an individual who introduces something new in the economy a method of production not yet tested by experience in the branch of manufacture concerned, a product with which consumers are not yet familiar, a new source of raw material or of new markets and the like."[6]

Schumpeter differentiates between an inventor and an innovator. An invention is one who discovers new methods and new materials whereas an innovation utilizes inventions and discoveries in order to make new combinations.

Schumpeter also says that the entrepreneurs are men of vision, drive and talent who spot out opportunities and promptly seize them for exploitation. By virtue of them initiative, earnestness and activity, they accomplish significant advances in national production. Entrepreneurs constitute the generating force or motive force of economic development.

(d) *Group Level Pattern Function*

According to F.W. Young[7] the entrepreneurial characteristics are found in clusters which may form themselves as entrepreneurial groups. He says that entrepreneurial activity is generated by the particular family backgrounds, experiences, as a member of certain kind of groups and as reflection of general cultural values.

(e) *Management and Leadership Skills Function*

Hoselitz[8] states that "a person who is to become an industrial entrepreneur must have additional personality traits to those resulting from a drive to a mass wealth... in addition to being motivated by the expectations of profit, he must also have some managerial abilities and more important he must have ability to lead". He is of the view that managerial skills and leadership are the important facets of entrepreneurship.

(f) *Organisation Building Function*

Harbinson[9] says that organisation building ability is the most critical skill required for the industrial development. Entrepreneurship means the skill to build an organisation. Harbinson's entrepreneur develops the new ideas of different innovators to the rest of the organisation.

(g) *High-Achievement Function*

McClelland[10] identified two features of entrepreneurship. Firstly doing things in a new and better way and secondly 'decision making under uncertainty.' McClelland introduced the concept of 'need for achievement' as a psychological motive. He emphasized the need for achievement or achievement orientation as the most directly relevant factor for explaining economic behaviour. This motive is defined as a tendency to service for success in situations involving an evaluation of one's performance in relation to some standard of excellence.

Besides many other social scientists have given their views on concept of entrepreneur. Leibenstein identified "gap-filling" as an important characteristic attributable to entrepreneurship. This "gap-filling" activity gives rise to a most important entrepreneurial function, namely "input-completing". He has to collect all the inputs to realise final products. The renowned management expert Peter F. Drucker[12] says, "Innovation is the specific tool of entrepreneurs, the means by which they exploit changes as an opportunity for a different business or a different service. It is capable of being learned, capable of being practised. Entrepreneurs need to search purposefully from the sources of innovation, the changes and their symptoms that indicate opportunities for successful innovation. And they need to know and to apply the principles of successful innovation."

Types of Entrepreneurs

In a study of American Agriculture, Clarence Danhof[13] has attempted a four-fold classification of entrepreneurs. The four categories of entrepreneurs are discussed below :

Innovating entrepreneurship is characterised by aggressive assemblage of information and the analysis of results deriving from novel combinations of factors. Men in this group who are very commonly found in developed nations are generally aggressive in experimentation and exhibit greater ingenuity in putting attractive possibilities into practice. *Imitative entrepreneur* is characterised by readiness to adopt successful innovation inaugurated by innovative entrepreneurs. They are also revolutionary in nature with the differences that they do not innovate the changes themselves, they just imitate techniques innovated by others. Such entrepreneurs are particularly important in under developed countries because they contribute significantly to the development of such economics. *Fabian entrepreneurship* is characterised by very great caution and skepticism in practicing any change. They try to bring in innovations only when failure to do so results in loss. They are by nature non-enterprising with a hard core of inertia governing their activities. The fourth category is the *Drone entrepreneurship.* There are people who refuse to respond to changes even of it means loss and low returns in relation to other producers. They typical traditional farmer in under developed countries constitutes a perfect Drone entrepreneur.

Prof. Vasant Desai[14] has given a broad classification of entrepreneurs which are discussed below :

According to the Type of Business

(a) *Business Entrepreneur :* Business Entrepreneur is individual who conceive an idea for a new product or service and then create a business to materialise their idea into reality. They tap both production and marketing resources in their search to develop a new business opportunity. They may setup a big establishment or a small business unit. They are called small business entrepreneurs when found in small business units such as printing press, textile processing house, advertising, ready-made garments or confectionery. In a majority of cases, such entrepreneurs are found in small trading and manufacturing business and entrepreneurship flourished when the size of the business is small.

(b) *Trading Entrepreneur :* Trading entrepreneur is one who undertakes trading activities and is not concerned with manufacturing work. He identifies potential markets, stimulates demand for his product line and creates a desire and interest among buyers to go in for his product. He is engaged in both domestic and overseas trade.

(c) *Industrial Entrepreneur :* Industrial Entrepreneur is essentially a manufacturer who identifies the potential needs of customers and tailors product or service to meet the marketing needs. He is product-oriented man who starts in an industrial unit because of the possibility of making some new product. He is found in any industrial unit such as the electronic industry, textile unit, machine tools, etc.

(d) *Corporate Entrepreneur :* Corporate Entrepreneur is a person who demonstrates his innovative skill in organising and managing a corporate undertaking. A Corporate undertaking is a form of business organisation which is registered under some statue or Act which gives it a separate legal entity. Corporate entrepreneur is an individual who plans, develops and manages a corporate body.

(e) *Agricultural Entrepreneur* : Agricultural Entrepreneurs are those entrepreneurs who undertake such agricultural activities as raising and marketing of crops, fertilizers and other inputs of agriculture. They are motivated to raise the productivity of agriculture through mechanisation, irrigation and application of technologies of dry land agriculture. They cover a broad spectrum of the agricultural sector and includes agriculture and allied occupations.

According to the Use of Technology

(a) *Technical Entrepreneur* : A technical entrepreneur is generally an entrepreneur of "craftsman type". He develops a new and improved quality of goods because of its craftsmanship. He demonstrates his innovative capabilities in matters of production of goods and rendering services. The greatest strength which the technical entrepreneur has is his skill in production techniques.

(b) *Non-Technical Entrepreneur* : Non-technical entrepreneurs are those who are not concerned with the technical aspects of the product which they deal. They are concerned only with developing alternative marketing and distribution strategies to promote their business.

(c) *Professional Entrepreneur* : Professional Entrepreneur is a person who is interested in establishing a business but does not have interest in managing or operating it once it is established. A professional entrepreneur sells out the running business and starts another venture with the sale proceeds. Such an entrepreneur is dynamic and he conceives new ideas to develop alternative projects.

According to Motivation

(a) *Pure Entrepreneur* : A Pure Entrepreneur is an individual who is motivated by psychological and economic rewards. He undertakes an entrepreneurial activity for his personal satisfaction in work, ego or status.

(b) *Induced Entrepreneur* : Induced entrepreneur is one who is induced to take up an entrepreneurial task due to the policy measures of the government that provides assistance, incentives, concessions and necessary overhead facilities to start a venture. Most of the entrepreneur are induced, entrepreneurs who enter business due to financial, technical and several other facilities provided to them by state agencies to promote entrepreneurship. A person with a sound project is provided package assistance to his project. In the recent past the government has taken many policy measures which have induced many people to start a small-scale industry.

(c) *Motivated Entrepreneur* : New entrepreneurs are motivated by the desire for self-fulfilment. They come into being because of the possibility of making and marketing some new product for the use of consumers. If the product is developed to a saleable stage, the entrepreneur is further motivated by reward in terms of profit.

(d) *Spontaneous Entrepreneur* : These entrepreneurs start their business out of the natural talents. They are persons with initiative, boldness and confidence on their ability which motivate them to undertake entrepreneurial activity. Such entrepreneurs have a strong conviction and confidence in their ability.

According to Growth

(a) *Growth Entrepreneur* : Growth entrepreneurs are those who necessarily take up a high growth industry. These entrepreneurs choose an industry which has substantial growth prospects.

(b) *Super-Growth Entrepreneur* : Super-growth entrepreneurs are those who have shown enormous growth of performance in their venture. The growth performance is identified by the liquidity of funds, profitability and gearing.

According to Stages of Development

(a) *First-Generation Entrepreneur* : A first-generation entrepreneur is one who starts an industrial unit by means of an innovative skill. He is essentially an innovator, combining different technologies to produce a marketable product or service.

(b) *Modern Entrepreneur* : A Modern Entrepreneur is one who undertakes those ventures which go well along with the changing demand in the market. They undertake those ventures which suit the current marketing needs.

(c) *Classical Entrepreneur* : A Classical Entrepreneur is one who is concerned with the customers and marketing needs through the development of a self-supporting venture. He is a sterotype entrepreneur whose aim is to maximise his economic returns at a level consistent with the survival of the firm with or without an element of growth.

Role of Entrepreneurship in Economic Development

It is not an easy task to define economic development. It is viewed as a process which implies the series of changes in social, technological and economic forces which are useful in accelerating the pace of development. Process also implies the optimum use of capital, modern methods of production, technical development, institutional reforms demographic and social framework which leads to an increase in the national income over a long period. This facilitates in improving and raising the living standard of the people.

Adam Smith the classical economist in his book, "*An Enquiry into the Nature and Cause of the Wealth of Nations*" published in 1776 assigned no role to the entrepreneur in economic development. He gave due importance to capital formation which was regarded as an important determinant of economic development. He laid emphasis on division of labour because it increases the productivity of labour through specialisation of tasks. His theory is based on the principle of '*Laissez-Faire*' in economic matters.

Another classical economist, Prof. David Ricardo discussed the theory of distribution. He regarded only three factors of production - land, labour and capital and the entire produce is distributed as rent, wages, interest and profit. According to him, profit leads to savings which ultimately goes to capital formation. Capital acts as the engine of growth.

Thus the attitude of classical economists was very cold towards the role of entrepreneurship in economic development.

The economic history of the presently developed countries tends to support the fact that the economy is an effect for which entrepreneurship is the cause. The people of under-developed countries have now realised that to achieve the goal of economic development there is need to enhance entrepreneurship. Both qualitatively and quantitatively, Schumpeter (1934) visualized the entrepreneur as the key figure in economic development because of his role in introducing innovations. Parson and Smelser (1956) entrepreneurship and increased output of capital as two necessary conditions for economic development. Sayigh (1962) described entrepreneurship as a necessary dynamic force.

The role of entrepreneurship on economic development varies from economy to economy depending upon its material resources, industrial climate and the responsiveness of the political system to the entrepreneurial function. According to McClelland's concept of personality aspects of entrepreneurship, people with high achievement motivation are likely to behave in an entrepreneurial way, as they would not be satisfied with their present status in the society, they would prefer entrepreneurial function.

India being an under-developed country requires decentralised industrial structure to reduce regional imbalances. Small-scale entrepreneurship in such industrial structure plays an important role to achieve balanced regional development.

References

1. Cochran, T.C., 1949 : Change and the Entreprenum, Harvard University Press. Cambridge.
2. Schumpeter J.A.1955 : 'Economic Theory and Entrepreneurial History'. Explorations on Enterprise, Huge G.T. Atkin (Ed), Harvard University Press, Cambridge.
3. Schumpeter J.A. 1954 : 'History of Economic Analysis'(Edited from manuscript by Elizabeth Boody Schumpeter), George Allen and Unurn Ltd., London, p. 555.
4. Ricardo David, 1962 : 'The Principles of Political Economy and Taxation', J.M.Dent and Sons Ltd., London, p. 73.
5. Marshall Alfred, 1946: 'Principles of Economics', Macmillan, London (Originally published in 1890)
6. Schumpeter J.A.,1961 : 'The Theory of Economic Development' (Translated by R. Opie), Oxford University Press, London, p. 66.
7. Young F.W., 1971 : 'A Micro Sociological Interpretation of Entrepreneurship' in Peter Kilby(Ed) "Entrepreneurship and Economic Development" The Free Press, New York p.147.
8. Hoselitz, B.F. : "Entrepreneuria and Economic Growth" American Journal of Economics and Sociology, Volume 12, No. I October 1952, p. 106.
9. Harbinson Frederick : "Entrepreneurial Organisation As a Factor in Economic Development'Quraterly Journal of Economics,Vol. LXX No. 3, Aug. 1956.

10. McClelland D.C. 1961 : "The Achieving Society" D.Van Nostrand Co. Inc. New York.

11. Liebenstein Harvey : "Enterpreneurship and Development" American Economic Review, Vol.LXIII No. 2, May 1968, p. 72-82.

12. Drucker P.F. 1985: Innovation and Entrepreneurship, Harper and Row. New York.

13. Wohl, R, 1952 : "Observation on Entrepreneurship in Agriculture, in Williamson and Buttrick(Ed), Economic Development Principles and Patterns, Harvard University Press, Cambridge, p.205.

14. Vasant Desai. 1991 : "Entrepreneurial Development", Vol. I. Himalaya Publishing House,Bombay, p. 81-84.

3

Forms of Industrial Organisation

A business unit may be started by an individual or by a group of perons. All such private business units consitute one sector known as the provate sector. When business units are established by Government or by other public bodies and government agencies, then they consitute the public sector. The concept of mixed economy has been extended and a combination of private and public sectors is known as joint sector.

It is crucial for the business concern to choose a proper form of organisation. From the point of view of ownership there are five main forms of organisation and each form has got its advantages which must be duly considered by the entrepreneur. Therefore, it is necessary to study in detail the characteristics, mertis and demerits of different forms of organisation.

Sole Trader or Proprietorship

Sole tradership or proprietorship is a business owned by one person. It is the oldest, simple and most popular form of business organisation. It is a form of business organisation established by an individual. He introduces his own capital, uses his own skill and intelligence in the management of its affaris with almost unlimited freedom and is entitled to receive all the profits and assume the risks of ownership.

Characteristics

(a) The business is owned by a single person; (b) The sole trader bears the entire business risk all alone; (c) He brings the entire capital; (d) He has an unlimited liability; (e) The business firm is not a separate legal entity from the sole trader; (f) If there are profits, the trader alone is entitled to them. On the other hand, if there are loses, he alone has to bear with them; (g) He is the organiser and manager of the business; (h) The sole trader may engage certain persons as employees; he may take the help of the members of his family; and (i) No legal formalities are necessary to set-up the business but there may be legal restrictions on a particular type of business but there may be legal restrictions on a particular type of business, e.g. if a man wants to start a photo studio he can do so without any legal formalities. But if he starts a restaurant or hotel, he will have to obtain licence from the proper authority.

Advantages

1. *Easy formation* : The sole trading concern can be established bery easily. No legal formatlity or other complcated procedure is required to be followed.
2. *Close contact with customers* : The sole trader develops close and personal contacts with his customers. This enables him to maintain goodwill and cater to the exact requirements of his customers.
3. *Business secrecy* : He can maintain secrecy regarding his business and thus safeguard against his competitors.
4. *Gets entire profit* : The sole trader being responsible for the management and control of his business, receives entire profit. This gives him incentive to work hard and efficiently and maintian economy.
5. *Quick decisions* : He can take decisions regarding his price policy, credit policy, discount policy, stock position, disposal of surplus funds, etc. as he has to consult no one.
6. *Smooth functioning* : There is none to oppose him, and therefore, he can function smoothly. He can control all his affairs personally.
7. *Social desirability* : From the social standpoint it ensures diffusion of business ownership and thus concentration of wealth and power in the hands of a few is avoided.

Disadvantages

1. *Limited capital* : The greatest limitation of the sole trader is

that the capital available for the business remains very limited. Thus he may not find adequate funds to expand the scale of his business.

2. *Limited management ability* : During the course of running of the business, serious problems arise and the sole trader may not be able to take suitable decisions. Also, he may not be expert in performing every function like purchasing, merchandising, advertising, accounting etc.
3. *Unlimited liability and risk* : The liability of sole trader being unlimited, he has to pay all his business obligations, firstly out of business assets and secondly if they are inadequate, out of his private property.
4. *Doubtful continuity* : There is always lack of continuity or stability in such business. Long illness, disability or death of the sole trader may cause his business to come to a standstill unless his relatives or heirs may wish to continue it.
5. *Uncertainty in purchase and sales* : He is unable to get full economies of bulk purchases and increased sales as he carries business on a small scale. Since he has no influence over the market he may become an easy victim to any slight change in the mood of the market.

From the above analysis it seems that the sole trader is misfit in the modern large scale business. But still it occupies a prominent place in the modern world. It can flourish where : (i) small capital is required; (ii) risk involved is not much; (iii) prompt decisions are of great importance; (iv) personal element plays an important role; and (v) managerial talent is required to limited extent.

The retail shops, tailoring shops, ready-made dressing concerns, book-shops, studios, etc. are mostly started by individual proprietors.

Partnership

With the limitations of the sole trader and the expansion of business, it became necessary for a group of persons to join hands together and supply necessary capital and skills. Thus partnership organisation has grown out of necessity. In this form of organisation, two or more persons, who are competent, agree to carry on lawful business and share the profits there of an agreed basis. The business may be carried on by all of them or any of them acting for all.

In India partnership organisations are governed by Indian Partnership Act, 1932. Section 4 of this Act defines partnership as, "the relation between persons who have agreed to share profits of a business carried on by all or any of them acting for all".

Persons who enter into partnership are collectively known as "firm " but individually known as " partners " and the name under which their business is carried on is called the " firms name".

Essential Features

The above definition contains the following elements :

(i) It is a relation between persons i.e. at least two persons must be there to constitute partnership.

(ii) There should be an agreement between them and they should be legally competent to enter into contract.

(iii) They should carry on some business which is not forbidden by the State.

(iv) Business to be carried on should be with profit motive.

(v) Business must be carried on by all or any of them acting for all.

All the elements stated above must be present before a group of persons constitutes a partnership. The fundamental features of partnership are discussed below :

1. *Number of Persons* : There should be at least two persons to form the partnership organisation. But the maximum number of persons in case of banking business is 10 and the case of other business is 20.
2. *Contractual Relationship* : The partnership is the relationship between two or more persons. It is a creature of a contract but not of status, e.g. a manager of a firm may get his remuneration which may be based on the profits of the firm but on that account he cannot be considered as a partner as the element of agreement is not there. Likewise a Joint Hindu Family firm is not a partnership.
3. *No Legal Distinction Between Firm and its Partners* : Since partnership is merely an association of persons, no separate legal entity is created. The partner binds the firm which his acts

done on behalf of the firm but he is also free to undertake personal business separately.

4. *Unlimited liability* : The liability of the owners of the firm is unlimited. The liability of the partner is called joint and several because any one of the partners or all the partners jointly can be called upon to pay the firm's liabilities.
5. *Principal-Agent relationship* : The partnership business is carried on by all or by any one of the partners acting for all the partners. It means, the partners not only own business, but also manage it. For the sake of convenience only some of them may be authorised to take part in the routine management of the firm, on behalf of all partners. Each partner is an agent for the other partners and for the entire firm as well as principal. A partner's business dealings are binding upon the other partners.
6. *Restriction on transfer of share* : No partner can transfer his share without the consent of remaining partners.

Forms of Partnership

Forms of partnership firms may be classified as following :

1. *Partnership at will* : Where no fixed period has been specified for the duration of partnership, it is known as "partnership at will". Such a firm is formed to carry on a lawful business for an indefinite period.
2. *Particular partnership* : A firm formed only for specified venture of temporary nature or only for certain period is called particular partnership. Such firm is dissolved immediately on the completion of a particular venture or on the expiry of such period.
3. *Limited partnership* : Such partnership firms where the liability of all the partners, with the exception of at least one partner (called a general partner) is limited are called "limited partnership firms". Such type of partnership has no legal recognition in India.

Types of Partners

There are different kinds of partners and they may be classified as under :

1. *Active or working partners* : There are some partners who not

only contribute capital to the business but also take active part in the administration of the firm are known as " active partners or working partners ".

2. *Sleeping or Dormant partners* : If a partner contributes only capital but does not participate in the management of the business is called sleeping or dormant partner. There are two other kinds of dormant partners :

   - Secret partners.
   - Silent partners.

   A partner who wants that his name should be kept secret is called " secret partner ". Such partners are, however, liable for the debts of the firm. Silent partners are those who do not have any voice in the management of the firm. But they share the profits or losses of the firm and bear the burden of its debts.

3. *Nominal Partners* : Those persons who only lend their names to the firm are known as nominal partners. They neither contribute any capital nor do take active part in the management. They are also known as ostensible partners or quasi partners. They are liable for all the debts for which their names and credit are used.

4. *Partners in profit only* : If a person is entitled to a certain share of profits without being liable for the losses, he is known as partners in profits only. Such partners are not allowed to take part in the management but will have to bear all liabilities to third parites.

5. *Partners by Estoppel and Holding out* : If a person conducts or behaves in such a way or represents to third parties through spoken or written words that he is a partner of the firm is called a " partner by estoppel ". If such a person who is considered as a partner by another and does not deny this fact that he is a partner being fully aware of the use of his name in the partnership, he is called a "partner by holding out". Such persons are liable to the third parties for the acts of the firm.

6. *Retired or Outgoing Partners* : A partner is known as retired or outgoing partner when he leaves the firm but the rest of the partners continue with the business. He is liable for all the debts of the firm which were incurred before his retirement.

7. *Incoming partners* : A person who joins an existing firm with the consent of all the other partners is known as incoming partner. He conrtibutes some capital to the firm and pays some premium to the existing partners. He is not liable for the debts of the firm incurred before his joining the firm.
8. *Minor as partner* : A minor can be admitted in the partnership firm but he cannot be a full-fledged partner. Though he cannot contract with the third parites, but he can be admitted to the benefits of partnership. His liability is limited to the extent of his share in the firm. He cannot take part in the conduct of the business of the firm. On attainment of majority he has to declare within six months whether he will continue as partner or not.

Partnership Deed or Agreement

A partnership can be formed either by oral or written agreement, but it is desirable to enter into written agreement which is called partnership deed or agreement. When such an agreement is framed it should be duly stamped according to Stamp Act. The partnership deed is not a public document.

Registration of Partnership Firm

Registration of partnership is not legally compulsory under the Partnership Act, 1932. It is optional, but the Act imposes certain disabilities on the partners of an unregistered firm hence registration is desirable in the interest of the firm and partners.

If the firm is also registered under the Income Tax Act, profits are divided among the partners then tax is charged on the incomes of the partners individually otherwise it will have to pay income tax on the whole of its income.

Effects of Non-Registration

1. The unregistred firm cannot enforce its claims against the third party in the court of law.
2. Any partner of such firm cannot enforce his claims against outsiders or against his co-partners of the firm.
3. Such firms cannot sue its partners.

Dissolution of Partnership

A partnership can be easily formed and can be dissolved easily. A distinction has to be made between "dissolution of partnership" and "dissolution of firm". Dissolution of partnership implies the end of original partnership agreement among the partners but it does not necessarily mean the end of the firm or its business. Dissolution of firm means the dissolution of partnership between all the partners of the firm. It puts an end to all the activities of the firm.

There are various circumstances which cause the dissolution of the firm.

1. *Dissolution by consent* : A firm may be dissolved at any time if the partners agree to close it or it becomes necessary in accordance with any prior agreement.
2. *Compulsory dissolution* : A firm is compulsory dissolved : (a) By the adjudication of all the partners, or of all the partners but one, is insolvent. (b) If the business carried on by them becomes unlawful.
3. *Contingent Dissolution* : Subject to any agreement between the patterns, a firm is dissolved by :
   - Death of a partner
   - Insolvency of a partner
   - Expiry of any period previously specified
   - If consitituted to carry out any venture, then on its completion.
4. *Dissolution by notice* : Where the partnership is at will, it may be dissolved by any partner giving a notice in writing to all other partners indicating his intention to dissolve the firm. Dissolution takes place from the date mentioned in the notice. In case no date is mentioned then it is dissolved from the date of the communication of the notice.
5. *Dissolution by the Court* : A suit being filed by any partner, the Court may dissolve a firm on any of the following grounds :

   (i) *On lunacy of a partner* : When a partner has become of unsound mind, either a guardian of lunatic partner or any other partner can move the court.

(ii) *Permanent incapability of a partner* : Where a partner other than the partner suing becomes permanently incapable of performing his duties as a partner.

(iii) *Misconduct of a partner* : Where a partner is guilty of misconduct which is likely to affect prejudicially the carrying of the business.

(iv) *Breach of agreement* : When a partner willfully or persistently commits breach of agreement relating to management affairs of the firm or the conduct of its business or if he conducts in such a way as it is not resonably practicable for the other partners to continue the business in partnership with him.

(v) *Transfer of interest* : When a partner has in any way transferred the whole of his interest in the firm to a third party without the knowledge of other partners.

(vi) *Recurring losses* : Where the business of the firm can not be carried on and to save at a loss.

(vii) *On any other ground* : On any other ground which renders it just and equitable.

Advantages

1. *Easy formation* : It can be formed easily without much expense and legal formalities. Only thing required is an agreement among persons desiring to form a partnership.
2. *Larger resources* : Under partnership several persons pool their capital, resources, skill, expertise, experience and services, etc. This helps to extend the activities of the firm. New partners can be admitted to secure more capital, managerial ability and organising capacity.
3. *Flexibility* : If there is a need to change the nature of the business it can be done without much difficulty. There is no legal restriction so long as the firm carries a lawful business.
4. *Division of labour* : A partnership enjoys all advantages of division of labour. Benefits of specialisation can be derived by the firm by assigning duties to different partners according to their qualifications and likings.
5. *Prompt decisions* : It is quite possible to take prompt decisions.

The decision at the same time is combined and more balanced. The decision of several partners combined together is likely to be very valuable.

6. *Division of risks* : The losses of the firm are divided and they are not to be borne by one person alone.
7. *Unlimited liability* : Since liability of each partner is unlimited, joint and several, partner are discouraged to take hasty steps in the conduct of the business. This puts a check on their reckless activities.
8. *Dissolution not difficult* : If any of the partners desire to free himself from the agreement, the business can be closed without legal hurdles.

Disadvantages

1. *Limited resources* : In spite of pooling resources by several partners the firm may not be able to raise adequate capital for expansion beyond a certain limit.
2. *Unlimited liability* : Since the liability of the partners is unlimited and they are jointly responsible for all acts and debts, they hesitate in undertaking a large enterprise and also it hampers further growth of the very business enterprise alredy undertaken by the firm.
3. *Continuity is uncertain* : There is always an uncertainity in continuing this type of organisation. Death, insolvency, insanity, incapacity of one of the partners may lead to dissolution of the firm.
4. *Lack of harmony* : It is a difficult task to maintain harmony among the partners for a long time. There is a possibility of difference of opinion in themselves. Mutual conflicts and lack of team spirit among themselves may lead to loss of reputation and dissolution of the firm.
5. *Lack of public confidence* : It may not enjoy the confidence of the public, because their accouts are secret and there is absence of publicity.

Joint Hindu Family Firm

In India we find a distinct form of business or organisation known as Joint Hindu Firm. It is operated by the Hindu Law. In India we have two schools of Hindu Law :

- Mitakshara
- Dayabhaga

Under the Mitakshara school which is applicable all over India except West Bengal and Assam, the property inherited by a Hindu from his father, grandfather and great grandfather is ancestral property. Thus son, grandson and great grandson become joint owners of ancestral property by reason of their birth in the family. They are known as coparceners in interest. The Hindu Succession Act 1956, has extended the line of coparcenary interest to female relative of the deceased partner or male relative claiming through such female relatives.

Under the Dayabhaga system which is applicable in West Bengal and Assam only, the male heirs become members only on the death of the father.

Characteristics

(i) The business of such firms managed by a senior member of the family known " Karta ", (ii) The Karta controls the income and expenditure of the family and is considered as a custodian of the joint property; (iii) He has the power to continue or close down the business, other members have no claim of participation in the management; (iv) He is liable not only to the extent of his share in the property of the family but he may also be held personally liable. Other members will be liable only to the extent of their share in the joint family property. The liability of Karta is unlimited; (v) The other members of the family cannot question the authority of the Karta and the remedy is get the family dissolved by mutual agreement; (vi) Joint Hindu Famil can enter into partnership with others. But outsiders cannot become members of the family.

Advantages

(1) Every member of the family is guaranteed a 'bare subsistence' irrespective of his work; (2) Younger members of the family can get the benefit of knowledge and experience of elder members of the family; (3) It teaches the members of the family to work not only for their own benefit but for their family without being selfish; (4) Members of the family who are sick, unemployed old and bodily infirm,

widows and orphans are looked after with due care by the other members of the family; (5) It provides an opportuinty to develop virtues of discipline, self-sacrifice and co-operation; (6) The principal of 'Division of Labour' can be secured by assigning the work to members of the family according to the specialisation; and (7) Management is centralised in the hands of the Karta who runs the business without interference of others, thus quick desicions are possible.

Disadvantages

(1) Karta alone manages the business of the firm but its benefits are shared by all the coparceners which discourages the Karta to work hard and earn more; (2) As the Karta is responsible for all the work, the coparceners become lazy and inactive; (3) Both reward and efforts are not well balanced; (4) Karta who works independently may misuse his freedom for his personal benefits; and (5) Quarrels over petty things may result in the breaking of the business.

This form of business organisation is losing ground with the gradual end of the Joint Hindu family system. It is being generally replaced either by sole tradership or partnership firm.

Joint Stock Company

The growth of joint stock company constitutes an important advancement in the modern emerging commercial structure. With the increase in business activities, the sole trading and partnership forms of organisation could not cope with the problems of financial resources and managerial skill.

The Joint Stock Company grew up as a convenient form of business organisation to solve the needs of capital and skill.

The main drawbacks of sole trading and partnership as studied earlier are limited capital, unlimited liability, absence of continuity, limited skill and capacity. In order to overcome these difficulties joint stock compnay became important and inevitable for large scale enterprises.

A company is a voluntary association of persons who contribute the capital to carry a specified business but their liability remains limited. This association should have legal recognition. According to Kimball and Kimball, " A corporation is by nature an artificial person created or authorised by the legal statue for some specific purpose". A company may be described as, " a voluntary association of many persons who contribute money or money's worth to a common stock and employ it in some trade or business and who share the profit and loss arising therefrom. The common stock so contributed is denoted in money and is the capital of the company. The persons who contribute it are members. The proportion of capital to which each member is entitled is his share". But this definition does not give the unique nature of the company as a legal body corporate. A company can also be defined which is as follow :

"A company is an incorporated association which is an artifical person created by law having common seal and perpetual succession".

Characteristics

1. *Artificial person created by law* : A company is constituted as a distinct and independent person in the eyes of law. When registered legally it attains a distinct personality of its own. It can sue and be sued. It can hold property, incur debts and enter into contracts.
2. *Continuous existence* : The continuity of the company is not affected by the death or lunacy or insolvency of its shareholders. Its life is not affected by the sale or transfer of its shares. Thus it enjoys perpetual succession.
3. *Limited Liability* : The debts incurred by the company are not the liability of the shareholder. The liability of the members is limited to the face value of the shares he has purchased.
4. *Common Seal* : The company cannot sign any document as it is an artificial person. Therefore every company has a common seal with its name engraved on it. When the seal is affixed two directors must sign it as *witness.*
5. *Transfer of shares* : The shareholders are at full liberty to dispose of all their shares or any part of their total holding to any person they like. No shareholder, however, can demand the return of his capital contribution during the existance of the company.
6. *Difference between ownership and management* : A company is managed by a Board of Directors elected by the shareholders. The shareholder is not a co-owner of the company or its property. He is given certian rights by law. He can only attend and vote at the meeting of the shareholders and receive dividend. Thus there is a separation between ownership and management.

Types of Companies

The types of companies can be classifed from their view points viz., (a) Nature of their formation, (b) From the view point of liability; and (c) From the functional point of view.

1. *Nature of their formation* : There are three ways by which companies can be formed, namely by Charter, by Statute and by Registration.
   (i) *Chartered Companies* : In the initial stages of the development, the companies were created by charter or a special santion granted by the Head of State. This system was quite popular in England during the early period. Such companies have no place in India after Independence.
   (ii) *Statutory Companies* : These are created by Special Act of Parliament or State Legislature. This is done when the company is to be established with some specific purpose and that requires proper regulation. The Companies Act does not apply to it. Examples are State Bank of India, Reserve Bank of India, Air-India, Life Insurance Corporation, etc.
   (iii) *Registered Companies* : Most of the companies in the industrial and commercial field are usually established under the Companies Act in force by way of registration with the Registrar of Companies.
2. *From the view point of liability* : Companies which are registered under the Companies Act are classified into three categories :
   (i) *Companies with Unlimited liability* : In such companies the members are liable to the full extent of the debts incurred by the company but such companies are not found in India.
   (ii) *Companies limited by guarantee* : In such companies, the liability of members is limited to the extent of the amount guaranteed to be paid by them in the event of the company being wound up. The guaranteed amount is usually specified in the Memorandum of Association of the company. These companies are formed not with the intention of making any profit but to promote art, literature, sports, eduction, religion, etc.

(iii) *Companies limited by shares* : In such cases the liability of members is limited to the extent of the nominal value of shares held by them. They are liable to pay only the balance unpaid on the shares allotted to them. For example a shareholder who has paid Rs. 40/- on a Rs. 50/- share can be called upon to pay balance of Rs. 10/- and nothing more. Such company is also known as a ' Share Company '.

3. *From the functional point of view* : From the functional point of view there are private and public companies. A public or private company may be a Government company.

(i) *Private Company* : According to Companies Act 1956, a private company is one, which by its Articles -

- Restricts the right to transform its shares;
- Limits the number of members to 50 excluding employees; and
- Prohibits any invitation to the public to subscribe to its shares or debentures.

This company can be formed by at least two persons by subscribing their names to the Memorandum of Association.

(ii) *Public Company* : According to Companies Act, a public company means a company which is not a private company. It can be formed by at least 7 persons. All the restrictions of a private company are not applicable on a public compnay. It must allot its shares within 120 days of the issue of the prospectus. It can commence business only after it receives a ' Certificate to Commence Business' from the Registrar.

(iii) *Government Company* : A Government Company is a company in which not less than 51 percent of the paid-up share capital is held by the Central Government or by any State Government or Governments or partly by the Central Government and partly by one or more State Government. Upto 49 percent of the share capital may, therefore, be held by private parties or financail institutions. A Government company can be a public or a private company. Most of the Government companies in India are private limited companies and all the shares are held by the government.

4. *Holding Companies and Subsidiary Companies* : A public or private company may be either holding company or a subsidiary company. The Companies Act 1956, defines a holding company as "any company which directly or indirectly through the medium of another company either holds more than half of the equity share capital or controls the composition of the Board of directors of some other companies". A company may become a Holding Company of another company in any of the following three ways :

   - By holding more than 50 percent of the issued capital of the other company; or
   - by holding more than 50 percent of its voting rights; or
   - by securing to itself the right to appoint the majority of the directors of the other company, directly or indirectly.

The other company in such a case is known as a " subsidiary company ". Though the two companies remain separate legal entites, the affairs of both the companies are managed and controlled by the holding company. A holding company may have any number of subsidiaries.

(i) *One Man Company* : A member may hold virtually the entire share capital of a company. Such a company is known as a 'One Man Company'. This can take place both in a private company and a public company. The other members of the company may be holding just one share each and remaining shares are held by one of the members only. Such other members may be just dummies for the purpose of fulfilling the requirements of law as reagards minimum membership.

Advantages

1. *Financially sound* : This form of organisation facilities mobilization of large amount of capital for investment in industries. Since its capital is divided into shares of small value a large number of people from different walks of life can contribute to its capital by simply purchasing it shares. In addition, it can borrow from banks and financial institutions to a larger extent.
2. *Limited liability* : The liability of the shareholders of a company

is limited to the face value of the shares they have purchased. When he purchased the shares in a company he knows the maximum loss he may suffer if the company fails. His personal assets cannot be called upon for the purpose of payment of liabilities of the company.

3. *Stability* : The organisation is a legal entity with perpetual succession. The life of a company does not depend upon either on management or the owners. Thus a company because of its continuity and stability, can build up a power of endurance and high level of efficiency.
4. *Transferability of Shares* : The shareholder can at any moment transfer his shares to others according to the procedure laid down in the Articles of Association. The asset position of the company is in no way affected by the transfer of shares by its members.
5. *Diffused task* : The burden of risk is diffused and is not to be shouldered by one or few persons but is spread over all the shareholders of the company.
6. *Democratic control* : The company is managed on the principles of democracy. The Board of Directors who manage the company are elected by the share holders. The directors are responsible and accountalbe to the shareholders. The directors retire by rotation and may be re-elected by the shareholders.
7. *Greater scope for expansion* : The company form of organisation can raise capital and increase in the scale and size of the business unit and undertake large scale operations. Expansion of company cannot be delayed for want of financial and managerial resources. A company also offers an excellent scope for self-generating growth.
8. *Managerial efficiency* : A company having financial resources in abundance can secure the services of highly qualified persons who are experts in different fields of business management. Thus the available skill is utilized for the benefit of the community.
9. *Social advantage* : A company form of organisation is an effective medium of attracting small and scattered savings of the community. Since the company's financial acounts are published and circulated, teh public has enough faith on them.

Disadvantages

1. *Difficulty in formation* : In the formation of the company lot fo legal formalities are involved. Besides this, itis expensive too.
2. *Fradulent management* : This form of organisation gives a chance to the dishnest promoters to get capital from the public. The unscrupulous promoters may present a rosy picture of the prospectus. In this way the innocent and ignorant investors are trapped.
3. *Concentration of power in few hands* : The management of the company which is supposed to be conducted according to the will of shareholders practically have no say in the affairs of the company. The directors of the company become self-centred and they do not care for the shareholders.
4. *Conflict of interest* : There is a conflict of interest between persons who are at the top of the company and the shareholders. The directors try to mislead the members by presenting fake reports.
5. *Excessive Government control* : It has to observe many provisions of the different laws imposed by the Government. At every step the company has to comply with its provisions lest the company and the management may be penalised. This at times effects the smooth functioning of the company.

Formulation of a Company

To establish any industrial or commercial enterprise on a corporate basis, one has to comply with certain economic and business factors and follow rules and regulations given under the company law. Therefore the formation of company passs through the following stages:

Promotion of a Company

Promotion means various initial steps to be taken for the establishment of a company, before it comes into existence. An idea which is developed into a concrete project accomplished by the incorporation and floatation of a company is called promotion. All the initial activities undertaken before the company is registered are called promotional eforts. The person who helps in the promotion of a company is called a promoter. These promoters are experts in the work of company formation. He is a person who transforms an idea into business, who brings together various persons concerned helps in raising capital and finally produces a growing concern - Company : A promoter is entitled to the remuneration of services rendered and expenses incurred by him. Such remuneration may be in cash or in the form of shares for securities or he may demand a job.

Stages in Promotion

1. *Discovery of an idea* : Promotion starts with a person or persons conceiving an idea about a business concern. The promoters may not necessarily be an inventor; they only perceive the possibility of organising a commercial enterprise. Their idea can take shape in three forms : (i) the idea of commencing a new venture; (ii) the idea of expanding a concern already established; and (iii) the idea of combining the existing concern.
2. *Investigation* : Next step is the investigation of the idea conceived by the promoters. The analysis of the projected idea can be divided into the following :
   - the probable costs involved
   - estimate of annual revenue obtainable; and
   - expected annual margin of surplus or profit.

In other words the promoters should find out the sources of supply and the extent of demand, the cost of operation, recurring expenditure and the compensation to owners for risks and services.

The investigation should be conducted with the help of experts, engineers, statisticians, etc. regardign costs, sales, price and probable earnings. They should conduct factual study so that it can be revealed whether the idea is feasible or not.

3. *Verification* : After investigation has been made the findings should be sent to independent experts. It helps to correct any shortcomings in the methods and contents of investigation.
4. *Assembling* : In the next stage te business idea is put in the form of proposition. He starts assembling the idea. It means projecting the original business idea, securing all the proerty needed in building up the enterprise, securing of patents, making tentative appointments of key personnel, etc. He enters into contracts with selles and owners of te property which are to be

approved by the company after it is registered under the companies Act.

5. *Provision of finance* : The next stage is arranging for funds to launch it as a growing concern. Financing for business idea implies financing planning. The promoters enter into arangement with bankers, make contract with underwriters for raising the permanent capital for the proposed company.

Incorporation of Company

The promoters have to apply to the Registrar of Joint Stock Companies with the necessary documents, declarations and fees as laid down in the Companies Act, so that the ensuing company may be registered. The documents to be submitted are :

(i) The Memorandum of Association to which at least seven persons (two persons in case of private company) have subscribed their names and each one of them has taken at least one share. It has to be duly stamped.

(ii) The Articles of Association is to be prepared, signed and filed.

(iii) A list with consent of persons who have agreed to act as directors.

(iv) Notice of the situation of the Registered office of the company.

(v) A Statutory declaration by an advocate or an attorney or a chartered accountant or secretary engaged in the formation of the company or any other officers of the company, to the effect that all the provisions of the Companies Act have been duly complied with, is to be filed.

(vi) Licensing required under other relevant Acts.

(vii) A Statement of Nominal Capital and where it exceed Rs. 25 Lakhs, a certificate from the controller of Capital Issues permitting the issue of capital.

All the documents are submitted to the Registrar with proper stamp duly and registration fees at the prescribed rate. The Registrar will scrutinise these documents and when satisfied will enter the name of the company in the Register of Companies maintained in his office. He will issue a Certificate of Incorporation, which gives the company legal existence from the date given on the certificate.

Memorandum of Association

It is the most important document and acts as its charter containing the fundamental conditions upon which the company can be incorporated. It sets out the powers and objects of the company to know what is its permitted range of enterprise. The memorandum of a company limited by shares must contain the following clauses :

(a) *Name clause.* In this clause the name of the company should end in "limited" in case of public company and the words "Private Limited" in the case of private company.

(b) *Domicile clause.* In this location of the registered office should be stated. This helps the Registrar, to have necessary correspondence with the company. It also helps in locating the jurisdication of Registrar of Companies and the courts.

(c) *Object clause.* This is one of the important clauses of the Memorandum as it determines the rights and powers of the company and indicates the sphere of its activities. This clause must mention the state or states to whose territories the objects extend. It should also specify the acts which the company proposes to undertake in future.

(d) *Liability clause.* This clause defines that the liability members of the company is limited to the face value of total number of shares taken. It gives an idea to every shareholder as to his total financial liability to the company.

(e) *Capital clause.* Under this clause the total amount of share capital with which the company is to be registered is stated. The number of shares and the value of each share should also be mentioned.

(f) *Subscription clause.* This clause contains the names of the signatories to the memorandum and the number of shares he has agreed to take.

Alteration of Memorandum

Any clause in the memorandum can be altered in accordance with the provisions of the Act only.

1. The name of the company can be changed by passing a special resolution and with the aproval of the Central Government. The change of name will be effective and complete only when

Registrar will issue a fresh Certificate of Incorporation.

2. The company can shift its registered office from one state to another and change its object clause by passing a special resolution and also by taking "Confirmation Order" from the appropriate courts. This can be done if such change is rendered necessary :
   - to carry on its business more economically and more efficiently;
   - to attain its main purpose by new or improved means;
   - to enlarge or change the local area of operations;
   - to carry on some business under which existing circumstances may advantageously be combined with the business of the company;
   - to restrict or abandon any of the subjects specified in the memorandum;
   - to sell or dispose of the whole or any part of the undertaking or any of the undertakings, of the company; or
   - to amalgamate with any other company or body of persons.
3. If the Articles authorise a company limited by shares it can alter its share capital by an orginary resolution in general meeting, so as to (i) increase it by issue of new shares; (ii) consolidate and divide its capital into shares of large amount; (iii) subdivide its shares into shares of smaller amount; (iv) convert its paid up capital into stock or reconvert the stock into paid-up shares; or (v) cancel shares which have not been taken or promised to be taken at the time of the resolution.
4. If the Articles authorise, a company by special resolution confirmed by the court may reduce its share capital in any way and in particular by (i) reducing or extinguishing the liability of members for uncalled capital (ii) writing off lost capital; or (iii) paying off capital which is in excess of the company's requirements.

Articles or Association

The Articles of Association contain rules and regulations or bye-laws which govern the internal management of the company. They are subordinate to the memorandum of Association. They contain the rules regarding (a) share certificates; (b) call on shares; (c)transfer and transmission of shares; (d) lien on shares; (e) general meetings and voting rights of members; (f) borrowing powers of the company; (g) dividends; (h) directors and their remuneration; (i) forfeiture of shares; (j) liquidation, etc.

A company is free to frame its own Articles or adopt Table A as given in the first schedule of the Companies Act 1956. In case a company does not get its Articles registered, Table A will apply. The Articles of Association must be stamped, printed, divided into paragraphs, numbered consecutively and signed by the subscribers to the Memorandum of Association in the presence of atleast one witness.

Alteration of Articles can be altered at any time by a special resolution without the permission of the court, provided that the alteration is in the best interst of the company as a whole. An alteration, regarding converting a public company into a private company should be approved by the Central Government.

Raising Capital or Capital Subscription Stage

When a company has been incorporaated it is ready for floatation. The promoters will seek capital required to commence business. the nedded capital is sometimes collected from private sources. A public company issues an invitation to the public to buy shares, debentures, etc. of the company. Generally the promoters who are the first directors of the company raise the capital by making arrangements with bankers and issue an invitation in the form of a prospects to the public to purchase shares in the company.

1. *Prospectus* : It is an important document usually issued to raise funds from the investors. A prospectus is defined as, "any prospectus, notice, circular, advertisement or other documents inviting offers from the public for the subscription or purchase of any shares in our debentures of a body corporate".

   The objects of a prospectus are :

(a) to inform the public that a new company has been formed; (b) to convince and create interest so that the people can make investment in the new company; (c) to create confidence in the public about the company, its directors and other factors which make for success; (d) to preserve records of the terms and conditions on which the public have been invited to buy its shares and debentures; and (e) to make the directors responsible for the facts mentioned in it.

To achieve the above-mentioned objective, the prospectus should be properly drafted and widely circulated. It must mention all the true facts and should not conceal any material fact. It may be prepared in the best possible manner which may project the best prospectus of the company.

2. *Statement in lieu Prospectus* : A public company may not raise its capital by public issue of shares and hence need not publish any prospectus. It may collect capital by issuing shares privately. If it does not issue a prospectus, it would have to file a "Statement in lieu of Prospectus' with the registrar as per Part I of the Schedule III of the Companies Act 1956 and it must be signed by all the directors.

   A prospectus, before it is issued to the public, must be filled with the Registrar, because until a prospectus of statement in lieu of prospectus if filed, no company can allot its shares or debentures.

3. *Allotment of shares* : After the prospectus is issued the prospectus investors have to apply in the prescribed form to the company for the number of shares they would like to buy. The application for the shares constitute the offers and when these offers are accepted it is called allotment. Allotment establishes legal relationship of persons with the company to whom the shares are allotted. If the applications for shares are recieved for more than the shares issued capital is said to be ' over subscribed'. When applications are for less number of shares, capital is said to be 'under-subscribed'. The directors then find out whether applications for minimum subscription as given in the prospectus are recieved or not.

   After the last date of receipt of applications the Board of Directors decide about the allotment of shares. It passes a resolution about the allotment of shares to specified persons.

   Letters of allotment are written to the allottees and Letters of Regret are written to those who have not been allotted any shares.

4. *Restrictions as to allotment* : According to the Companies Act, Allotment cannot be made unless the following conditions are fulfilled :

(a) A prospectus or statement in lieu of prospectus must be filed with the Registrar;

(b) The minimum subscription as provided in the prospectus, has been subscribed or applied for ;

(c) The company must receive in case the application money amounting to at least 5 percent of the nominal value of share; and

(d) The money recieved has to be kept deposited in a schedule bank.

5. *Irregular allotment* : If the Shares are allotted without fulfilling the above mentioned conditions, it is known as Irregular allotment, and the applicant can reject the allotment within 2 months after the statutory meeting of the company and if the allotment is made after this meeting, then within 2 months of such allotment. The applicant can claim refund of the money of the company goes into liquidation. He can also claim compensation from the directors.

6. *Inability to allot* : A company for want of minimum subscription is unable to allot shares within 120 days of the issue of prospectus, it must refund the amount to the applicants within the next 10 days. After this the directors will be personally held liable to repay all the amount with interest at the rate of 6 per cent per annum.

7. *Return of allotment* : The company must submit a return of allotment with the Regstrar, within one month. The returns should specify the numbers of shares allotted, the nominal value of the shares, names adresses of the allottees, amount paid and due on the shares.

Certificate to Commence Business

After the above-mentioned formalities are over the public company apply to the Registrar, for grant of a certificate to commence business. this can only be issued if the following conditions are fulfilled:

- The minimum subscription is alotted;
- The directors have paid for their qualification shares as stated in the prospectus; and
- A declaration that a prospectus or statement in lieu of prospectus

has been filed with the Registrar.

The Registrar on being satisfied, with the above declaration shall issue a 'certificate to commence business' which will entitle to start its business within one year of its incorporation. Failing to do so, the court of law may order the company to be wound up.

Co-operative Societites

In this form of organisation the basic aim is to render service to its members. It aims at encouaging self-help among the needy and pursuing common economic interests by way of co-operative trading and mutual help. It can be defined as a voluntary association of persons of moderate means and incomes who associate together to provide mutual assistance and service while promoting their common business and economic interests.

Characteristics

1. *Voluntary association :* The membership of the society is voluntary and anyone having a common interest is free to join it. There is no bar on the basis of caste, creed or religion. He can leave the society any time by giving proper notice. He can withdraw his capital but cannot transfer his shares to another person. The minimum number required to form it, is ten and there is no maximum limit.
2. *Equal voting rights* : Democracy is the rule of co-operatives and all members have equal voice in the management of its affairs. The rule is ' one man one vote '. Therefore, each member has one vote irrespective of the number of shares held by him.
3. *Democratic management* : Usually co-operative societies operate on local bases which enable all the member to take part in its activities in some way or the other. Since each member exercises an equal right with others, the management committee is in real sense an elected body.
4. *Service motive* : It is basically formed with the object of rendering maximum service to its members. Unlike other organisations its aim is not to earn profits.
5. *Disposal of profits* : A co-operative society does not distribute all its surplus in the form of dividend on shares held by its members. It gives them in the form of bonus which need not be

in proportion to the capital contributed by the members. In fact, the entire surplus is not distributed to its members but a portion of it, is utilised for the general benefit of the members.

6. *Cash trading* : Generally they conduct business on cash basis and allow no credit. This is done so that the society does not face the danger of bad debts.

7. *State control and corporate status* : The co-operative society is required to be registered under the co-operative Societies Act 1912 and thus becomes a corporate body subject to control and supervision of the government.

Type of Co-operatives

Co-operation being a way of life may be formed practically for every purpose and in very walk of life. The different types of business co-operatives are given below :

(a) Consumer's Co-operative Societies.
(b) Producers' Co-operative Societies
(c) Co-operative Marketing Societies.
(d) Co-operative Credit Societies
(e) Co-operative Housing Societies
(f) Co-operative Farming Societies.
(g) Miscellaneous Societies.

Advantage

(i) *Easy formation* : Any ten persons may form a co-operative society for the promotion of their economic interest. Not much is required on legal formalities and registration is also very easy.

(ii) *Open membership* : Any person can become a member of the society and can take its advantages.

(iii) *Democratic management*: All the members take part in its affairs. Every member has one vote and thus he has a say in the management.

(iv) *Limited liability* : The Liability of the members is limited to a certain proportion of their capital contribution as mentioned in the bye-laws of the society.

(v) *Perptual succession* : The co-operative society is a separate legal entity and its life is not affected by the death, insolvancy or conviction of its members.

(vi) *State patronage*: The policy of the government is to encourage co-operatives in evry field. They get certain concession from the government. Cheap loan is available to the societies; they are exempted from paying stamp duties and registration fees; income-tax benefit is also given below a specified amount of income.

(vii) *Non-economic benefits* : Co-operation is a way of life. It helps in educating the people to live together. It educates them regarding thrift, self-help, moral values and develops a feeling of co-operation.

Disadvantages

(i) *Limited resources* : They are not able to raise huge amount of capital because their members are men of meagre income and are limited to local areas.

(ii) *State interference* : In our country the co-operatives have grown through the blessings of the government. But the moment it takes an official form they stop growing which is very big curse.

(iii) *Inefficiency of management* : The societies are not managed efficiently because they do not get specialised and professional managers to look after their affiars because they cannot pay high remuneration.

(iv) *Lack of secracy* : They co-operative society is not in a position to maintain secrecy which is leaked out to the members and officials of the co-operative department.

(v) *Infighting among members* : Many a times members of the management committee are elected on the basis of politics rather than efficient service. Factionalism among the members affects its normal working.

4

Management of Companies

The company management is totally different from that of sole tradership or partnership concern. The company consists of the a large number of shareholders who are heterogeneous in character and it is not possible for them to control the affairs of the company. Therefore, they delegate their powers to the elected members known as Directors. These directors are collectively known as " Board of Directors ". The powers and duties of the Board of Directors are, apart from the provisions in the Companies Act, determined but the company's Memorandum and Articles of Association.

As we know, that the joint stock companies are owned by shareholders but managed and controlled by a small group of shareholders who are elected as directors and thus there is a divorce between ownership and management. There are a number of reasons for this divorce between ownership and management in joint stock companies. Firstly, there is a distinction between the shareholders and the legal personality of a company so much so that a shareholder is allowed to carry on business competing with that of a company. Therefore, it will not be desirable for him to know the secrets of the company for his personal gains. Secondly, the shareholders are very large in number and it would be impossible for them to personally carry on the management of the company. Thirdly, the shareholders belong to all walks of life and they cannot be expected to have competence and skill to deal with the complex problems of modern business. Fourthly, the shareholders live far and wide and are unable to attend the meeting and general meeting. If they are able to attend the meeting, they may remain passive spectators or their voice may not be effective enough to be heard by the Board of Directors. It is due to these reasons that the shareholders play a passive role in the management of the company and assume the role of investors by providing part of the funds and bear the risks of business. Since a company is an artificial person, it is necessary that the exercise of powers must be delegated to proper authority. The effective powers of management are exercised by the Board of Directors.

The Board of Directors is the top administrative organ of the company. The delegate their powers to the chief executive and the secretary who serve as a link between the Board of Directors on one side and the operating organization on the other. The chief executive interprets and executes the policy decision laid down by the Board. The chief executive further delegates some powers to the departmental or functional managers who direct the operations of the various departments. The pattern of the company management may be seen from the following chart.

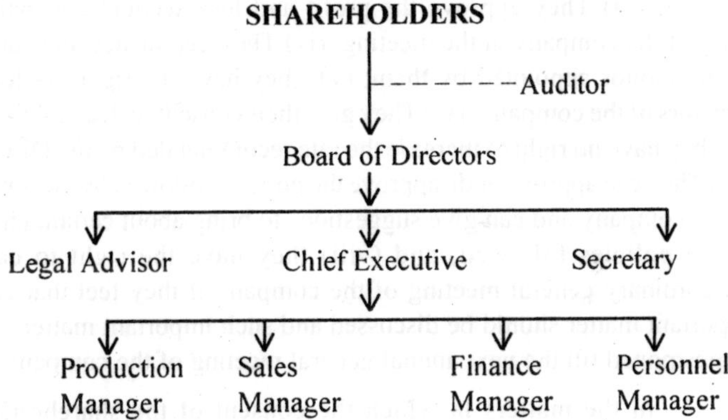

Most of the companies in India follow the above mentioned chart. Now we shall discuss the role of all these organs in the management of companies.

Shareholders

The Shareholders provide the required capital for the company and bear the risk and since they are the owners of the company, they have certain power to control over the affairs of the company. The rights of the shareholders can be classified in two categories :

Individual Rights

Following rights are exercised by a shareholder as an individual:

(i) To receive dividends when declared; (ii) To receive notices for meetings of the shareholders and to attend them; (iii) To vote in meetings in persons or by proxy; (iv) To inspect the records of the company; (v) To share the assets of the company on dissolution; (vi) to transfer his shares; and (vii) Articles of Association of the company.

Group Rights

The following rights are exercised by the shareholders collectively when they meet in the meeting of the company :

(i) They decide the board policy of the working of the company; (ii) They have the right to receive the profit and loss account, and balance-sheet duly audited, and directors report 21 days before the date of the meeting; (iii) They approve the profit and loss account and balance-sheet of the company in the meeting; (iv) They get the accounts audited by an auditor appointed by them; (v) They have the right to elect the directors of the company; (vi) They give their consent to declare dividend but they have no right to increase the rate recommended by the Directors; (vii) They can approve or disapprove the policies followed by the directors of the company and can give suggestions to bring about certain changes in the policies followed; and (viii) they have the right to call an extraordinary general meeting of the company if they feel that certain important matter should be discussed and such important matter cannot be postponed till the next annual general meeting of the company.

In the matters in which the consent of the shareholders is necessary the directors alone cannot take any decision. The powers of the shareholders can be enhanced by making suitable provisions in the Articles of the company but they cannot be reduced.

Board of Directors

A company though legal entity in the eyes of the law, is an artificial person. It can act only through some human agency. Such persons through whom a company acts and carries its business transactions are called Directors. Every company and its subsidiary must have at least three directors and at least two-thirds of the total number of directors retire by rotation. In such retiring directors, one-third retire at the end of every year but are eligible for re-election. A private company must have at least two directors.

Appointment of Directors

Procedure for Appointment : Under the Companies Act the intending candidate for the office of the directors has to file with the Company a notice of his intention to contest for the post of directorship at least 14 days before the meeting. This is not applicable to the retiring directors or in a private company. The company must then inform the members at least seven days before the meeting bout the candidature of a person for the office of the director by serving individual notices on members or through advertisement in two newspapers. On being elected he has to file his consent to act as a director within thirty days of such election.

Share Qualification for Directors : The Articles of a company usually requires its directors to hold a certain number of shares. Such shares are called ' qualification shares '. He can obtain qualification shares either by transfer or by subscribing them directly. These shares should not be obtained within two months after his appointment as director. The nominal value of such shares should not exceed Rs. 5,000 or nominal value of one share where it exceeds Rs. 5,000/-.

Number of Directorship

A person cannot hold office at the same time as director in more than twenty companies.

Remuneration of Directors

According to Indian Companies Act the total managerial remuneration to the directors and/or manager must not exceed 11 percent of the net profits of the company for that financial year. A director may receive remuneration :

(i) by way of a fee or each meeting of the Board or a committee of the Board, attended by him, which is Rs. 250 for attending each meeting of the Board;

(ii) by way of a monthly, quarterly or annual payment with the approval of the Central Government; or

(iii) by way of commission if the company by special resolution authorizes such payment.

The whole time director or managing director cannot get remuneration in excess of 5 percent of net profit or one such director and 10 percent for all of them together. The part-time directors who does not receive any monthly sum as remuneration may be paid 1 percent of the net profit if the company has no manager, he can get 3 percent of the net profit of the company.

If any director receives any remuneration, directly or indirectly in excess of these limits without the prior sanction of the Central Government, he has to refund such excess to the company. The company cannot waive the recovery of any such without the permission of the Central Government. If the remuneration is determined by a special resolution, such a resolution has to be renewed after every five years.

Meeting of Directors

In case of every company, a meeting of its Board of Directors must be held at least once in every three months and at least four such meetings must be held in every year. The quorum for a meeting of the Board is one-third of its total strength or two directors, whichever is greater.

Powers and Functions of Directors

Individually the directors have no powers and they have to act as a Board. But the Board has the power of delegating certain authority to an individual director or to a committee of directors. The Board of Directors of a company is entitled to exercise all such powers and to do all such acts and things as the company is authorized to exercise and do. These powers have been given to them under the Companies Act 1956 or in the Memorandum or Articles of the company. These powers can be divided into two categories :

Statutory Powers : The Companies Act 1956 provide Statutory powers of the directors which can be divided into three parts.

Powers which cannot be delegated. Under Section 292 of the Act, following are the powers which can only be exercised by the Board and in no case be delegated to others. These powers are (a) to make calls; and (b) to issue debentures.

Powers which may be delegated. Under the same section, Board can delegate certain powers to a committee of directors or other managerial personnel. They are (a) to borrow money; (b) to invest funds of the company; and (c) to advance loans.

Powers which can only be exercised by the board with the consent of shareholders of the company in its general meeting. These powers are (a) to sell, lease or dispose of the undertaking of the company; (b) to remit or give time for repayment of any debt due to the company by a director; (c) to invest them in the trust securities; (d) to borrow money in excess of the paid-up capital and free reserves of the company (Apart from the temporary loans obtained from the banks); (e) to contribute to charities, etc. not related to the business or welfare of its employees, amounts exceeding in any financial year Rs. 50,000 or 5 per cent of the average net profits of the three preceding financial years whichever is greater.

Executive Powers : The Board of Directors which is the chief executive authority and the highest organ of top management, exercises certain powers, which are of great importance, to direct the company to achieve the given objectives. These powers are as follows :

Making Contracts : Important contracts like purchase of land, purchase of patents, construction of buildings, etc. are generally made by the Board.

Recommending Rate of Dividend : The Board recommends the rate of dividend to the general meeting. The shareholders are required to approve it, but they do not have power to increase the rate of dividend recommended by the Board.

Issue of Additional Securities : The decision to issue additional securities and debentures and to augment the resources of the company is taken by the share holders in the general meeting. But once the decision is ratified, the Board has to decide the terms, conditions, time and amount of issue. Formulation of major policies. The Board formulates the major policies of the company and lays down broad guidelines relating to various sections such as finance, marketing, personnel, research and development, production, etc.

Appointment of Senior Personnel. The Board selects a number of senior executives for the company such as secretary, finance manager, accounts officers and various other sectional managers. The Board also decides about the payment and services conditions of these senior executives.

Other Powers : The Board has also to review the work of the executives and see the company is being run efficiently. It has to decide the organisational structure of the business and to make changes as and when required. Thus it exercises several powers while directing and controlling the operation of the company.

Legal Restrictions of Directors

The Companies Act 1956 lays down a number of restrictions on the powers of directors so that they may not misuse them. Such restrictions are given below :

Assignment of Office : Under section 312 of the Act the director is prohibited from assigning his office.

Number of Directorship : No person can become director in more than 20 public companies or their subsidiaries. This number does not include private limited companies and also excludes companies in which a person is an alternate director.

Loans to Directors : Under the Act it is necessary to obtain the previous approval of the Central Government or a company making a loan to , or giving any guarantee or providing any security in connection with a loan made by any other person, to any director of the leading company. Such restrictions also apply the following cases also : (i) any firm in which any such director or relative is a partner; (ii) any private company of which such director is a director or a member; (iii) any body corporate at whose general meeting any director or two directors control 25 per cent of the total voting powers; and (iv) any body corporate, the Board of directors, the managing directors, or manager of which is accustomed to act in accordance with the directors or instructions of the Board of Directors, or of any director or directors of the lending company. These restrictions do not apply to any loan made, guarantee given or security, provided by a private company or a banking company or holding companies to their subsidiaries.

Office of Profit : Any director can hold any office or place of profit under the company of its subsidiaries, provided the consent of the shareholders is accorded by a special resolution.

Disclosure of Interest : Every director has to disclose, if he is interested or concerned in any contract entered into by the company before the Board of Directors. The disclosure must be made at the first meeting of the Board after he became so interested.

Board's Consent of Contracts : Except with the consent of the Board of Directors of a company, a director cannot enter into any contract with the company (a) or the sale, purchase or supply of any goods, materials or services; or (b) or underwriting the subscription of any shares or debentures of the company.

Furthermore, in the case of a company having paid-up share capital of not less than rupees one crore, no contracts in which the directors are interested shall be entered into without the approval of the Central Government.

Liabilities of Directors

Usually the liability of the Directors is limited like that of the other shareholders, but their liability can be made unlimited by a provision in the Memorandum of Association of the company. Before the Directors accepts the office, notice should be given to him that his liability will be unlimited.

The liability of Directors may be discussed under these categories :

Liability to Third Parties :

Under the Act: Liability of directors to third parties may arise in connection with the issue of prospectus which does not contain the particulars required by the Act, or which does not contains material misrepresentations. They may also incur such liability where the allotment of shares has been irregular.

Apart from The Act. Directors are the agents of the company and are not personally liable on contracts entered into as agents on behalf of the company. But if the directors fail to exclude personal liability, by signing a negotiable instrument mentioning the company's name, they are personally liable to the holder of such instrument. They are also personally liable if they act their own name.

Liability to The Company

The directors are liable for ultra vires acts : The directors should act within their powers as defined in the articles of Associations and if they go beyond their powers they will be personally liable.

The directors may be held liable for gross negligence or breach of trust. Directors are expected to show fair and reasonable diligence in the discharge of their duties and act honestly.

Liability of breach of statutory duties

The directors are expected to maintain proper accounts, filing of returns or observance of certain statutory formalities. If they are guilty of frauds they may be held personally liable.

A director who is habitually absent from meeting will become responsible for the acts.

Other Managerial Personnel

In addition to the Board of Directors, a company may employ or appoint a managing director or a manager. But in no case a company can appoint both of them at the same time.

Managing Director

Usually the directors elect one of them as the managing director of the company. He is a whole-time officer who is responsible for the entire management of the company. Only an individual can be appointed as managing director and not as association of persons or a body corporate and he must be a member of the Board of Directors. The Companies Act defines the managing director in the following words. " A director who, by virtue of an agreement with the company or of a resolution passed by the company at the general meeting or by its Board or by virtue of its Memorandum or Articles of Association, is entrusted with substantial powers of management which would not otherwise be exercisable by him, and includes a director occupying the position of a managing director, by whatever name called. " The managing director functions in a two-fold provisions of the companies Act apply to the managing director :

(i) His appointment should be approved by the Central Government.

(ii) In case of a public company, he can only be appointed within three months of the incorporation of the company;

(iii) He can be appointed for five years at a time ;

(iv) A person cannot be appointed as managing director of more than two companies at the same time. In case of second company, his appointment must be unanimously approved by the members of the Board;

(v) The remuneration of a managing director is subject to the maximum limit of 5 per cent of net profit, the Central Government may, however, increase this limit;

(vi) Under Section 318 of the Act the company has to pay the managing director compensation for the loss of office if he accepts to hold office before the expiry of his term. But the compensation should not exceed the remuneration which he would have earned for the remaining term or 3 years whichever is shorter. He is not entitled to any compensation in the following cases : (a) if he resigns office because of reconstruction or amalgamation of the company with other company and he is appointed managing director or other officer in the new company; (b) if the company is wound up of wing to his negligence or default; (c) if he is guilty of fraud or breach of trust or gross negligence or mismanagement of the affairs of the company; or (d) if he instigates or takes part directly or indirectly in termination of his office.

Manager

Manager is an individual who is given the charge of the whole management of the affairs of the company. Under the Act no company can employ a firm or a body corporate or association as its manager and only an individual can be appointed as the manager. According to the Act the manager is defined as follows : ' An individual who subjects to the superintendence, control and direction of the Board of directors, has the management of the whole, or substantially the whole of the affairs of a company, and includes a director or any other person occupying the position of a manager by whatever name called, and whether under a contract of service or not'. According to the above definition even a director can be appointed as the manager of the company.

Disqualification of a Manager

Under section 385 of the Act, the following persons cannot be appointed as manager of a company :

(a) A person who is an undischarged insolvent or one who has been adjudged insolvent within the preceeding five years of the proposed appointment;

(b) A person who suspends payments to his creditors or has suspended such payment, at any time within the preceeding five years; and

(c) A person who is, or has been convicted at any time within the preceeding five years by a court in India of an offence involving moral turptude.

The Central Government has the power to remove any of these disqualifications if it desires to do so.

Managing Agents

The managing agents played a very important role in the early stage of industrial development of the country. He occupied a very important position in the management of companies. He was usually given the task of managing all the affairs of the company. But as the time passed the managing agents started misusing their position and the system developed a number of evils and, therefore, there was a demand for abolition of the system. In view of the mounting criticism of their functioning the Government of India appointed in January 1965 a committee called Managing Agency Enquiry Committee headed by Dr. I.G. Patel to report whether the managing agency system could be abolished as provided in section 324. The committee selected for enquiry five major industries, namely cotton textiles, jute, sugar, cement and paper. It submitted its report in March 1966. On the recommendation of the report a comprehensive Companies (Amendment) Bill was passed by the Parliament in 1969 and it provides that the managing agents will cease to exist with effect from 3rd April 1970.

Company Secretary

The secretary is one of the most responsible officials to the company. He is an employee of the organisation with a number of responsibilities assigned to him. The Companies Act defines company secretary as " Secretary means any individual appointed to perform the duties which may be performed by a secretary under this Act and any other purely ministerial or administrative duties, if such individual possesses such qualifications as may be prescribed ".

Secretary of a company is the principal officer having the responsibility of carrying on the day-to-day routine activities and the execution of the policies formulated by the management. He also acts as the connecting link between the management on the one hand and the members and the public on the other. He handles staff matters, personally deals with outside callers, conveys the decisions of the management to the staff, maintains public relations, etc.

The Act has made provision for the compulsory appointment of the qualified Secretary in every company having paid-up capital of not less than 25 Lakh rupees. It further provides that secretary shall be a whole-time officer and shall work for not more than one company.

Rights of the Secretary

A company secretary has the following rights :

(A) As the head of the secretarial department the secretary has the right to exercise control and supervision of the activities of the department; (ii) As the principle officer under the Act he has the right to sign documents requiring authentication of the company; (iii) As a servant of the company he has the right to demand his outstanding salary as a preferential creditor in the event of winding up of the company. (iv) He has the right to control and manage the departments that comes under him; and (v) he has the right to register the transfer of shares if the Board of directors authorise him to do so.

Duties of Secretary

As he is principal officer of the company he has to perform numerous duties of varied nature depending on the nature and size of the company. He has to be very careful in performing his duties because a slight lapse on his part can bring disrepute to the company and he may be personally liable for certain acts and omissions. His duties are discussed below :

Statutory Duties : (i) Under the Act he is required to maintain all the books, documents and records in the registered office of the company; (ii) to deliver return of allotment of shares to the Registrar; (iv) to issue share or debenture certificate; (v) under the Estate Duty Act he should give information to the Estate Duty Controller on the expiry of any shareholder and submit any information required by the controller; (vi) under Indian Stamp Act he has to see that proper stamps have been affixed on all documents; and (vii) under the Income Tax Act he has to see that requisite income-under the Income-tax has been deducted, returns filed and tax deposited with government. Similarly he has to keep in mind the provisions of the Act which affect the working of the company and he must function within the preview of the various Acts.

Duties Towards Directors : The Secretary acts as the mouthpiece of the Board of directors and conveys all the decisions to the staff and shareholders of the company. The secretary has to attend the meetings of the Board and provide information needed to frame a policy. He convenes meetings of the Board and prepares notices, agenda for them and fixes up the date and time of the meetings. He has to take down the minutes of the meeting. He has to appraise the directors regarding the provisions of the various acts which may be helpful in framing policies. He has also to see that all the instructions given by the Board have been duly implemented.

Duties towards Shareholders : He is a link between the Board and the shareholders and he has some duties towards the latter also. He entertains all the enquiries from the shareholders and satisfies them with reasonable replies. He issues notices of meeting to shareholders, arranges them and records the proceedings of the meeting. He also issues share certificates, share warrants, dividend warrants and makes arrangements for the payment of dividends. At times it is his duty to see that no secret of the company is disclosed to them prematurely.

Duties towards Office : He organises, trains the staff, motivates, controls and brings, about a proper co-ordination among them. All the sectional heads are directly responsible to him. At times he may look after the activities of all the departments or may supervise and co-ordinate the activities of certain departments. He has to see that all the departments works smoothly and efficiently.

Besides the above, the secretary performs multifarious duties. His position is of trust. He has to keep confidential matters secret. He has to execute the policies framed by the Board of Directors. He has to see all the documents of the company are prepared in time.

Liability of Secretary

The Companies Act lays down certain specific liabilities of a secretary for his failure to perform duties entrusted to him by the Act. These liabilities which have been provided by the Act itself, are both statutory and contractual. A secretary cannot be held liable if he acts with reasonable care and skill but may be held liable for his negligence and fraud. The secretary is in a fiduciary relationship towards the company and, therefore, must not all his personal interests to clash with the interests of the company. Secretary will be held liable if he uses the common seal of the company for his personal use. Under the Act he may be held liable if he makes a default in maintaining minute books at the registered office, failure to maintain a register of directions, failure to make entries in the register of directions, failure to make entries in the register of members on the issue of a share warrant, etc.

Books of the Company

A Joint stock company has to maintain certain books relating to members, director, financial and other transactions. These books are kept with the secretary. They are of two types :

(1) Statutory books; and (2) Optional or Non-statutory books.

Statutory Books

These are the books which have to be maintained, as required under the Companies Act, by every company at its registered office. If a company fails to keep any of these books, it attracts the penalties provided for the management under the Act.

Some of these books are as follows :

1. Register of Investments not held in company's own name (open to members and debenture holders).
2. Register of charges.
3. Register of members.
4. Index of members where their number is more than fifty, unless the register of members itself affords an index.
5. Register of debenture holders.
6. Index of debenture holders where their number is more than fifty, unless the Register of debenture holders itself affords an index.

7. Foreign register of members and debenture holders.
8. Minute books containing minutes of proceedings of general meetings.
9. Books of accounts.
10. Register of contracts.
11. Register of directors, managing directors, etc.
12. Register of director's shareholding.
13. Register of loans.
14. Register of investments in shares and debentures of other companies.

Optional Books

Usually, company maintains several books for the purpose of keeping proper record though not required compulsorily by the Companies Act. They are also known as non-statutory books. Some of these books are as follows :

1. Register of transfers
2. Register of documents sealed.
3. Register of certification.
4. Register of balance tickets.
5. Share application and allotment book.
6. Register of share warrants.
7. Director's attendance book
8. Register of probates and letters of administration.
9. Log book.
10. Dividend mandates register
11. Register of lost certificates
12. Agenda book
13. Debenture interest book
14. Common seal book.

Auditors

A company carries on business with the capital furnished by

share holders who are not in control of the money supplied by them. They want that their investments should be safe and utilised properly. For this purpose the accounts should be checked and audited by a competent authority. The usual provision regarding the appointment of auditors and for the audit of accounts are normally contained in the Articles. Because of the importance of audit, the Companies Act makes it compulsory for every company to appoint qualified auditors to make a systematic examination of books and records of the company.

Any person who is a chartered accountant within the meaning of the Chartered Accounts Act 1949 can only be appointed as an auditor of a company. The first auditor or auditors of the company shall be appointed by the Board of Directors within one month of the company's registration and auditors so appointed shall hold the office until the first annual general meeting. The subsequent appointment of auditors are made in annual general meeting of the company.

Right and Duties

Every auditor of a company has a right of free and complete access at all times to the books and accounts and vouchers of the company, whether kept at the head office of the company or else where shall be entitled to enquire from the officers of the company such information and explanations as the auditor may think necessary for the performance of his duties. He is entitled to receive a notice of and to attend every general meeting of the shareholders and be heard on any part of the business which concerns him as auditor. The duties of an auditor are summarized below :

(1) An auditor must be acquainted with his duties under the articles and the Act; (2) He must act honestly within skill and care and should not be influenced by others in the discharge of his duties; (3) He must see that the books show the true financial position of the company; (4) He must report all materials facts and points to the shareholders; (5) He is not bound to give advice nor he is concerned with how the business is being carried on; (6) He is justified in trusting the servants of the company, provided he uses reasonable care; (7) If anything suspicious occurs, he is bound to probe deep into it; (8) He must check the cash in hand and the bank balance; and (9) He must verify the existence of the company's securities and see that they are in safe custody.

Company Meetings

Meetings play a very important role in the functioning of the company. Number of meetings are held by the company and the secretary has to make arrangements for them. The meetings of a company may be classified as (a) meetings of the Board of Directors, (b) meetings of the shareholders, (c) meetings of debenture holders; and (d) meetings of the creditors. The following chart shows kinds of meetings.

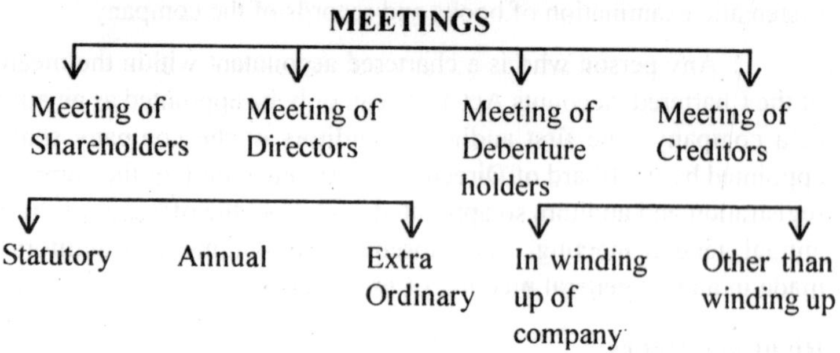

Kinds of Company Meeting

Meetings of Board of Directors

The Companies Act states that the meeting of the Board of Directors of every company must be held at least once in every three months and at least four such meetings must be held in every year. The company secretary has to make arrangements for such meetings in accordance with the provisions of Articles and Companies Act 1956. The secretary prepares the notice and agenda for the Board meetings and despatches them to every director at his usual address in India. The requisite quorum for a Board meeting is one third of the total strength of the directors or two directors which ever is higher. If there is no quorum, the meetings stands adjourned automatically.

Shareholders Meetings

As mentioned earlier the meetings of the shareholders is of the following types :

Statutory Meeting : Under Sec. 165 of the Companies Act a Public company has to hold the statutory meeting within a period not exceeding six months and not less than one month from the date on which the company becomes entitled to commence business. Private companies are not required to hold such meeting. At least 21 days before the day of that meeting, the Board of Directors must forward to every member report called the statutory report, along with the notice of the meeting.

The secretary should prepare the report carefully and get it certified by at least directors and also by the auditors of the company as the report relates to shares allotted, cash received and the receipts and payments of the company. A copy of the statutory report should be filied with the Registrar of Companies for registration also before such meeting is held.

Annual General Meeting : Section 166 of the Act provides that every company must in each year hold an annual general meeting and specify it as such in the notices calling it, provided that not more than 15 months shall elapse between two annual general meetings. The first annual general meeting must be held within eighteen months of incorporation. In case of some difficulty the Registrar of Companies has powers to give an extension of 3 months except in case of first annual general meeting. Every annual general meeting must be held during business hours on a working day. The notice of 21 days must be given to the members of the company. The notice should mention the matters to be discussed at such meeting.

The following business matters are transacted at annual general meeting of the company :

(a) Consideration and adoption of accounts and the reports of the Board and auditors;
(b) Election of directors in place of whose who retire;
(c) Appointment and fitting remuneration of auditor; and
(d) Declaration of dividend.

It is usually provided in the Articles of companies that Chairman of the Board of Directors shall also be the chairman of such meeting.

Extraordinary General Meeting : Every general meeting which is neither statutory meeting, nor annual general meeting, is an extraordinary general meeting. It is usually convened by the Board of Directors for transacting some important business. It is defined as a meeting held between two annual general meetings. Only the business for which it is convened can be transacted at this meting. Every member of the company must be given a notice of the meeting at least 21 days before the day of meeting stating the object of the meeting. Such a meeting is called by the Board of Directors but the shareholders of the company cannot call for such a meeting. They can do so if the requisition of the meeting is signed by members holding 10 per cent of the paid up capital carrying voting rights in respect of matters to be discussed, and where the company has no share capital, the requisition has to be signed by members holding 10 per cent of the total voting powers. The Board of Directors have the duty calling the meeting within 21 days of the deposit of requisition. If the Board does not convene the meeting with 45 days of requisition, the members themselves may hold such meeting and may claim the expenses from the company which, in turn, will recover the expenses from the directors. Notice of such meeting is to be given in the same manner as in the case of annual general meeting.

Some Aspects of Company Meetings

There are certain important aspects in connection with the company meetings. They are discussed below :

Chairman : There must be a Chairman in every meeting who is ultimately responsible for the proper conduct of the meeting. The first Chairman of the meeting is provided for in the Articles of the company and in other meetings the chairman of the Board of Directors becomes their Chairman.

The Chairman's position is of great importance and has to perform a number of duties relating to the meeting. He must ensure that the meeting is properly convened and constituted and proper notice has been issued. He must ensure that requisition quorum is present in the meeting. He has to see that various items in business are taken up in the order in which they appear in the agenda. He must preserve order, conduct the meeting properly and ascertain the sense of the meeting. He has to decide the order of speakers and guide the discussion tactfully and patiently that the meeting transacts the business on agenda peacefully and in shortest possible time. He has a right to adjourn the meeting and exercise his casting vote in case of tie.

Proxy : Any member of a company entitled to attend and vote at a meeting has a statutory right under the Act to appoint another person, to attend and vote for him. The term proxy is applied to the person so appointed. It is required under the Act that an instrument appointing a proxy must be in writing and must be deposited with the company not less than 48 hours before the time for the meeting. Unless a provision to the contrary is made in the Articles, a member cannot appoint a proxy of a company has no share capital. Similarly in the case of private limited company, a member can nominate only one proxy and the proxy cannot speak in the general meeting and also cannot vote except on the poll.

There are two type of proxies, viz., special proxy and general proxy. When a proxy is nominated to vote only on a particular resolution it is called a "special proxy", but if he is nominated to vote for all the resolutions it is called a general proxy.

Quorum : A quorum is minimum number of persons whose presence is necessary for the transaction of business. Before the commencement of the meeting it should be seen whether the quorum is complete or not. The quorum for meetings of members is generally fixed by the Articles. If the Articles are silent regarding the number, the quorum of a general meeting consists of five members for public company and two members for a private company.

Ascertaining the Sense of The House : Discussion takes place in the company meetings on certain issues and it usually happens that the members are divided on a particular issue. When there is no unanimity, the chairman wants to ascertain the sense of the House. For this purpose he has to put the question to vote. This can be done by (i) acclamation; (ii) Voice voting; (iii) show of hands; (iv) ballot; (v) division; and (vi) poll.

By Acclamation : Motion of thanks to the chair are approved by acclamation of the members present. But this method is not adopted if there is a sharp difference of opinion among the members.

Voice Vote : In this case the Chairman puts the motion before the meeting and persons who are in favour of the motion say " Yeas " and those who are against it say " No ". The chairman hears both the voices and then declares the result of voice voting. In case any member is dissatisfied he may demand a vote by show of hands.

By Show of Hands : Under this, Chairman calls upon those in favour of the motion to raise hands and on counting them ask all those against the motion to do likewise. On that basis he announces the result of voting. It is to be noted that under Section 177 of the Companies Act, there is a provision that , " At any general meeting a resolution put to vote of the meeting shall, unless a poll is demanded under section 179, be decided on a show of hands". Proxies are not allowed to vote under this method. 'Standing Vote' is a variation of this method according to which members stand up in their seats to be counted for or against the motion.

Ballot : In this case every member present at the meeting records his vote on the ballot paper and deposits it in the ballot box. The ballot papers are then counted and the chairman declares the result. This method ensures secrecy in casting of votes.

By Division : Under this method the Chairman request all the members present in the meeting to divide themselves into two groups. One in favour of the motion and another against it. After counting the number of persons in each group the chairman gives his verdict.

By Poll : Section 179 of the Companies Act provides for a poll to be taken if the members are not satisfied with the result of voting by show of hands. Poll may be demanded by (a) not less than five members of a public company having voting rights at the meeting; (b) by one member, in case less than seven members are present, and by two members if more than seven members are present in case of private company; or (c) by any one member having at least one-tenth of the total voting power.

If the Chairman knows that the show of hands would not truly represent the sense of the meeting, it is his duty to order poll. It is to be noted that there were a demand for poll is made the decision on a show of hands stands uneffected.

Motions : The term motion implies a proposal made at a meeting by any member. A motion should always be in writing and necessary notice must be given before it is brought in the meeting for discussion. The person who proposes the motion is called a mover and the motion should be signed by him. The motion should be clear and unambiguous and must relate to the matter placed on agenda. The motion is placed in the meeting and discussed by all the members present. When the motion is passed it becomes a resolution. Motion and resolution are two terms which should not be misunderstood. " Motion is proposal put to the meeting for consideration, whereas resolution is the decision of the members which has been arrived at after due deliberations".

Amendments : An amendments is a proposed modification in the terms or wording of the motion which is yet to be discussed by the meeting. Amendments in the motion can be done by (a) adding some new words to the motion; (b) replacing some words of the motion by some other words; (c) deleting some words; or (d) changing the position of certain words. When the amended motion is put before the members for discussion it is called substantive motion.

Resolutions : As it has been mentioned earlier, when a motion is discussed by the members and they vote in favour of it, it becomes a resolution. Under the Act provision has been made for three kinds of resolutions which can be passed in any meeting of the company, are :

Ordinary Resolution : When a motion is passed by a simple majority of the shareholders at a meeting, it is known as ordinary resolution. Such resolutions are passed to do the routine type of business of the company viz., declaration of dividend, appointment of auditors, issues of shares at discount, adoption of the statutory report etc.

Special Resolution : A special resolution is one which requires 21 days notice and the conditions required are given below. The notice should indicate the reason to move a special resolution by virtue of Section 189(2) of the Companies Act. A resolution shall be special resolution when –

– the intimation to propose the resolution as a special resolution has been specifically mentioned in the notice calling the meeting or other intimation given to the members of the resolution ;

– the notice required under the Act has been duly given of the general meeting; and

– the number of votes cast in favour of the resolutio[illegible]s three times the number cast against it, either by a show of ha[illegible] or on a poll in person or by proxy.

Special resolution is necessary in certain specific cases viz., change of registered office from one State to another; change in the name of the company; alteration of the articles of association; reduction of share capital, etc. A copy of the special resolution must be filed with the Registrar within 15 days of its passing.

Resolution Requiring Special Notice : Section 190 of the Companies Act has made provisions for certain resolutions to be passed after a special notice is given for the same. The members should give the notice to the company at least 14 days before the date of meeting. The company in its turn gives 7 days notice to members through advertisement in a newspaper or in any other words allowed by the articles. Such resolutions have been given in the Act after abolishing extraordinary resolutions which earlier existed.

Special notice is required by the Act in certain matters viz., to appoint an auditor other than a retiring auditor; for passing a resolution at an annual general meeting to the effect that a retiring auditor shall not be re-appointed; to remove a director before the expiry of his period of office, etc.

Minutes

The proceedings of all the meetings whether they are Board meetings or general meetings should be recorded, so that they can be consulted whenever necessary. Such records of business transacted at meeting are known minutes. Section 193 of the Companies Act provides that every company must keep minutes containing a fair correct summary of all proceedings of general meetings and Board meetings in books kept for this purpose. But it should be very clear that minutes are not conclusive evidence but only prima facie evidence. The pages of the minute-book must be consecutively numbered and the minutes must be recorded within 30 days from the date of the meeting. Each page of every such book must be initialled or signed and the last page of the record of proceedings of each meeting dated and signed by the chairman of the next Board meeting or in case of a general meeting, by the chairman of that same meeting.

The minute must contain each and every aspect of the proceedings. Officers appointed in any such meetings of the Board are to be included in the minutes. The minutes must contain the names of the directors present at the meeting and if any director does not agree with the resolution passed at the meeting, his name and his dissent must be noted down in the minutes. The minute-book must be kept at the registered office of the company and any member has a right to inspect them during business hours. Minutes of the directors' meetings are confirmed at the next succeeding directors' meeting, whereas the minutes of the shareholders' meeting are usually confirmed at the next directors' meeting following the shareholders' meeting.

5

Business Combinations and Monopoly

In the field of business, every entrepreneur aims at earning profits through different forms of business organisation. With the economic and industrial development in the country, a large number of producers came into the field and there was cut-throat competition among themselves. This reduced their profits and they were made to think how to reduce wasteful and unhealthy competition among themselves. They started thinking of coming together to solve the crisis. This very tendency of coming together and forming " combinations " is only a group of persons joining together to earn more profits by bringing about economies of production, management, finance and marketing. Haney has defined combination as follows, " To combine is simply to become one of the parts of a whole and a combination is merely a union of persons to make a whole or group for the prosecution of some common purposes ". Thus, when two or more business units combine for some common purpose, it is termed as combination. The firms may combine to control the market, stabilise the prices, eliminate wasteful competition or obtain the economies of large scale production.

Causes of Combination

There are many reasons for the growth of business combinations. They are the outcome of several complex forces and at times they are overlapping. The different causes have been given below :

Cut-throat Competition. Every business unit tries to earn the maximum profit. But in the present day economy, intensity of competition is one of the most important factors which had led to the development of business combinations. With the improvement in the technique of production and marketing, various firms had to face a stiff competition in the line to secure a steady market. Some firms who could benefit by large scale production, reduced their prices, but it was alone not a good sign, because during the recession, the market became dull for all the products. During such periods, the large units could not diversify because they had installed heavy equipments with huge outlays. Thus business had to form combinations to avoid cut-throat competition which had become acute and wasteful.

Individual Ability. It is a bare fact that technical skill, administrative capacity, business talent, etc. cannot be possessed by one individual. Thus to get the entire benefit of individual ability, various business units come together for combinations to get the best out of all.

Benefits of Large Scale Production. It has already been seen that production on large scale basis can bring about economy. The bulk purchases of raw materials, spreading of overheads over large quantities of output will definitely reduce the cost of production and increase the profits. Economy and efficiency of management can be had. Similarly, in the field of marketing and advertising, there can be numerous advantages over small firms.

Control of Market. As to avoid intense competition and to secure steady market, various business units combine together to maximise their profits by controlling the market. This leads to monopoly. It is successful in those products which enjoy inelastic demand.

Influence of Tariffs. It is said that protective tariff is the mother of all types of combinations. In order to protect the domestic units, the Government imposes heavy duties on the imported goods. It results in the growth of business units in the country causing severe competition among themselves. Competition among the business units becomes so intense that the need for combination is felt. It has been felt that custom tariffs enable the protected industries to monopolise the market by forming cartels. In 1932, the Government afforded protection to the sugar industry. In 1937, they formed a Sugar Syndicate for selling sugar produced by member producers.

Trades Cycles. A constant change in the conditions of the market affects the demand for products. The demand of goods are fluctuated by the occurrence of trade cycles. During the boon period, there is mushroom growth of business units and cut-throat competition complete them to join together. During the period of depression, economic activity is reduced to a low level. The small firms who find it difficult to continue during this period, think of coming together with the larger firms to survive the onslaughts of depression. Depressions are, therefore, characterised not only by a large number of closures but also by a number of combination of business.

Rationalisation. The various schemes of rationalisation can be implemented, if the regulation of prices and output, optimum utilisation of plant and machinery, utilisation of scarce raw materials, etc. are taken up in a joint and co-ordinated manner. It involves the combination of less efficient business units together to undertake one joint programme for developing new markets instead of competing with each other. Competition in the same line can be avoided.

Joint Stock Companies. The development of Joint sock Companies has facilitated the growth of combinations. A few persons who have majority of shares of different companies agree to join together so that the business units can easily be combined.

Types of Combinations

Combinations may be of different forms, but they are classified into four main categories - (i) Horizontal Combination, (ii) Vertical Combination, (iii) Lateral Combination, and (iv) Diagonal Combination.

Horizontal Combination. It is also known as ' parallel ' or ' unit ' or ' trade ' combination. Under this, concerns carrying on the trade of the same line join hands with the object of eliminating compention, achievement of large scale production and reduction in the cost of production. They are most similar in character and compete on the same line. A combination of four cotton mills doing similar business belongs to the category of horizontal combination. Associated Cement Company Ltd., The Indian Jute Mills Association and the Indian Cotton Mills Federation are examples in point. This can be illustrated in the given diagram.

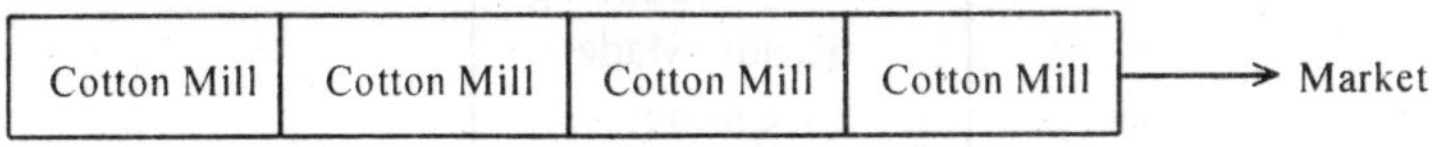

Cotton Mill	Cotton Mill	Cotton Mill	Cotton Mill	→ Market

When such units join together they can carry on restrictions on the supply of product, fixation of a common price, selling in a cooperative basis and other adjustments of similar nature and thus avoid the intensity of competition. They can derive economies of large scale production by making common purchases of raw materials, pooling resources for research, standardisation of products, credit at soft terms, organising common advertising campaigns in place of wasteful competitive advertising, effective use of waste, transport economies, engaging top brains in management and distribution of products.

But in actual practice, it has been found that such combinations lead to monpoly and they can exploit the consumers. It does not guarantee market of the products nor it can ensure supply of raw materials at the time of scarcity.

Vertical Combination. It is also termed as ' sequence ' or industry ' combination. In the vertical combination, the combining units represent different successive stages of production either in the same industry or various industries connected in a sequence. In the words of Haney, vertical combination unites organisations which are on different planes and which represent the successive stages or ' trades ' within an industry. The organisations combined are not competing side by side, but stand end to end, the one receiving the products of the other as its own material. In other words, the combination is devised in such a manner that the finished products of one concern is the raw materials of the other. For instance, if a cotton textile industry, cotton ginning factory combines with cotton spinning factory and spinning factory with weaving factory and the weaving factory combines with the factory producing readymade clothes. This would known as vertical combination. It can be explained with the following diagram :

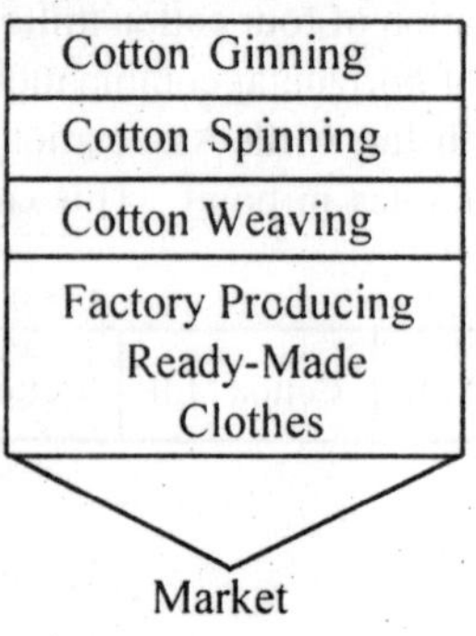

This type of combination is suited to those business units which posses the following characteristics :

(a) Where the finished product of one unit constitutes the raw material of another unit; (b) Where one process is complementary to the other; (c) Where balanced production is necessary like spinning and weaving; and (d) Where the quality of the product is important, thus necessitating a control over the supply of raw materials.

Vertical combinations eliminate the wasteful and unnecessary expense involved in carrying on the connected processes. They eliminate middleman's profit and are assumed of regular supply of raw material of required quality. But there are certain limitations also. The combining units may have to face a difficulty, if there is any dislocation in the intermediate processes. Such units cannot take the advantage of large scale production because the combining units produce different kinds of products. Such combinations are only possible in large industries.

Lateral Combination. It is also known as ' allied ' integration. When certain business concerns are engaged in manufacturing different kinds of products though they are allied in some way or the other, then that combination is known as lateral or allied combination. It is of two types - (i) Convergent lateral combination, and (ii) Divergent lateral combination.

Convergent Lateral Combination takes place when various business units combine together with a large concern to supply its requirements of raw materials or basic materials. Thus the different items manufactured by the combining units become the raw materials of a single major firm which can be regarded as the centre of this type of combination. An example is given below :

In the above diagram, there are four units namely - ink, types, cardboard and paper which work independently, but they are used as raw materials by the printing press.

Divergent Lateral Combination takes place when a single major concern supplies its product to the other combining units which use it as their raw materials. Thus the product of one business unit becomes the raw material of many other units. To the business concern which is supplying the raw material, the market is ready and to the other firms, the supply of raw materials is almost guaranteed. For example, a leather industry may combine with other units manufacturing shoes, suit-cases, belts, bags, sandles, etc. This can be explained with the help of the given diagram :

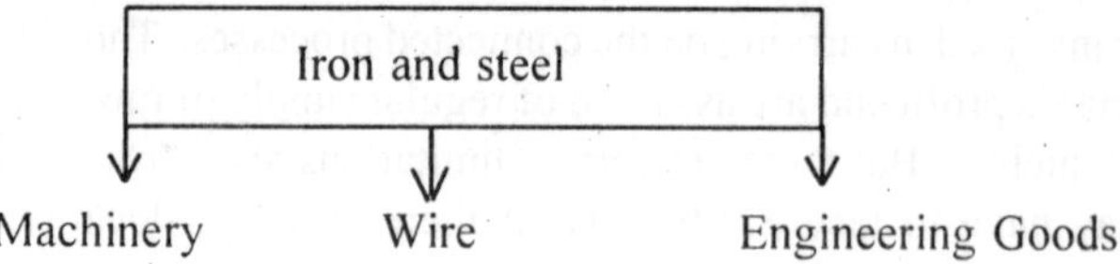

In the above diagram, the combination may be in iron and steel unit which supplies iron and steel to a number of allied firms for the manufacture of number of products like tubing, wire, machinery, automobiles, engineering goods, etc.

Diagonal Combination. It is also known as ' service ' combination. Diagonal combination takes place when a business unit supplying essential auxiliary goods and services combines with a unit of operating in the main line of production. For instance, a business unit producing coal combines with a unit producing electricity. Then this will be known as diagonal integration. Similarly, an advertising agency may combine with a large engineering firm, a transport company with a large agro-enterprise, etc. The main advantage of such combination is that the main business unit becomes self-sufficient in auxiliary goods and services and does not have to depend upon others for them.

Forms of Combinations

Today, in the business sphere, varieties of combinations are found. They have been classified as given below :

Association

An association is a union of some business enterprises. The business enterprises organise to form an association for achieving some common objective. The business units may remain members of the association as long as it serves their purpose and is convenient to them. The agreement between them should be informal and they should not be forced to follow a certain course of action.

Trade Association. A trade association is formed when business units engaged in a particular trade or industry come together for promotion of their interests. It is a non-profit organisation, voluntary in character and work to promote the economic interests of its members. They try to solve the problems of their members like procurement of raw materials, labour problems, transport bottlenecks, etc. These associations may be organised at the local level or state level or at the national level. The general purpose of trade associations is usually to improve the positions of their members by establishing better conditions in the trade and protecting the trade against adverse influences. The basic advantage of these associations is that they do not effect the functioning of the individual business units and they are free to do whatever they like. There are number of trade associations in the country. On the national level, there is All India Manufacturers' Organisation (AIMO), Association of Indian Engineering Industry (AIEI), Indian Sugar Mills Association (ISMA), and so on.

Chambers of commerce. A Chamber of Commerce is a voluntary association of merchants, fianciers, manufacturers and others engaged in the business in a particular area or region for promoting the general economic interests of all the members. They work to foster the growth and development of commerce and industry of the respective areas and regions in which they operate. Their ultimate object is to promote and protect the general trade interests of all the members irrespective of the trade they are engaged in. The basic difference between a trade association and chambers of commerce is that the former is concerned with the interests of a particular trade whereas Chambers of Commerce serves the interests of all businessmen engaged in various trades from the region it represents.

Some of the functions of Chambers of Commerce are :

(i) Collecting and passing on the information to the members;

(ii) Serving as the spokesman of the business community by commenting on various government policies like commenting on general budget, export and import policies, etc.,

(iii) Making representations to the government regarding the enactment of any legislation that will obstruct the business and aiding the government in framing a legislation that will help in the growth of trade and industry;

(iv) Settling disputes arising out of trade or commerce by means of arbitration;

(v) Organising trade and industries fairs within and outside the country;

(vi) Providing a platform for discussion, lectures, seminars etc. on matters of common interest; and

(vii) Sending delegations to various countries to promote trade.

Informal Agreements. The trade associations and chambers of commerce are usually formed to exchange views on matters of common interest. They may reach at certain agreements connected with trade associations. Such agreements are usually verbal agreements with the members reach an informal understanding regarding price regulations, division and control of market and other aspects concerning their trade. Such agreements kept secret and are known as " working agreements " or " price agreements ". Such agreements require the surrender of some freedom by the combining business units, though the individuality of conducting incorporation formalities to be conducted. No penal action is imposed if a member fails to abide by the rules framed by informal agreements.

Federation

L.H. Haney, has defined federation as " an alliance for mutual support, or a union by agreement of independent and autonomous powers for mutual benefit in relations external to any member and it implies that outside of such external relations the members retain their independence and autonomy. Thus a federation, both in political and business life, is relatively loose form of combination based upon mutual consent". Usually federations were formed when informal agreements could not achieve the objective of meeting competition in respect of price, output, etc.

Pools. A pool is a federal combination, based upon the federation of members who by mutual consent combine together to attain some common purpose and retain considerable autonomy over the conduct of their business units. It is entirely a separate form of business organisation.

It is more definite and highly developed form of combination than the agreement. According to the nature of activities, the pool is divided among the members on some predetermined conditions without effecting their separate existence. Usually under pooling, certain factors on the supply side or demand side are combined by a number of business units in order to regulate price. The agreement may also relate to the control of output, income distribution, etc. For example, an industrial pool is, " a form of business organisation established through federation of business units whose members seek a degree of control over prices by combining some factors on the price-making process in common aggregate and apportioning that aggregate among members". Thus the combining units not only agree to co-ordinate some of the activities by pooling method but some machinery is also arranged to see that the objectives with which such arrangement has been made are fulfilled.

Types of Pools. According to the nature and objects, pool organisations may be classified in the following classes :

(i) *Output pools.* The very name indicates that an output pool is formed to maintain prices at a reasonable levels by controlling and regulating the total output in the market. It aims at avoiding over production. It is formed by manufacturers of the same industry producing similar products. Every individual member is given a quota for production and the prices are fixed by the association.

(ii) *Traffic Pools.* Under this system, the traffic among the transportation companies is avoided by regulating the routes, area of operation and ports of call. They are generally formed by shipping companies and road transport agencies. The members are required to carry their business in fixed areas with uniform freight rates and fixed volume of business to be carried on. This helps in avoiding duplicate services and eliminating wasteful competition. About the Shipping Conferences, it has been said, "A Conference of this type is a combination shipping lines organised for the purpose of regulating and restricting competition on definite routes". The deferred rebate system is adopted to avoid competition for non-member lines.

(iii) *Market pools.* Under this system, the prices are maintained at a reasonable level and competition is avoided. The markets are divided among the members of the market pool. The division is made in three ways - (i) by customers; (ii) by products; and (iii) by territories.

Such type of pools influence the demand side of price determination. Such pools may not necessarily be found in our country but can be arranged at the international level.

(iv) *Income and profit pools.* Under this system, the members of the combining units may pool their entire income or total profits earned by them and after deducting the expenses the balance may be distributed among the members on an agreed basis. In the profit pool, the members pool their net earnings and after deducting the expenses of the pool, they are divided among the members on the pre-determined basis.

(v) *Patent Pools.* These pools have generated from U.S.A. Such pools are organised with aim of bringing together the patent rights held by various business concerns in the country. The General Electric Company formed the Ratio Corporation of America to take over the patents of numerous concerns. Similarly many American Oil Companies pooled together their refining patent rights.

(vi) *Export Pools.* Such pools are organised by the exporters of a country to meet the competition of their counterparts in other countries. Under such pooling arrangements, the association fixes the price, divides the available shipping space among the members, frames rules and regulations regarding packaging and maintains strict quality control of the goods meant for export.

(vii) *Price Pools.* Under this system, the members of the pooling association enter an agreement to fix price of goods and services. For fixing the prices, usually, the ' basing point system ' is used. Under this system, a certain place is fixed as the basing point where a certain price is ascertained. Then the price of the produce anywhere else would be ascertained on the basis of the price fixed at the basing point plus transport and other charges from the basing point to the place of delivery. If the area covered is very large, then several basing points may be ascertained and then it is called 'multiple basing point system'.

There are numerous advantages of pools. Some of them are as follows :

(a) It is formed easily and without expense; (b) It does not lead to over-capitalisation as it does not require raising of capital; (c) It does not affect the internal functioning of the business units; (d) Pools help in stabilising the prices and trade conditions; (e) There is lot of flexibility and adjustments that can be made under changed circumstances; (f) It helps in eliminating competition among the members.

On the other hand, pools are not free from limitations. They may be as follows :

(a) It is unstable form of organisation; (b) It reduces initiative in the management; (c) They often lead to monopolies which are detrimental to the interest of the customers; (d) They fix the price and regulate the output which may lead to hardships to the consumers.

Cartels : The greatest development of cartels took place in Germany, where it was termed as " Kartells ". It is a pool with which some common sales agency is attached. It is a device to secure monopoly of the market. According to the definition given by Von Beckereth, " A cartel is a voluntary agreement of capitalistic enterprise of the same branch for a regulation of the sales market with a view to improve the profitableness of its member's business". The basic aim of the cartels is to dominate the market by eliminating competition. The federation of dealers fixes the price, pools the output and allocates production quotas. Besides this, it establishes a sales agency (known as syndicate) to which the outputs is sold.

There are many types of cartels. They may be formed to fulfil different aims and objectives. Term Fixing cartels regulate the terms and conditions of sales such as conditions of delivery, mode of payment, place of delivery, transportation, etc. Price fixing cartels regulate the prices of the goods of their members. No member can sell below the fixed price. Market assigning cartels allot certain markets to each producer. Zonal or territorial cartels assign all customers or buyers within a region to an individual or a group of producers. Quota fixing cartels allocate certain output quota to every member and he cannot increase the output. This is done to restrict the supply. Super or international cartels are formed under an agreement cartels of one country and the cartels of another country.

Cartels which have a common selling agency come to form a different type of organisation known as ' Syndicate '. A syndicate is established to perform the economic function of distribution of goods. A syndicate is a method of pooling products, produced by the member of business firms without interfering within the internal functioning of individual member concerns. A syndicate may take the form of a joint stock company. All the members sell their products to the syndicate at a base price covering the cost of production. Sales are, however, made to the syndicate at a higher price called accounting prices. The profits earned by the syndicate are shared by the member firms in proportion to their quotas. Thus the syndicate assumes risk, takes the responsibility of selling the products and commands complete monopoly so far as supply side is concerned.

The cartels offer certain advantages which are as follows :

(i) Each producer is able to secure at least a reasonable profit; and (ii) The producers concentrate on the production side only while the selling aspect is done by the syndicate. Thus it saves them from advertising and transportation expenses.

But the cartels suffer from certain limitations. They are :

(i) The creation of cartels leads to monopoly and the consumers are exploited by them; (ii) The cartels may permit certain inefficient units to function thus bringing down the total efficiency; (iii) They may also fail to stabilise demand or arrest fluctuations on demand.

Partial Consolidation

Under such combinations, the combining business units surrender the freedom for all practical purposes to the combined organisation, but retain their individual entitles. The various types of partial consolidations are given below :

Trusts : They were formed to eliminate the shortcomings of pooling arrangements. It aims at centralised direction and management. It is defined as, " A form of business combination established through temporary consolidation, in which the stockholders of the constitutent organisations under a trust agreement transfer a controlling amount of their stock to a board of trustees in exchange for a trust certificate. These trust certificates show their equitable interests in the income of the combinations". Thus we can see from the definition that the stock-holders of the constituent organisations transfer a controlling amount of their stock to a Board of Trustees as per agreement. The holders of trust certificates are known as beneficiaries. Trusts are also established for religious or charitable purposes and are known as common trusts. A business trust means an agreement by which the business is entrusted to the care of trustees by a number of business concerns. In such cases, the owners of the business become the beneficiaries. In business trusts, the property is not transferred to the trustees but is retained by these units.

There is another form of trust known as the ' Voting Trust ' under which the majority of the stock-holders may transfer their stock or a right to receive dividend direct from the company will be retained by them, while the voting right will be given to the trustees. Therefore, it is known as voting trust.

The trust form of combination possesses the following advantages :

(i) They have proved to be more stable and shown more continuity than the pools and cartels; (ii) The trust brings about complete centralisation of direction and management of the various companies joining it; (iii) It facilitates in obtaining the advantages of economies of management, sales, purchases and administration and eliminates the duplication of plants thus bringing about reduction in costs; and (iv) It makes possible to have a huge aggregate of capital.

The trusts, however, suffer from certain limitations also :

(i) It is difficult to form a trust; (ii) It is inflexible because it cannot be changed so easily; (iii) It may lead to over capitalisation which has its own problems; and (iv) It may lead to monopoly and exploit customers by charging different prices in different markets.

Holding Companies. Holding companies came into being after the trusts were declared illegal in U.S.A. It is defined, as " a form of business organisation (established through partial or temporary consolidation) which is created for the purpose of combining other corporations, by owning a controlling amount of their stock". The Companies Act, 1956, defines a holding company as " any company, which directly or indirectly through the medium of another company either holds more than half of the equity share capital or controls the composition of the Board of Directors of some other companies ". Thus a holding company controls the majority of the shares of other company and such other company is known as a subsidiary of the holding company. The subsidiary companies are independent and have their own name and seal but they are effectively controlled by the holding company. Under one holding company, there can be any number of subsidiary companies.

Types. They can be of the following types :

(i) *Primary of Parent Holding Company.* It is at the top of the holding company structure and is not a subsidiary of any other company. It has a number of subsidiaries under its control.

(ii) *Offspring or Consolidated Holding Company.* It is formed to unite a number of existing companies which become its subsidiaries.

(iii) *Intermediary Holding Company.* It is a holding company which controls its subsidiaries but is itself a subsidiary company controlled by another holding company.

(iv) *Pure Holding Company.* Such holding companies are established to control the subsidiaries. They do not interfere the functioning of its subsidiaries. They are also known as non-trading companies.

(v) *Mixed Holding Company.* It is a company which carries manufacturing on its own but at the same time it controls its subsidiaries of similar nature.

(vi) *Investment Holding Company.* It is not interested in controlling the subsidiaries but aims at making profits by financing different industrial units through under writing reorganisation.

A holding company has the following advantages :

(i) Its formation is easy and one has to simply purchase the shares of a company until it comes to a controlling amount; (ii) Business risks are easily eliminated by undertaking projects through its subsidiaries; (iii) The centralisation of control and direction of subsidiaries helps in obtaining economies of large scale operation and organisation; (iv) It is possible to maintain secrecy of holding company's control over other companies which may be advantageous to the investors; (v) It helps in pooling the vast capital resources for use in business; and (vi) Each subsidiary company retains its identity and if there is any goodwill attached with its name, it will not be lost through combination.

The holding company has the following disadvantages too :

(i) The financial liability of the members of the holding company is very small of their financial power and hence they have no responsibility for their economic power; (ii) It may suffer from over-capitalisation which may lead to frauds, manipulation, etc.; (iii) A holding company may exploit its subsidiaries by forcing them to make excessive charge for specialised services that are unnecessary for the subsidiaries or by compelling them to make unwarranted dividend payments by neglecting depreciation and maintenance or by diverting the funds of one company to another without looking in the interests of the companies; (iv) There is every possibility that the secrets may be misused by the Directors especially when the value of shares of the subsidiaries fluctuates according to the rate of dividend; and (v) It may form a secret monopoly which may be determental to the interest of the consumers.

Community of Interests. According to Owens, it is " a harmonious relationship established between two or more companies as a result of the ownership of their stock by the same persons ". Haney has defined it as " a form of business organisation in which without any formal central administration, the business policy of several companies is controlled by a group of common stockholders or Directors". This is a special type of combination. The community of interest is created by appointing the Directors of one company on the Board of other companies. When a group of shareholders control shares in a number of companies, they shall be able to elect majority of Directors on the Boards of various companies. Through these Directors, the group of shareholders can develop harmonious relationship in the functioning of these companies. All the companies will function as independent units but as a matter of fact, there is community of interests involved which unites them together.

In our country, community of interest was created by the managing agency system under which one agency could manage a number of companies under an agreement. But this system has been declared illegal since 1970.

The community of interests may take the following three forms :

(i) Interlocking directorate and multiple directorships.
(ii) Managerial integration.
(iii) Financial integration.

If one person holds a number of directorships subject to the limit imposed by the Companies Act, 1956, it is known as ' Multiple directorships ' Whereas ' Interlocking Directorate ' simplies that when a few businessman with controlling shares in a number of competing concerns become directors in all these concerns and are able to frame the policies of these companies accordingly.

The basic advantage of community of interest is that it can be created without any formality and publicity. But it has some limitation also. It leads to concentration of power in the hands of few business leaders who may exploit the resources of the companies for their own benefit. They may not be able to function effectively because the directors may lack mutual confidence and goodwill. It chiefly works secretly which may not be beneficial to the companies. It usually leads to financial manipulation and there is a general decline in the efficiency of management.

Complete Consolidation

Notes has defined complete consolidation, " as a part of a plan for combining competing corporate interest, a purchasing corporation is organised with a share capital sufficiently large for the purpose, which purchases the properties, plants, stock-in-trade, goodwill of the several corporations and result of this process becomes the absolute owner of the properties of all the corporation ". Haney has defined it as, " a form of business organisation which is established by the outright purchase of the properties of constituent organisations and the merging or amalgamating of such properties into a single business unit ". In other words, complete consolidation is the unification in which the business units loose their independent legal entity. Complete consolidation can be achieved in two ways viz. ' merger ' and ' amalgamation '.

Merger. A merger is a consolidation in which one business unit merges with another unit and latter one retains its status and identity and no new concern is formed. For example, if two units, 'X' and 'Y' decide to get themselves absorbed with the third unit 'Z' the legal entity and existence of 'X' and 'Y' units is no more, and only 'Z' remains it will be denoted as merger.

Amalgamation. When two or more business units combine together to form a new company with the liquidation of previous ones, it is called amalgamation. For example, if two units, 'A' and 'B' combine to form a new company 'C' and the two comapnies 'A' and 'B' cease to exist, it will be called amalgamation.

Some of the advantages of complete consolidation are as follows :

(i) It is the simplest form of combination and brings about

directness in organisation; (ii) It brings about economy in management and better managerial ability is available; (iii) It brings about economies of large scale operations like production, marketing, financing etc.; (iv) It facilitates pooling of capital resources of the units which may be helpful in strengthening the financial condition of the combined unit; (v) It combines responsibility with power; and (vi) From the legal point of view, it does not violate the provisions of Companies Act.

But it also suffers from certain limitations :

(i) Its formation is very expensive; (ii) It requires to have consent of three-fourth majority of shareholders of the constituent companies to form a complete consolidation; (iii) Nothing can be kept as secret; (iv) A combining units after consolidation become too big to be effectively and efficiently managed; (v) The combining units loose their identity and hence whatever goodwill is developed is lost; and (vi) it may lead to over-capitalisation. The purchasing unit may spend vast sums of money on the assets which may prove to be unproductive later and suitable returns may not be available.

Advantages of Combination

Combination of business units offers various advantages which are given as follows :

1. It develops a feeling of co-operation, understanding and mutual adjustment which is difficult to achieve and the firms are competing among themselves only. The combined units are in a better position to solve their problems more easily and speedily which is not possible in individual units.

2. It eliminates wasteful and cut-throat competition and makes the best possible use of all the available resources.

3. All economies of large scale production can be easily secured. Standardisation of products, processes and materials can be had, by-products, processes and materials can be had, by-products can be utilised, higher efficiency of plant and machinery can be secured. Effective control over raw materials and supplies can be exercised. There can also be economies of bulk purchases of raw material. All these things help to reduce the cost of production and maximise profits.

4. It helps in achieving economy in the distribution of goods by taking up collective marketing of goods, advertisement and publicity, development of international markets, etc. All these things lead to increased sales turnover and lowering of overhead costs.
5. They are able to raise credit easily by bringing about efficiency in expenses, ploughing back of more profits, etc. It also enhances the credit-worthiness of such units and it becomes easy to obtain loans from the financial institutions.
6. The combinations offer stability and ability to withstand trade cycles.
7. Orders can be received at the central office and distributed among the producing units according to the states from which they emanate. Thus, goods can be despatched to customers from the nearest producing unit, thereby saving freight expenses and avoiding cross freights.

Disadvantages of Combination

There are numerous disadvantages of combination of which some are discussed below :

1. Combinations sooner or later leads to monopoly. Cartels are important medium through which the monopolies extend their domination from the national to the international market. The holding company or the merger is the highest form of monopoly combination. Monopolistic combinations charge monopoly prices, exploit the suppliers by paying them rock bottom prices.
2. They usually exploit the consumers by charging exorbitant prices.
3. It leads to concentration of power and wealth in the hands of few. This is anti-social because it leads to rich becoming richer and the poor becoming poorer.
4. It may lead to inefficiency. The combining units may become unmanageable size, thus leading to general reduction in efficiency. Some combinations are unstable because the agreements may be secret and difficult to enforce in the court of law. Also because the directors attached to many concerns are not able to give due attention to all the units and, therefore, the efficiency of the concern may suffer.

5. They may also exploit the labour under the grab of rationalisation and scientific management. There may be displacement of labour due to modernisation or automation.
6. A monopolistic organisation has great power and they bribe the legislators, executives, etc. and can easily secure favourable decisions and actions. They may adversely affect government policies due to finance monopolism.

The Control over Monopoly

As we have seen from the above discussion that combinations give rise to monopoly which create harmful effects on the different sections of the economy. Therefore, it was considered to develop such measures to control monopoly. The following ways and means for controlling monopoly are given below :

1. Legislation has been tried with mixed success in many countries. In our country, Monopolies and Restrictive Trade Practices Act was passed in 1969 which came into force Ist June, 1970.
2. Development of consumer organisatoins to fight against monopoly.
3. Publicity to expose evils of monopoly and to create strong public opinion against monopoly.
4. Strong steps and measures to encourage fair and healthy competition in the market place to prevent exploitation of workers, consumers and community as a whole.

Nationalisation

If all the above measures fail, then this is the last resort to get rid of monopoly combination. The Government declared the managing agency system as illegal and thus abolished the monopoly business. It nationalised the major commercial banks and thus suppressed the financial monopoly of Indian business. Today all financial institutions, life insurance business, general insurance, oil companies, etc. are under the control of the Government. They all have been brought under the ownership and management of the State sector in order to safeguard the public interest.

Government and Monopoly

Economic power with reference to industrial organisation means possession of creative energy or strength of factor or production such as land, labour, capital and organisation. And concentration of economic power means bringing all such power so generated by the factors of production under common control either in the field of production of distribution of product or service.

Article 39 of the Constitution of India deals with the Directive Principles of State Policy which states, " that the ownership and control of the material resources of the community are so distributed as best to subserve the common good". Added to this, the Indian Parliament has accepted the " Socialistic pattern of Society " as the objectives of future social and economic policies. Thus to control the growth of monopoly, the Government has made provisions under various legislations such as Companies Act 1956, Industries (Development and Regulation) Act, 1951, the Capital Issues (Control) Act, 1947 etc. The Industrial Policy Resolution, 1956 states that, " it is urgent to reduce disparities in income and wealth which exit today and to prevent private monopolies and the concentration of economic power in different fields in the hands of a small number of individuals. Accordingly, the state will assume a predominate and direct responsibility for setting up new industrial undertaking ". In view of this, the Government of India has started setting up public enterprises in all fields with a view to breaking the monopolies in the private sector.

Mahalanobis Committee

In October 1960, this Committee was appointed by the Planning Commission under the Chairmanship of Prof. P.C. Mahalanobis on the statement made by the then Prime Minister, Pandit Jawahar Lal Nehru, in the Lok Sabha that it was desirable for constituting an expert committee to enquire into the nature of distribution of additional incomes generated. The committee was called " Distribution of Income and Levels of Living Committee ". The committee was asked to - (i) review the changes in levels of living during the First and Second Plan periods; (ii) study recent trends in the distribution of income and wealth in particular; (iii) ascertain the extent to which the operation of the economic system has resulted in concentration of wealth and means of production. The first part of the report was submitted in 1964. The committee gave a broad connotation to the concept of concentration and analysed the share of large companies in total share capital and their reliance on public financial institutions.

Monopolies Enquiry Commission

On the basis of the recommendations made by the Mahalanobis Committee, the Government of India constituted a five man commission in April, 1964 under the Chairmanship of Mr. K.C. Das Gupta. The commission was asked to inquire into the extent and effect of concentration of economic power in private hands and the prevalence of monopolistic and restrictive practices in important sector of economic activity. It was also asked to suggest such legislative and other measures that might be necessary in the light of such enquiry to regulate such concentration. The commission submitted its report at the end of October 1965.

The Commission analysed the causes of concentration of economic power and reported that such causes were many and varied. The main causes were supply of managerial skills by the managing agency system in different forms, centralised control through the joint stock companies, protecting and aid to industrialists to produce war materials during World War II, the passing on of several British concerns into the hands of wealthy Indian industrialists, foreign exchange allocation, licencing policy, control of capital issues, regulation of imports, foreign collaboration, assistance of banks and other financial institutions to the big business houses were all responsible.

The Commission observed that the dangers from concentrated economic power and monopoly do exist to a large extent either at present or potentially. To avoid or minimise these dangers, it recommended certain legislative and non-legislative measures. The important recommendation made by the Commission is that " a permanent body should be set up with the duty and responsibility for exercising vigilance and for taking action to protect the country against the dangers that we think do exist ". This body may be known as Monopolies and Restrictive Trade Practices Commission with powers to institute an enquiry in connection with any matters relating to monopolistic and restrictive trade practices. The Commission felt that the Director of Investigation should have the power to institute an enquiry on receipt of complaint from the public or on his own. If the charges are proved that restrictive practice is being carried on, then the Commission would issue orders to discontinue such practice. The non-legislative measures recommended by the Commission include (a) non-acceptance of the election funds by the political parties from big houses; (b) removal of corruption from the administrative machinery; (c) streamlining the licensing policy so that licences may be obtained easily; (d) taking care in the issue of import licences; (e) promoting small scale industries; and (f) encouraging consumer co-operative societies.

Monopolies and Restrictive Practices Act, 1969

On the recommendations of the Monopolies Inquity Commission, a Bill seeking to set up of a Monopolies and Restrictive Trade Practice Commission was introduced in Rajya Sabha in August, 1967. The Bill was passed by the Parliament in 1969 and came into effect from Ist July, 1970. The objectives of the Act were to ensure that operation of the economic system does not result in the concentration of economic power to the common detriment and to prohibit such monopolistic and restrictive trade practices are injurous to the welfare of the public.

The Act provides for the appointment of Monopolies and Restrictive Trade Practices Commission by the Central Government. It will have a minimum of two and a maximum of eight members and its Chairman will be a judge of the Supreme Court or of a High Court. It also provides for the appointment of the Director of Investigation and the Registrar of Restrictive Trade Practices, to assist the Commission in its work. The duty of the Director is to carry out preliminary investigations into the complaints of restrictive trade practices and the Registrar would look after the registration of restrictive trade agreements.

According to the Act, a " dominant undertaking " means an undertaking which either by itself or alongwith other undertakings produces, supplies, distributes or otherwise controls not less than one-third of the total goods of any description produced, supplied or distributed in India or provides or otherwise controls not less than one-third of any services rendered in India.

A ' Monopolistic Trade Practice ' is defined as any practice which has or may have the effect of maintaining prices at an unreasonable level through curtailment of control of the production or supply of certain goods or services or unreasonably preventing or lessening competition in the production or supply or services or limiting technical development or capital investment to the common detriment or allowing the quality of any goods produced, supplied or distributed in India to deteriorate.

A ' Restrictive Trade Practice ' is one which has the effect of preventing distorting or restricting competition in any manner. It particularly includes a practice that tends to obstruct the flow of capital or resources into the stream of production or that which tends to bring about manipulation of prices, or conditions of delivery or to effect the flow to supplies in the market for goods and services in such a manner as to impose on the consumers unjustified costs or restrictions.

A ' Monopolistic Undertaking ' means a dominant undertaking or an undertaking which together with other independent undertakings control the production or supply or distribution of not less than one-half of any services that are rendered in India and indulges in any monopolistic trade practice.

The Act does not apply to Government companies, any public corporation, trade union, and undertaking the control of which has been taken over by person or persons in pursuance of any authorisation made by the Central Government and Co-operative Societies.

References

1. L.H. Haney : Business Organisation and Combination
2. B.F. Shields : The Evolution of Industrial Organisation
3. R.N. Ownes : Business Organisation and Combination
4. L.H. Haney : Business Organisation and Combination

6

Industrial Estates

Role of Infrastructure in Industrial Development

In a developing country like India there is an imperative need of basic infrastructure facilities for a sustained industrial development. It has been observed that while planning for the establishment of an enterprise emphasis is given to the financial and technical aspects and very little attention is given to the development for infrastructural facilities. Infrastructure facilities is also termed as ' social overhead capital.' It includes numerous facilities besides transportation, electricity, water supply and other public services. The main constituents of infrastructural facilities are as follows :[1]

1. **Transport :**
   (i) Roads
   (ii) Railways
   (iii) Shipping
   (iv) Ports and Harbours
   (v) Airport

2. **Communication :**
   (i) Post
   (ii) Telegraph
   (iii) Telephone
   (iv) Radio
   (v) Television
   (vi) Cinema

3. **Energy :**
   (i) Coal
   (ii) Electricity - (a) Hydel; (b) Thermal; (c) Nuclear
   (iii) Wind
   (iv) Solar
   (v) Oil
   (vi) Gas
   (vii) Bio-Gas

4. **Intermediatory Goods :**
   (i) Minerals
   (ii) Steel
   (iii) Metals other than steel
   (iv) Basic Chemicals
   (v) Fertilizers and Pesticides
   (vi) Machinery and Machine Tools

5. **Natural Resources :**
   (i) Irrigation
   (ii) Forests

6. **Science and Technology :**
   (i) Teaching
   (ii) Basic and Applied Research
   (iii) National Laboratories

7. **Information Systems :**
   (i) Mass Media
   (ii) Libraries
   (iii) Fairs and Exhibitions
   (iv) Books and Journals
   (v) Computers

8. **Finance and Banking :**
   (i) Money Market
   (ii) Capital Market

9. **Human Resource Development :**
   (i) Health and Community Welfare
   (ii) Education facilities

Industrial Estates :

The concept of Industrial Estate emerged at the end of the 19th century and early of 20th century. It was only after the Great Depression it started picking up. But it was only after the World War II that it started gaining popularity throughout the world. The meaning of Industrial Estate varies from place to place. In USA, these estates are termed as Technology Parks.

However, Dr. Willium Bredo[2] defines it as, "An Industrial Estate is a tract of land which is sub-divided and developed according to a comprehensive plan for the use of a community of industrial enterprises.

Dr. P.C. Alexander[3] defines it as, "a group of factories constructed on an economic scale in suitable size with facilities of water, transport, electricity, steam, bank, post office, canteen, watch and ward, first aid and provided with special arrangements for technical guidance and common service facilities."

The United Nations has defined[4] Industrial Estate as, "a planned clustering of industrial enterprises offering standard factory buildings erected in advance of demand and a variety of service and facilities to the occupants."

On analysing the above definitions, four important points emerge. They are :

- It is well organised and pre-determined effort in construction and selection and establishment of industrial units.
- Construction of industrial buildings in advance of demand thereby clearly indicating the industrialisation and development.
- Standardization in the construction of industrial buildings.
- Provision of various services and facilities to the occupants such as Tool Room, facilities for storing raw materials and finished products, etc.

In India, there has been development of Industrial Estates in various parts of the country in order to speed-up industrialisation and promote Small Scale Industries. The basic objectives[5] are :

(1) To develop the small scale industries by providing facilities, assistance and guidance to small industrialists at every stage of establishment, operation and management.

(2) To decentralize industries from big cities, urban areas and highly industrialized centres to other places.

(3) Encouragement of industries and employment in industrial backward

regions.

(4) To provide all facilities (infrastructural and others) at one place for the smooth running of industry.

(5) To provide entrepreneurs built up factory sheds so that they can start their industry without any inconvenience or delay.

(6) To create conducive and favourable industrial climate for the rapid industrialisation of the country.

Types of Industrial Estates[6] :

Industrial Estates are multi-purpose in nature. They are of various types. A brief description is given below :

(a) **Industrial Estates for General Purposes :**

These are estates where all types of industries are encouraged for admission which is made possible by the provision of standard factory buildings and common service facilities.

(b) **Ancillary Industrial Estate :**

These are estates in which different small-scale units manufacture component part and stores, which are required by a large industrial undertaking, on a sub-contracting basis. These are located generally in close proximity to the large industrial unit to facilitate technical supervision and assistance and economic transport.

(3) **Single Trade Industrial Estates :**

These provide factory accommodation to industrial units belonging to the same trade, such as leather, wood, diamonds, etc.

(4) **Functional Industrial Estates :**

These are estates in which the functions of one industry are sub-divided among a number of small scale units located at one place, each functioning according to a co-ordinated manufacturing programme.

(5) **Industrial Estates Based in Metropolitan Cities, Small Towns and Rural Areas :**

The business environment of metropolitan cities makes small industries viable to grow and prosper. Such cities have a well developed infrastructure and there is no shortage of trained labour and markets for their products.

Industrial Estates in small towns are established for dispersal of industries so as to remove regional imbalances. This helps in developing infrastructural facilities in towns, which would otherwise have remained backward.

Industrial Estates in rural areas are established for rural industrialisation and provision of alternative employment opportunities to seasonally unemployed agricultural workers. Sometimes these estates are developed to support a traditional craft of skill in a particular area.

(6) Government, Private and Assisted Industrial Estates :

Usually the Industrial Estates are developed and managed by the Government to promote industrialisation and also for dispersal of industries. But recently the Government has encouraged the private sector to participate in the development of industrial estates. It may be in the form of a company or on co-operative basis. The Government helps them by providing land at cheap rates, low electricity tariffs, etc.

The small-scale industries in the Industrial Estates in or country are engaged in manufacturing a host of items, many of them are manufactured with the help of modern technology.

References

1. Rao, V.K.R.V., "Infrastructure and Economic Development" Commerce, Annual Number (1980) page-9.
2. Bredo Willium, Industrial Estates : Tool for Industrialisation, California International Industrial Development Centre, Standard Research Institute, USA (1960) p-1.
3. Alexander P.C., Industrial Estates in India, Small Industries Training Institute, Hyderabad, India (1963), pp 5-8.
4. UNIDO, Policies and Programmes for the Establishment of Industrial Estates, International Symposium on Industrial Development, Athens (1967).
5. Mehta, Anil., Organisation and Working of Industrial Estates, Problems and Prospects, Deep and Deep Publications, New Delhi, pp 34-35.
6. Ibid, pp 35-40.

7

Industrial Productivity

Industrial Productivity is the key of economic development. Since ages, agriculture formed the mainstay of all economic activities. It was only after the Industrial Revolution that the man started observing faster changes. Though agriculture continues to play a major role in the India economy and its importance cannot be under-rated, industrial productivity plays a pivotal role in economic transformation of the country.

Producers or Manufacturers are interested in achieving the maximum output as against minimum input. This is because the wants are unlimited and the resources are scarce. Thus, where maximum results are achieved by using minimum resources is termed as efficiency. Thus productivity is a relationship between output and input.

Thus we can say that productivity -

(a) is a relationship between input and output;
(b) measures the effectiveness of the management under changing environment;
(c) measures the efficiency of the resources used in production; and
(d) measures achievement against targets.

Productivity is multi-dimensional in nature. It strives for greater efficiency; optimum utilisation of the capital invested, physical and human resources; and full capacity utilisation of machines used. Productivity enhances efficiency of performance in every field, contributes significantly in raising the standard of living and satisfies the social needs of the community as a whole.

Productivity is often confused with production. Productivity is the ratio of output against the inputs. Output can be products or services and inputs cover all forms of resources - capital, physical and human. Productivity incorporates production and measures the rates of production. A general measure of productivity is :

$$\text{Productivity} = \frac{\text{Output}}{\text{Input}}$$

Definitions :

According to European Productivity Council, "Productivity is an attitude of mind. It is the mentality of progress, of the constant improvement of that which exists. It is the certainty of being able to do better than yesterday and continuously. It is a constant adoptation of economic and social life to changing conditions. It is the continual effort to apply new techniques and methods. It is the faith in human progress."

According to International Labour Organisation, "The ratio between the volume of output as measured by production indices and the corresponding volume of labour input as measured by indices and the corresponding volume of labour input as measured by employment indices."

According to Peter F. Drucker, "Productivity means a balance between all factors of production that will give the maximum output with the smallest effort."

Measurement of Productivity :

From the above definitions of productivity, we can say that it is the combination of effectiveness and efficiency which determines the productivity. Effectiveness is concerned with performance whereas efficiency is related with resources utilisation.

Productivity Ratio :

$$\text{Productivity} = \frac{\text{Output Obtained}}{\text{Input Used}}$$

$$\text{Productivity} = \frac{\text{Performance Achieved}}{\text{Resources Consumed}}$$

$$\text{Productivity} = \frac{\text{Effectiveness}}{\text{Efficiency}}$$

Measurement of productivity with the above ratio can be categorised as :

(a) Single/Partial Factor Productivity
(b) Total Factors Productivity.

(a) **Single/Partial Factor Productivity Measure :**

It is the average productivity of a particular factor e.g. productivity of land, labour, capital employed etc.

(i) Land Productivity $= \dfrac{\text{Net Output}}{\text{Number acres of Land}}$

(ii) Labour Productivity $= \dfrac{\text{Output}}{\text{Labour (manhours spent)}}$

(iii) Machine Productivity $= \dfrac{\text{Total production in length weight etc.}}{\text{Machine hours worked}}$

(iv) Material Productivity $= \dfrac{\text{Weight or Volume or Number or length of finished goods}}{\text{Weight, Volume, number of length or raw material used}}$

(b) **Total Factors Productivity Measure :**

Usually a single or partial productivity measure may not be able to give a correct picture where there are numerous inputs with various combinations. Therefore, a weighted combination of all input factors such as labour, capital, equipment, fuel and various other input factors used in the process of production is termed as total factors productivity measure.

Total Productivity $= \dfrac{\text{Total Output}}{\text{Labour + Capital + Raw Materials + Other Miscellaneous factors}}$

Productivity is a measure of how the given resources are utilised to achieve the pre-determined objectives.

Difficulties in Measuring Productivity :

(a) The single factor productivity measure is not a clear indicator because in the production process there are numerous inputs of varying degrees and they are used in combinations which create difficulties.

(b) Productivity ratio does not reflect the quality of the output.

(c) Time is an important variable. A particular model suited at a particular time period may not be suitable after a specified period.

(d) Usuage of different production techniques, tends the data to become uncomparable.

(e) There are certain factors which are not computable but have a major effect on the productivity. The impact of socio-economic and political system effects productivity but is very difficult to measure.

(f) It is difficult to measure productivity of intangible goods.

Determinants of Productivity[1]

There are numerous factors which affect industrial productivity. These factors are complex and interwoven that it is very difficult to evaluate the influence of each individual factor on the overall productivity of an individual unit. It is rather difficult to assess whether increased productivity is due to efficient utilisation of plant and machinery or intensive efforts of human resources on the application of latest technology and using better methods of production. However the factors which affect productivity are discussed below :

1. *Technological Factors :* There is no denying fact that advances in science and technology and its application to production has largely contributed to the increase in production, continuous technological improvements keep the productivity rising. According to M.M. Mehta, "the most dominant factors that have contributed to the spectacular advances in industrial productivity are the application of mechanical power, varied improvements in equipment, ranging from the steady accumulation of small changes to the introduction of highly specialised and semi-automatic and automatic machines, of parallel improvements in the organisation of production processes, from more efficient layout to assembly line production, better and more efficient integration of plant and machinery, the steady flow of raw materials and components, the greater degree of specialisation both of work and output and more efficient co-ordination and integration of productive process."

The major reasons for technical advancement are the availability of plentiful opportunities for technical and scientific research, the application of the fruits of these researches to processes of production, the willingness of the management to accept the advances made, availability of the technically trained personnel and so on.

2. *Financial Factors :* Financial factors play a very major role in enhancing industrial productivity. Modern technology is highly capital intensive and its application requires abundance of capital. It must be available for meeting fixed capital and working capital requirements. "It is a matter of common observation that where capital is relatively abundant and the borrowing facilities easily available, the firms will have greater incentives to adopt the new technical improvements and innovations than where such facilities are lacking. The movement of mechanisation has made the greatest progress where capital is relatively abundant and the supply of labour relatively scarce. Those countries that have lagged behind in the introduction of new technical improvements are those that are handicapped by relatively scarcity of capital and rigid banking laws."

3. *Labour Factor :* The worker or the labour occupies a distinct place in the production process and plays an important role in raising productivity. Productivity of labour depends on three sets of factors :

(i) The ability of the workers which includes factors like the physical ability, inherent and acquired skill, training and experience, aptitude and capacity and his intelligence and outlook.

(ii) The attitude and willingness of the worker are influenced by factors like the wages and incentives, social background, feeling of responsibility, political affinities and general outlook.

(iii) The working conditions and the environment greatly influence the labour productivity. It includes the factors like the layout of the working area, better lighting, ventilation, better air-conditioning, improved safety devices, types of tools, equipment etc. Application of ergonomics are very important to improve labour productivity.

4. *Natural Factors :* The natural factors such as physical, geographical or climatic have a considerable influence on industrial productivity. The relative importance of these factors depends on the nature and character of the industry, type of output, location, and to what extent these physical conditions can be controlled and modified.

5. *Managerial Factor :* There is need to emphasise the role of the managerial factor in raising the industrial productivity. Proper organisational set-up, qualified managerial personnel, use of modern management techniques, cordial human relations are all factors that help in raising the levels of productivity.

6. *Marketing Factor :* Productivity is not only concerned with the production of goods and services only but also with the marketing side. The market should be vast and stable otherwise there will be no investments. Mehta has rightly said, "Apart from the advantages derived from the fuller utilisation of plant and equipment, such as reduction in overhead costs and fixed charges, the stability of market stimulates investment and strengthens the morale of the workers, producers and investors alike." He further says that, "Generally speaking, productivity is higher in industries where there are fewer changes in tastes, designs, texture or quality and lower in those which specialise in variety products."

7. *Sociological Factors :* The social and moral values accepted by the society guide the habits and behaviour patterns of the people/concerned and consequently their productivity. The caste system, joint family system, occupational mobility, inter-regional mobility, attitude towards change, social responsibility of the management and workers are some of the factors affecting productivity.

8. *Government Factor :* The rules and regulations and the various determinants of the economic policy create an atmosphere for improving productivity. The policy of liberalisation has strengthened the Indian economy. The industrial policy has helped in bringing the latest technology available in the world. The Export-Import Policy has given a boost to our exports. These policies of the government greatly help in increasing productivity at all levels in different sectors of the economy. Besides the above there are other factors which influence Productivity like size of the plant; availability of Power; availability of raw materials; research and development; and office automation.

Productivity Movement in India :

The productivity movement in India started in the fifties with the arrival of teams of International Labour Organisation and later on the recommendations of Productivity Delegation to Japan and the First Seminar on Productivity in 1957, an autonomous body the National

Productivity Council (NPC) was formed in February 1958 with its head quarters in New Delhi. The major activities of NPC are :

1. Planning, organisation and presenting training programmes directly and through Local Productivity Councils and other bodies.
2. Organising Seminars and Conferences at local, regional, national and international levels.
3. Stimulation and promotion of productivity consciousness by dissemination of information relating to productivity.
4. Encouraging inter-plant visits which help in exchanging views on problems and their solutions.
5. Undertaking research into the problems of productivity.
6. Sponsoring teams of productivity studies abroad.
7. Inviting foreign technicians and productivity experts for guidance.
8. Publication of *Productivity, Productivity News,* NPC Information, booklets and books related to productivity, etc.
9. Fuel efficiency service.
10. Supporting the activities of Asian Productivity Organisation.

Reference

1. Based on M.M. Mehta, "Measurement of Industrial Productivity," World Press Ltd., Calcutta (1955).

8

Scientific Management

The growth in the national income of any country depends, to a major extent, on the application of sound management principles and practices. Management is an activity process of getting things done through an organisation and the efforts of other people. The basic aim of management is to provide dynamic leadership towards accomplishing the common socio-economic goals. Regardless of the activity to be performed, the management performs the following basic functions : planning, organising, motivating, and controlling. Whenever any work is to be accomplished by unified and co-operative human efforts, management becomes essential to impart direction to the group efforts towards a common purpose or objective. Now-a-days management is required not only in business, industrial and commercial activities, but on all human behaviour and activities.

Scientific management, as the name implies, means the application of the scientific methods for the solution of the problems of management. It is the use of scientific approach in solving the problems of management instead of depending on traditional methods or guess work. In the words of Frederick W. Taylor, the ' Father of scientific management movement ', it means " knowing exactly what you want men to do and seeing that they do it in the best and cheapest way ".

For a number of years in planning for the industry or a business the philosophy of management was that of following the traditional method of doing things or adopting practices followed by other firms or simply depending on individual intention or guess work supported by experience. But with the rapid changes in the production techniques ushered in by the Industrial Revolution there was tremendous growth on the scale of business operations which brought about fundamental changes in the industrial organisation. The Industrial Revolution brought about separation between ownership and control and the employee. This greatly expanded the responsibilities of management. A new philosophy of management capable of coping with the growing magnitude of management responsibilities was much needed. The scientific approach to management was the only answer to the growing need.

The origin of scientific management may be traced to as early as 1832, when Charles Babbage, a Professor of Mathematics at Cambridge University visited a number of factories in Europe and discussed the principles of scientific management in his book. " The Economy of Manufacturers " published in that year. But later, it was only F.W. Taylor who took interest in the application of scientific management acceptable university.

Scientific management was first applied in industries of R.S.A. by Frederick W. Taylor. He first took up a job as a machinist in an industrial establishment and then joined in Midvale Steel Company as a foreman. He rose to the position in different companies in different positions gave him opportunity to study the existing methods of production and their defects. He saw that the workers were wasting time while performing any task and they paid no attention to the wastage been done. Secondly the techniques used to carry out any manufacturing process was very crude. The tools and apparatus used were indifferently fitted and the labourers were doing work for which they were not suited. The managers were also not aware of their responsibilities for the delays and wastage. He conducted a number of experiments and published a number of papers on scientific management. He published two books ' Shop Management ' in 1903 and ' The Principles of Scientific Management ' in 1911.

Definition of Scientific Management

Scientific management has been defined by a number of writers. Taylor has defined it as ' knowing exactly what you want men to do and seeing that they do it in the best and cheapest way '. Another author Mr. Pearson defines scientific management as " that form of organisation and procedure in purposive collection effort which rests on principles or on policies determined emperically and casually by the process of trial and error". According to Dr. Tones, it is, " a body of rules, together with their appropriate expression in physical and administrative mechanisms and specialized executives, to be operated in co-ordination as a system for the achievements of a new strictness in the control and processes of production". On analysing the above definitions we can conclude that scientific management includes a number of elements concerned with business which are dynamic and constantly changing. Thus we can conclude in the words of Taylor that it involves, " science, not rule of thumb; harmony, not discard; co-operation, not individualism; maximum output in place of restricted output and the development of each man to his greatest efficiency and prosperity". Regarding the application of scientific management Taylor himself said that, " It can be applied with profit to the management of our homes, the management of business of our tradesmen, large and small; of our churches, our philanthropic institutions, our universities and our governmental departments."

Principles of Scientific Management

Taylor while developing his theory of scientific management stated a set of four principles of management :

1. The development of a science for each element of a man's work which will replace the old rule of thumb method.
2. The selection of the worker to be done on the scientific basis for each particular task, and then to train, teach and develop the worker whereas on the past the worker had to train himself as best as he could.
3. Co-operation of the management with the workers as to ensure all of the work being done in accordance with the principles of science which has been developed.
4. Equal division of work and equal division of responsibility between management and workers.

The principles of scientific management could be divided into the following four phases :

1. Mental revolution
2. Scientific selection of workers
3. Improvement in working methods
4. Organisational set-up

The above four phases are briefly discussed as follows :

Mental Revolution : The theory of mental revolution was developed by Taylor who said that the change in the mental attitude of both the workers and the management is very much necessary to implement scientific management. Usually the workers do not increase the output because they think that their interests are opposed to those of the management. The workers should realise that their efficiency will only increase when they discard the old methods of doing the work and adopt scientific methods of doing the work and adopt scientific methods suggested by the management after scientific investigation. Similarly the management should also change their mental attitude towards the workers. They should realise that if output increases cost will go down, increased wages still leave higher profits for them. They should be fair to the workers. Both the workers and the management should try to increase the production because ultimately it will benefit both and entire community. Taylor observes, " In its essence, scientific management involves a complete mental revolution on the part of the working man engaged in any particular establishment or industry and it involves and equally complete mental revolution on the part of those on the managements side - the foremen, the superintendent, the owner of the business, the Board of Directors and without this complete mental revolution on both sides, scientific management does not exist ".

Scientific Selection of Workers : The selection of right type of worker for the right job raises the efficiency of the workers. The scientific selection is very important aspect of scientific management. Under the traditional methods the workers are recruited by the foreman or supervisor. But under scientific management selection is made by personnel department and the workers are selected on the basis of their aptitude and capacity. After selection of the workers, proper training is imparted to him and he has to be told what type and how the work is to be carried on. Thus scientific selection and training helps to increase the efficiency of the labour which in turn helps in increasing the production and maintain harmonious relationship with the management.

Improvement in Working Methods : Taylor was of the view that in order to increase output there was a necessary to improve the working methods. In order to improve methods of working the following aspects should be taken into account.

Standardization of Tools, Equipment, and Materials :

Fixation of standards of work is one of the most important aspects of scientific management. Taylor and Gilbreth developed the standardization of working methods which helped in increasing the production and efficiency of the worker. Standardization involves simplification and helps in achieving the best results in a given time. Standards are dynamic and they change with the advancement of technical knowledge. Taylor laid great stress on the use of right type of tools and equipment. He also suggested of setting a " Tool Room " in every industry. By standardizing tools and equipment cost of production can be brought down and also production increased. Similarly the standardization of materials is also necessary in order to produce quality goods. There will be practically no wastage of the materials and the effectiveness of the machines will also increase.

Routing and Scheduling

Routing consists of determining the different stages through which the product should pass, before coming out as a final product. Therefore in any firm where scientific management its introduced, proper planning for routing should be prepared in order to determine the most economical way of completing the task. Scheduling aims at fixing a specific time limit to carry out any task. Generally the date of completing and delivering the final product is fixed. Outlining the importance of scheduling, Richard N. Owners says, " Operating departments can use the information pertaining to the amount of work planned to schedule personnel, extra shifts, overtime, machine repair and other work. Foreman can determine themselves whether their work operations are on schedule. Purchasing department can make its plans for the purchase of supplies, tools or equipment. The machine shop can know when special fixtures, moulds or tools will be required. The planning department knows at each stage whether an order is on schedule and whether corrective action is necessary".

Factory Environment

It is determined by the climatic conditions prevailing in the factory such as ventilation, heating, cooling, lighting, the colour of the walls, floor space, noise, etc. Under scientific management conditions of work are made healthy and cheerful.

Organisational Set-up

Production planning is the most important factor in any

industrial establishment. Under scientific management Taylor introduced planning department in his organisation. It is also called " Taylors plan of Functional Foremanship ". In his work Taylor found the following sub-divisions and re-arrangement of functions profitable :

In the Planning Department :

(i) The order-for-work or route clerk
(ii) The instrument card clerk
(iii) The time and cost-clerk

In the shop :

(iv) The gang boss
(v) The speed boss
(vi) The inspector
(vii) The repair boss

And for the entire work :

(viii) The shop disciplinarian.

The basic aim of planning is to keep employees, machinery, equipment and material most profitably employed, and thus fully utilize plant facilities and stabilise employment. According to Taylor, "Establishing a planning department merely concentrates the planning and much other brain work in a few men especially fitted for their task and trained in their special lines, instead of having it done, as therefore in most cases by high priced mechanics well fitted to work their trades, but poorly trained for work more or less clerical in its nature ".

Under Taylorism two most important methods of scientific management are (i) Motion study and (ii) Time study.

Motion Study.

It is the science of eliminating ineffective and wasteful motions. Motion study consists of selection and substitution of effective for non-productive wasteful motions. Its end objective is to find a simple, easy and better way of doing a job. Frank. B. Gilberth who developed the method of motion study defined it as under : " Motion study is the science of eliminating wastefulness resulting from unnecessary, ill-directed and inefficient motions. The aim of motion study is to find and perpetuate the schemes of least waste methods of labour. According to Kimball and Kimball, " Motion study may be defined as the study of movements, whether of a machine or an operator, in performing an operation for the purpose of eliminating useless motion and of arranging the sequence of useful motions in the most efficient order. It is on effect a refined form of routing and may be closely connected with the routing of work through the plant." Motion study includes not only the motions employed by a worker to do a job, but also the tools he uses, the places where he works and the materials he works with.

There are numerous advantages of motion study and some of them are that (i) it helps in increasing the output because it eliminates useless motions. It involves betterment of working conditions with better tools and equipment; (ii) It helps in reducing cost because there is greater output by each worker; (iii) since workers produce more they are benefited of more wages everyday; and (iv) since there are certain changes in the use of tools, equipments and materials, it leads to greater motivation and improved morale.

The disadvantages of motion study are that : (i) the worker has to do the job according to set pattern and this kills the creativeness of the worker; (ii) the worker at times is unable to work according to the set pattern because it may restrain his free movements; (iii) motion study does not take into account the differences among the individuals; and (iv) sometimes a rigid pattern has an adverse effection on the worker which may not help in increasing the production.

Time study

It is a known fact that Time Study and Motion Study are complimentary to each other. It is said that, "Motion and Time Study is the analysis of the methods, of the materials, and of the tools and equipment used or to be used, in the performance of a piece work ". F.W. Taylor considered the method of time study as the most important aspect of scientific management. Time Study includes motion study, standardization of job and selection of workers on a scientific basis. It can be seen from the following definition : " to subject each operation of a given piece of work to a close analysis in order that every unnecessary operation may be eliminated in order to determine the quickest and best method of performing each necessary operation; also to standardise equipment methods and working conditions; then, and not until then, to determine by scientific measurement the number of standard hours in which an average man can do the job". Taylor developed the concept of time study in order to fix wages by fixing standard time. Time study has helped in determining the best possible time in which a job can be efficiently carried out. It helps in production planning, finding out the capacity of the plant, efficiency of the worker and the cost of production.

Criticisms of Scientific Management

In spite of having a number of advantages to both the employees and the employers, scientific management is criticised on various grounds.

Opposition of Employers

1. Firstly they oppose on the ground that if they accept scientific management, they will have to incur huge expenditure on the entire overhauling of the plant.
2. Secondly in conducting time and motion studies a lot of money has to be spent which is beyond the means of small industries.
3. Thirdly they object over the establishment of a planning department. A large staff has to be employed to maintain the department and it adds to the cost of production as the work of planning department is totally non-productive.

Objections of Employees

1. Scientific management through standardization and simplification kills the creativity and initiativeness of the workers and creates monotony.
2. It is undemocratic as it gives complete control over the workers to " functional bosses " and reduces the interest and responsibility of the workers.
3. It is stated that scientific management forces the worker to depend upon the employer's conception of fairness and gives the worker no voice in hiring or discharge, in setting the task, in determining the wage rate, or determining the general of employment.
4. By introducing new plants and machinery and other labour saving devices it renders workers unemployed.
5. Another important objection is that the benefit to the workers from increase in wages and bonus is far less than the total benefit which accrue to management because of increased profits.

9

Rationalisation

The nature and scope of rationalisation is very wide. It is not applicable to a single industrial unit, but to the whole industry because it consists of all aspects of the industry taken together. It means application of scientific methods to bring about improvement in all the spheres of the industry. The term rationalisation has been defined in different ways and words by various authorities and organisations. Some of the definitions are given below.

The National Board for Economy and Efficiency (RRW) in Germany defined the term thus : " Rationalisation is the employment of all means of technique and ordered plans which serve to elevate the whole industry and to increase production, lower its costs and improve its quality. Its aim is to raise the general level of prosperity by cheaper, more plentiful and better quality goods ".

The International Economic Conference which met at Geneva in May, 1927 under the auspices of the League of Nations, defined rationalisation as, " the method or technique and organisation designed to secure the minimum waste of either efforts or material. It includes the scientific organisation of labour, standardisation of both materials and products, simplification of processes and improvements in the system of transport and marketing". The Conference also laid down the objectives of rationalisation : (i) Securing the maximum efficiency of labour with the minimum of efforts; (ii) facilitating by a reduction in the variety of patterns, the design manufacture, use and replacement of standardised parts; (iii) avoiding waste of materials and power; (iv) simplifying the distribution of goods; and (v) avoiding in distribution, unnecessary transport, burden-some financial charges and useless interposition of middlemen".

In May, 1937, the Advisory Committee of the International Labour Organisation gave the following definitions :

(i) Rationalisation in general, is any reform tending to replace habitual, antiquated practices by means or methods based on systematic reasoning;

(ii) Rationalisation in the narrowest sense, is any reform of an undertaking, administration or other services, public or private, tending to replace habitual antiquated practices by means or methods based on systematic reasoning;

(iii) Rationalisation, in a wider sense, is a reform which takes a group of business undertakings, as a unit, and tends to reduce the waste and loss due to unbriddled competition by concerted action, based on systematic reasoning;

(iv) Rationalisation, in the widest sense, is a reform tending to apply means and methods based on systematic reasoning to the collective activities of large economic and social group".

As different interpretations have been to its scope and objects, Prof. Sargent Florence defines rationalisation as a movement, " to eliminate waste and inefficiency scientifically and logically by some sort of joint action between all the firms within one industry".

According to Urwick, rationalisation is both an attitude and a process. "As an attitude, it records the belief that a more rational control of world economic life through the application of scientific methods is possible and desirable, as a process, it implies the application of the methods of science to all problems arising in the organisation and conduct of production, distribution and consumption".

In the publication, "Social Aspects of Rationalisation", the I.L.O. defines this term as , "Rationalisation means that instead of the traditional processes, established routine, empirical rules and improvisations, use is made of methods that are the fruits of patient scientific study and aims at the optimum adjustment of means to ends, thus securing that every effort produces the maximum useful results".

The National Commission on Labour in its report, have discussed the concept of rationalisation in the following words :

"Rationalisation, in its early connotation, meant rational use of inputs in a planned and rational distribution of its output to meet current market demands and simultaneously to bring about a reduction in costs. More recently, it has acquired a wider meaning in industrial and commercial management and includes determination of manning patterns in industry. In its more complete form, rationalisation implies a basic change in the structure and control of industrial activity, with the word ' industry ' used in its generic sense. Elimination of waste and promotion of efficiency by means of a coordinated, well integrated and all round view of industry will fall within the purview of rationalisation. In its application, it is a process, which brings together the advantages of planned production, pooling of research and scientific and technical know-how, centralised regulation of finance, modernisation of productive processes and sales and optimum utilisation of man power. It is, thus closely akin to a broad productivity drive through every available technique".

An analysis of the definitions quoted above indicates that there is a wide difference on the meaning and scope. But there are certain common features in all. It involves technological and managerial reorganisation of the industry so as to obtain economics of large scale operation, eliminating all types of wastes, increasing the productivity and efficiency of labour and increasing the wages of labour by bringing down the costs.

Aspects of Rationalisation

For a clear conception of rationalisation, one should have an idea of various aspects of rationalisation. They are categorised into four classes : (1) Technological, (2) Organisational; (3) Financial; and (4) Social.

Technological Aspect

It mainly aims at obtaining maximum, technical efficiency by adopting latest technological know-how and eliminating obsolete machinery. It involves the following features :

Standardisation. It is a process under which not only the methods and techniques of production are standardised but also products which are manufactured. The standard is the best possible shape with specific description and it clearly eleminates duplication and waste. For achieving efficiency and economics of operation, standardisation is necessary as it increases the productive capacity of the existing plant due to decrease in the number of various types and sizes. Standardisation aims at producing a few goods on a mass scale so as to reduce the cost of production.

Simplification. "Simplification is an act of rendering industrial processes simple or making less complex or less difficult". It chiefly involves the job simplification or product simplification so that unnecessary processes or goods can be eliminated. The manufacturer, the trader and the consumer are benefited by this simplification. It means greater productivity, less waste and simpler costing system for the manufacturer. To the trader, it means carrying of small stocks. To the consumer it gets the advantages of improved quality and reduced price.

Mechanisation and Intensification. It means more dependence on the machine than on manual labour in the process of manufacture. It saves labour cost and reduces the cost of production. Intensification is the speeding of industrial machinery removing slackness and inefficiency. Workers generally oppose intensification because it increases their work load.

Specialisation. It is the result of standardisation and simplification. When repetitive work on a mass scale is carried out, the natural consequence in course of time is specialisation. Specialisation leads to greater proficiency in production and increases the quality of the product. It can be obtained in every field of production and distribution. Specialisation is also referred to as ' Simulation ' as simultaneous links are established between material, machine labour, process and method.

Organisation Aspect

Rationalisation tries to bring about adjustments in demand and supply and stability in industry by trying to avoid competition, and laying stress on production in the most efficient units. It envisages a few large units with centralised control and management in place of large number of uneconomic units. Rationalisation from the organisational aspect means regulation of competition if not elimination. It leads to co-operative methods of action in order to achieve economies of operation both external and internal. These things tend towards a bigger and larger industrial unit.

Financial Aspect

Rationalisation of industry will be of no use if adequate finance is not available. Adequate financial strength is very much necessary for maintaining efficiency of manufacturing industries. If finances are not available, then the management will not be able to adopt new policies regarding the function of the enterprise. Financial aspect means reducing or eliminating unnecessary expenses and achieving economies in administrative and overhead expenses. That is, the units should neither be over-capitalised or under-capitalised, but should be fairly - capitalised. The cost of securing finance should not be burden on the unit. The emphasis should be on self-financing rather than outside finance. The unit is should create sufficiency reserves by ploughing back its profits. When merger of different units takes place, there is large capital available for modernisation. This may lead to over-capitalisation. Care should be taken so that the unit is neither over or under capitalised.

Social Aspect

Rationalisation, which is chiefly concerned with mass production and material prosperity of the community should also see the welfare of the society. In other words, the benefits of rationalisation should percolate to the whole society and should not benefit a small group in the community. Rationalisation should entail various provisions and measures like adequate incentives, recognition of efficient workers, organisation of satisfactory schemes of promotion, etc. to encourage and boost the morale of the workers. This will help in creating better relations between labour and management. Rationalisation is not only a material progress but includes the upliftment of the society as a whole. According to Dr. Myers, rationalisation, " demands the consideration of business not only in its own purely selfish, technical and commercial aspects, but also in its wider, economic social and generally human aspects, without all these aspects, it will be pseudo-rationalisation of business affairs ".

Rationalisation and Scientific Management

There are many people who feel that rationalisation and scientific management are more or less the same and the two are synonymous because both the concerned with the replacement of obsolete techniques with the latest ones. It is stated that, both aim to use scientific methods to industrial production and organisation with the objective of increasing efficiency and productivity. To a certain extent, it is true, but there are fundamental differences between the two which are discussed below :

1. Both of them differ in their approach to the problems of industries. Rationalisation tries to achieve an equilibrium in demand and supply. This means eliminating of weak and inefficient units, regulating the entry of new firms and organising large units to achieve economies of the operation. This involves combination and co-operation among the different units to bring stability in prices by adjusting production to demand. On the other hand, scientific management is not concerned with the adjustment of production to total demand and cannot protect any unit from wasteful and cut throat competition.
2. Rationalisation has a wider scope than the scientific management and the former includes the latter. Rationalisation has to consider the problems of the whole industry because it has to adjust total production to total demand whereas scientific management is applicable to only single unit.
3. Rationalisation entails all the aspects of economic organisation viz. increasing production upto the optimum level, bringing about economies of operation, organisational efficiency, financial, social, etc. It should benefit to the whole society and not a particular group of people. Scientific management is chiefly concerned in increasing production in a single business unit.
4. Scientific management is basically concerned in bringing about improvement in existing industries and their goods. Its stresses to improve the productivity of the existing business units and to better the quality of the existing goods. Rationalisation is not only concerned in improvement of the existing units but also in creation of new units. It is concerned in reducing the number of products by avoiding duplication, standardising and simplifying the goods and limiting their production to a few number so that quality goods can be produced on a mass scale.
5. Combination is an integral part of rationalisation. Without combining units economies of operation, distribution and finance cannot be achieved. In order to avoid competition and wasteful production, rationalisation has to be there whereas this has nothing to do with scientific management. It is concerned with the

improvement in production and bringing about better co-ordination among the various departments of unit.

In the end, we can say that, "Rationalisation has the objective of the greatest good to the greatest number whereas scientific management is concerned with the greatest good to the limited number who may be employers alone or both employers and employees".

Rationalisation and Combination

Rationalisation refers to such a number of firms belonging to a particular industry come under one banner with a view to eliminate wasteful competition or in other words, it means the formation of some kind of business combination. There are thinkers who believe that there is no difference between the two. Prof. Clay calls rationalisation as an "industrial combination with the object to securing certain productive economies ". Sir Josiah Stamp calls rationalisation as a " device to control production by means of amalgamation and to fix prices and a tool to eliminate competition". But these views are definitely partial and they should not be regarded as one. Both aim to eliminate cut-throat competition, but if it is done to earn profits, then it is combination and not raionalisation. It has now being accepted that ratonalisation has a social objective towards the society whereas combinations are formed to establish monopolies which are not in the interests of the society.

Rationalisation and Automation

Automation is the continuation of the process of mechanisation of production. Automation implies to replacing the direct man power for metal or manual work or both the automatic machines. Though rationalisation and automation are two different concepts but their effect on employment and labour is similar though not of the same magnitude. At one stage, automation is regarded as a broad concept of rationalisation. Usually both depend on the nature of technological advancement. "In its present connotation automation involves the application of automatic control mechanism with an element of self-regulation. In the process, the mechanism gets integrated with computers, mechanical brains and the like to assess with remarkable speed and accuracy, market forces of supply and demand and adjustment to price mechanism, as well as the efficient running of an undertaking which will include inventory control and production or quality control".

Standardisation of products and saving of labour costs are the results of automation. Goods and services are produced at a lower unit cost. A number of organisations in the public and private sectors have introduced automatic machines and computers.

Advantage of Rationalisation

Rationalisation schemes, if exercised in a proper and systematic manner will definitely bring improvements in the functioning of the industry and benefit the entire community as a whole. Some of its advantages are discussed below :

Advantages to the Producers

It offers a number of advantages to the producers :

(i) It brings about a reduction in the cost of production and increases the profits to the manufacturers. It economises the distribution and transportation costs of goods too; (ii) By eliminating wasteful and cut-throat competition among the various producers, it brings co-ordination and co-operation which helps in framing a perspective plan for the industry, (iii) The producers are able to avert losses because they can bring adjustments in the demand and supply of goods; (iv) It leads to pooling of research and technical know-how which creates a healthy atmosphere of constructive co-operation; and (v) It brings about specialisation, standardisation and simplification of products which, in turn helps the producers to produce only those goods which are best suited to them. Each unit will produce only those goods which will help in obtaining a number of economies.

Advantages to the Workers

It also provides a number of advantages to their workers :

(i) It helps in increasing productivity which in turn helps in better remuneration to the workers, (ii) Under rationalisation, various welfare programmes for the workers are introduced which in turn help the workers to increase their morale. It also helps in increasing labour defficiency; (iii) Rationalisation tries to eliminate every possible cause of waste of human effort, scientific and judicious selection, training and promotion. All these things help in increasing the productivity of the workers; (iv) It assures greater security of job. In the short period, there may be some sort of unemployment, but in the long run, rationalisation helps in increasing production which means more employment opportunity and more job security; (v) It helps in raising the standard of living of the workers.

Advantages to the Consumers

Consumers also stand to gain by rationalisation in the following ways :

(i) It helps in better utilisation of the country's resources, economically and efficiently; (ii) It enable proper allocation of scare resources among the various producers; (iii) The stability on the economy which is beneficial to the society; (iv) It helps in preventing wastes of materials, machines and human efforts which is of great advantage to the society; (v) Productivity of the economy is increased thus resulting in higher national income leading to a higher per capita income and enabling the people to raise their standard of living.

Disadvantages of Rationalisation

1. It is said that rationalisation leads to formation of monopolies, trusts and cartels which control the production and distribution of goods and thereby leading to concentration of economic power in the hands of few, which is not in the interest of the society.

2. Rationalisation often leads to unemployment and increase in the work load of the labourers. This lead to unrest among the labourers who resort to lock-out and strikes.

3. The gains achieved through rationalisation may not be properly distributed among the employers and employees. The wages of the workers are enhanced, but not in that proportion, as the earning capacity of the industry.

4. There is always a possibility of over-capitalisation, in the industry when rationalisation takes place. Over capitalisation creates a huge financial burden on the unit which becomes very heavy in times of depression.

5. Rationalisation usually leads to increase in the size of the industrial organisation which may be difficult to manage. There may be lack of co-ordination and control which may result in heavy losses. It is to be borne in mind that increase in the size of the organisation

does not necessarily increase the management ability.

6. Rationalisation units often lead to financial mismanagement. It has been observed that large combined units indulge in all sorts of malpractices in order to evade income tax and corporation taxes.

Attitude of Employers

There has been different attitude of the employers regarding the implementation of schemes of rationalisation on various grounds. Some of them are :

1. Rationalisation involves huge capital outlay without assuring adequate returns on the investments. Their contention is that rationalisation does not help in over coming business cycles. They are of the view that finances are not available even if they are keen to implement rationalisation.
2. They also contend that in determining a ration of sharing the benefits of rationalisation between them and workers may be very difficult and may lead to labour unrest.
3. The threat of nationlisation always haunts the industrialists. Their view is that under rationalisation, they have to spend a huge amount of money and if the industry is nationalised, then they are not going to benefit from it.
4. They also oppose on the ground that once the rationalisation policy is accepted, the industry will have to reorganise continuously in future and when new techniques of production develop, it will make the entire machinery obsolete and place a heavy financial burden on the industry.

But the above arguments put by the industrialists do not carry much weight and it should be understood by them that they have to change according to the needs of the community, if they have to keep themselves in business. Also rationalisation increases the earning capacity of their industry. Regarding finances, they can be made available from banks, investment companies, insurance companies, stock exchanges and many other government agencies.

Attitude of Employees

As we know that rationalisation involves closure of uneconomic and inefficient units, concentrating production with latest and modern devices, labour saving techniques and other aspects which are best suited to increase the productivity. The workers are mostly effected by the implementation of the rationalisation schemes. They oppose it on the following ground :

1. With the introduction of sophisticated techniques of production, the quantum of work done by the workers is reduced. This leads to large scale displacement of labour. Similarly, rationalisation seeks to bring about adjustment on demand and supply, output is reduced in certain units leading to displacement of workers. There is no doubt about it that rationalisation causes unemployment among workers though may be in the short run.
2. There is an increase in the work load on the workers by intensification. This extra work load results in the deterioration of both physical and mental health of the workers. It causes strain and is a source of fatigue.
3. The gains obtained from rationalisation are not distributed in an equitable and fair manner and the workers always get a poor share.
4. The workers oppose rationalisation on the ground that management will exploit them in the name of rationalisation. They fear that the employers will spend less on ancillary aspects like working conditions, suitable training, etc. because their financial commitments would be heavy in rationalisation.

But the advocates of rationalisation observe that the unemployment created will be of short duration. In the long run, it creates more employment opportunities. It is argued that rationalisation involves the adoption of modern techniques of production which leads to lowering of prices and will increase the demand for the products of the rationalised industry, and later there shall be an increase in wages of the workers. This will lead to increase of economic activity thereby expanding business and expanding employment. This is clear from the words of the Balfour Committee of Industry and Trade (1929) : " Rationalisation, in its early stages, may involve an increase in the number of the wholly unemployed, but it is considered that in the long run, the industries which have regained this prosperity will more than be able to reabsorb those who have been displaced". J.A. Hobson observes that, " There can be no ground for holding that rationalisation, as whole, tends to a distribution of income favourable to the workers either through raising wages of lowering prices. All economic evidence tends to show that rationalisation carries with it a net diminution of employment, and substitution of a large proportion of low skilled for high skilled workers and a distribution of the product which increases the proportionate share of capital and reduces that of labour ".

Rationalisation in India

The rationalisation movement which initially started in Germany after the World War I spread to almost all the European nations, although its nature and scope varied from country to country. Though the need for rationalisation in major industries in our country needs to be implemented, it has been generally misunderstood, both by the employers and the employees. Most of the industrialists think that it is a combination of units to replace manual labour by machine whereas the trade unions oppose on the ground that it leads to unemployment. The I.L.O., in their book, ' Industrial Labour in India ', observed : " Rationalisation is being undertaken in India in many undertakings, but little is known about the forms it has taken, except in the case of the cotton mills of Bombay and Ahmedabad where it has mainly meant increasing the number of machines in the charge of one worker, either in the spinning or in the weaving or in both the departments.

Rationalisation movement started in India in Bombay cotton textile industry in 1928. Later, the movement spread to Ahmedabad and Kanpur textile industry. It was only after independence and in the light of the planned development of the country, the problems of rationalisation started engaging the attention of the Government and it was very much concerned with the various aspects of industries. A Sub-Committee of the Industries Development Committee of the Planning Commission consisting of employers' and employees' representative under the Chairmanship of Shri Gulzari Lal Nanda, in 1951, discussed the issue of rationalisation in detail and arrived at the following conclusions :

1. Rationalisation should be introduced in the Indian Industries with a special care to avoid retrenchment of workers and to keep it to the minimum, if it is there. This was to be achieved by :

   (a) not filling the vacancies caused by death, retirement, etc; (b) absorbing the surplus workers in other departments without breaking the continuity of service and without reducing their total earnings; (c) granting gratuities for voluntary retirement; (d) extending machinery wherever possible to absorb some workers made surplus.

2. Work load should be standardised and if there is any dispute, it should be investigated and the standards should be fixed by experts, selected by both the parties.
3. The Government should prepare a scheme for the rehabilitation of the retrenched workers.
4. An equitable share in the gains of rationalisation should be given to the labourers.

All the above views were embodied in the Second Five Year Plan which observed that, " In the context of growing unemployment, rationlisation has an adverse psychological effect on workers. Even so, to freeze the existing techniques of production is not in the interests of a developing economy. Rationalisation should, therefore, be attempted when it does not lead to unemployment and is introduced in consultation with the workers and is effected after improving working conditions and guaranteeing a substantial share of gains to workers". In 1957, the Government evolved a model agreement on rationlisation emphasising the principles outlined above and presented before the 15th Indian Labour Conference. According to the agreement there should be mutual consultation between the management and the union in order to implement the scheme of rationalisation. It further provides that whenever management desires, to introduce technological improvement, involving retrenchment on the total number of workers employed it shall give reasonable notice to the worker's union. It further provides that if the scheme of rationalisation results in retrenchment, steps should be taken to expand the plant or production so that the workers displaced may be re-employed. If there is any dispute arising out of the implementation of the scheme of rationalisation, it should be referred to the arbitration.

There is an urgent need to rationlise the industries of the core sector viz., cotton textile, sugar, jute, coal, etc. Many industries are running below their optimum capacity. Our products find no place in the international markets because of their poor quality and high cost of products. In view of loosing the foreign market, several committees and commissions have, from time to time, recommended, the implementation of rationlisation schemes in various industries. Regarding finances there may be certain problems, but the Government has started granting loan for modernisation. Trade union should also accept the rationlisation, as it ultimately leads to the betterment of workers.

References

1. International Labour Review, August, 1937.
2. Logic of Industrial Organisation.
3. L. Urwick, The Meaning of Rationlisation.
4. Government of India, Report of the National Commission on Labour 1969.
5. R.M. Hudson, Simplification and Standardisation.
6. Govt. of India - Report of the National Commission on Labour.
7. J.A. Hobson : Rationalisation and Unemployment.

10

Industrial Policy Reforms

The Government has been giving due attention towards the industrial development of the country. In order to have a sustained and balanced growth, it has being coming out with Industrial Policy from time to time.

The first Industrial policy Resolution was enunciated in 1948 in which the state took the major responsibility in the development of industries. Later the Industrial Policy Resolution 1956 was announced under which the state assumed the direct responsibility for industrial development. To meet the demands of the changing times it was modified through industrial policy statements in 1973, 1977, 1980, 1985 and 1990. The encouraging results of the Industrial Policy Statements of 1985 and 1990, economic changes that took place in many countries and the severe economic crisis over the nation called for a bold set of measure to bring the economy back on the rails and to accelerate the pace of development.

The Industrial Policy Statements of 1991 is a policy design to achieve the following objectives :

(i) To build on the gains already made in the industrial sector.

(ii) To correct the distortions or weaknesses in the pattern of Industrial growth.

(iii) To maintain a sustained growth in productivity and gainful employment; and

(iv) To attend technological dynamism and international competiveness.

Main Features

The Industrial Policy Statement 1991 was presented in Lok Sabha on 24 July 1991 by the Minister of State for Industries, Mr. P.J. Kurien. The salient features of the policy are :

I. Industrial Licensing Policy

(i) An industrial licence was mandatory for investments above certain specified limit. This limit which was Rs. 5 Crores was raised for non-MRTP/non-FERA Companies to Rs. 15 Crores in case of projects in non-backward areas and to Rs. 50 Crores in backward areas, subject to certain conditions, in June 1988.

Under the new policy the industrial licensing has been abolished for all projects except for those which are important for security, strategic, social and environmental reasons and items of elite's consumption. The compulsory licensing provisions would therefore apply only in Annexure II. These industries are such as coal and lignite, petroleum, distillation and brewing of alcoholic drinks, sugars, cigars and cigarettes of tobacco, motor cars, plywood, industrial explosives, hazardous chemicals, drugs and pharmaceuticals, entertainment electronic, paper and newsprint, asbestos, electronic aerospace, animal fats and oils, air-conditioners, refrigerators, microwave ovens and domestic washing machines. However, the compulsory licensing provisions would not apply to any of these such items which are reserved for exclusive manufacture in small scale sector. It is also stated that the existing units exempted from industrial licensing will also enjoy exemption in respect of substantial expansions.

(ii) The new industrial policy statements says that areas where security and strategic concerns predominate will continue to be reserved for the public sector. The industries reserved for the public sector are spelled out in Annexure I. These industries are arms and ammunition and allied items or defence equipment, atomic energy, mineral oils, mining of iron ore, manganese ore, chrome ore, sulphur, gypsum, gold and diamond, mining of cooper, lead, zinc and tin and railway transport.

(iii) The new industrial policy statement seeks to give automatic clearance for the imports of capital goods in such cases where foreign exchange availability is ensured through foreign equity or if the CIF value of imported capital goods required is less than 25% of total value of plant and equipment upto a maximum value of Rs. 2 Crores.

(iv) The new industrial policy statement provides that in locations other than cities of more than one million population there will be no requirement of obtaining industrial specified approvals from the central Government except for industries specified in annexure II. In respect of cities with population greater than one million, industries other than those of non-polluting nature such as electronics, computer software and printing will be located outside 25 km of the periphery, except in prior designated industrial areas.

(v) All existing registration schemes such as Delicensed Registration, Exempted Industrial Registration and DGTD Registration have been abolished. Entrepreneurs will henceforth only be required to file an information memorandum on new projects and substantial expansion.

(vi) The existing and the new industrial units will be provided with a bread-banding facility to enable them to produce any article without additional investment in plant and machinery.

(vii) Financial institutions in India had the option to convert 20 percent of their loans into equity in all cases where the aggregate financial assistance from the financial institutions exceeded Rs. 5 Crores. This gave the financial institutions scope for acquiring considerable equity holding in such units. The new industrial policy statement states that this convertibility clause will no longer be applicable for terms loans from the financial institutions for new projects.

II. Foreign Investment Policy

(i) According to the policy statement approval will be given for direct foreign investment upto 51 per cent foreign equity in high priority industries. Annexure III spells out 34 high priority industries. Such approvals will be available if foreign covers the foreign exchange requirements for imported capital goods.

In further relaxation of the policy, on 25th October, 1991 the Government decided to permit direct foreign investment by Non-

Resident Indians (NRIs) upto 100% of the equity in 34 industries figuring in annexure III of the new industrial policy. There will be automatic clearance for such investments proposals from NRIs subject to the condition that the project's capital goods imports would be met from the foreign equity.

(ii) The new policy states that payments regarding import of components, raw-materials, intermediate goods and payments of knowhow fees and royalties will be governed by the general policy applicable to other domestic units, the Payments of dividend would be monitored through the Reserve Bank of India so as to ensure that ouflows on account of dividend payments are balanced by export earnings over a stipulated period.

(iii) The new industrial policy states that in order to provide access to international markets, majority foreign equity holding upto 51% will be allowed for trading companies primarily engaged in export activities. While the thrust would be on export activities, such trading houses will be at par with domestic trading and export houses in accordance with the Import export Policy.

(iv) According to the new industrial policy a special Empowered Board would be constituted to negotiate with a number of large international firms and approve direct foreign investment in select areas. This would be a special programme to attract substantial investment that would provide access to high technology and world markets.

III. Foreign Technology Agreements Policy

(i) The new policy accords automatic approvals for foreign technology agreements in high priority industries (annexure III) upto a lumpsum payment of Rs. 1 Crore. 5% royalty for domestic sales and 8% of sales over a 10 year period from the date of agreement or 7 years from commencement of production. The prescribed royalty rates are net of taxes.

(ii) The policy provides for an automatic approval for technology agreements in industries other than those specified in annexure III, provided no free foreign exchange is required for any payments.

(iii) No permission will be necessary for hiring of foreign technicians, foreign testing of indigenously developed technologies. Payment may be made from blanket permits or the foreign exchange according to Reserve Bank of India's guidelines.

IV. **Public Sector Policy**

The Government of India announced a New Industrial Policy in July 1991 which contains the following four major decisions in respect of the public sector :

(i) Reduction in the list of industries reserved for the public sector from 17 to 8 and introducing selective competition in the reserved area.

(ii) Disinvestment of Shares in Public Sector Undertakings (PSEs) to raise resources and encourage wider participation of general public and workers in the ownership of the PSEs.

(iii) Policy for Sick public enterprises to be same as that for the private sector; and

(iv) Improving performance through the performance contract or Memorandum of Understanding (MOU) system by which managements are to be granted greater autonomy and held accountable for results.

The policy was further elaborated in the statement made by the Prime Minister in Parliament on 20th December, 1991 in which he stated that while the mixed economy system will continue in the country no further nationalisation would be resorted to; that there will be reduced budgetary support to sick or potentially sick public enterprises with a view to eliminating it as early as possible; but that while dealing with sickness, human hardship would be avoided to the extent possible through the National Renewal Fund.

The Eighth Plan visualizes an important role for an autonomous and efficient public sector in providing essential infrastructure and strategic support for achieving the targeted rate of economic growth during the plan period (1992-97).

The Plan Document enumerates the following policy initiatives in this regard :

(i) Restructuring involving modernisation, rationalisation of capacity, product mix changes and selective exit and privatisation.

(ii) Increase in autonomy and performance accountability through an effective system of MOUs between the administrative ministries and public enterprises launched since the seventh five year plan.

(iii) Changes in management in specific enterprises to promote leadership, resourcefulness and innovation.

(iv) A major effort by the state Governments to streamline the working of their public sector enterprises which are beset with interference and adhoc investment and employment decisions.

(v) Technological upgradation through an integrated R & D effort and import of technology.

(vi) Re-orientation of approach in Ministries and other Government agencies corresponding to liberalisation and dismantling of regulations.

National Renewal Fund

As announced by the Prime Minister, the National Renewal fund (NRF) became operationalised in 1991-92. the objectives of the NRF are :

(i) To provide assistance to firms to cover the costs of retraining and redeployment of employees arising as a result of modernisation and technological upgradation of existing capacities and from industrial restructuring.

(ii) To provide funds for compensation to employees affected by restructuring or closure of industrial units, both in public and private sectors.

(iii) To provide funds for employment generation schemes in the organised and unorganised sectors in order to provide a social safety net for labour. The Department of Industrial Development, which administers NRF, has now taken up the first set of cases relating to the National Textiles Corporations units.

MRTP Act

The Monopolies and Restrictive Trade Practices Act, 1969, has had a very adverse effect on competition and industrial growth. The new policy acknowledges that with the growth and complexity of industrial structure and the need for achieving economies of scale for higher productivity and competitive advantage in the international market, the Interference of government through the MRTP Act on the investment decisions of large companies has become deleferious in its effects on Indian industrial growth.

With a view to preventing concentration of economic power, the MRTP Act had laid down that dominant undertakings with assets of one Crore or more and other undertakings which either by itself or together with interconnected undertakings had assets of Rs. 100 Crores or more should obtain the prior permission of the Central Government for establishment of new undertakings, expansion of existing undertaking, merger, amalgamation to take over. The new industrial Policy has replaced these provisions.

The Process of industrial de-regulation and structural reforms were carried out further in 1992-93 and the direction for future policy action was firmly established.

The following measures were undertaken during 1992-93 regarding industrial reforms :

1. Rates of import duties on project imports, capital goods and general machinery were substantially reduced.
2. The Capital market was liberalised and Government control over capital issues was withdrawn. The Office of the controller of Capital Issues was abolished. The Securities and Exchange Board of India (SEBI) has been converted into a statutorily empowered Board to regulate the functioning of the capital market and stock exchanges. The companies were free to price their equity issues at their own risk and at self-determined premia, within the guidelines laid down by SEBI for investor protection.
3. Taxation of Capital gains was restructured to allow for inflation accounting. Double taxation of partnership was abolished and financial assets such as equities and debentures exempted from wealth tax. These fiscal measures have improved the incentives for industrial investment and encouraged flow of resources towards industry.
4. The condition that the dividend payments should be balanced by export earnings over a specified period of time was withdrawn in

respect of all foreign investment approvals except for some notified consumer goods industries. The list of high priority (Annexure III) industries where foreign investments upto 51 per cent were allowed automatically was revised, rationalising the earlier grouping and adding new items. The software industry was now included in the list .

5. Automatic approval of RBI for raising foreign equity upto 51 per cent will be available to (i) companies wishing to raise foreign equity as part of an expansion programme in the high-priority (Annexure III) industries; and (ii) companies predominantly engaged in high-priority industries to raise the equity base without an expansion programme.

6. The restriction regarding use of foreign brand name or trademark in goods sold in the domestic market withdrawn.

7. FERA liberalised. All restriction on FERA companies in the matter of borrowing funds or raising deposits in India as well as taking over or creating any interest in business in Indian Companies have been removed. Indian companies and Indian nationals are now allowed to start joint ventures abroad and accept directorships in overseas companies. FERA companies are also exempted from restriction on the establishments of branches, liason offices and acquisition of the whole or a part of any undertaking or company in India excepting agriculture and plantations.

8. Liberalised Exchange Rate Management System (LERMS), a dual exchange rate system was introduced in the Budget of 1992-93. Under this system, 40 per cent of foreign exchange earnings to be surrendered at the official exchange rate. Remaining 60 per cent to be converted at a market determined rate. The foreign exchange surrendered at official exchange rate is utilised to import essential items. The foreign exchange converted at the market rate is available to finance all other imports.

9. Manufacture of industrial alcohol was delicensed and veneers brought under the compulsory licensing list.

10. Most of the conditions stipulated in the letters of intent and industrial licences issued earlier to firms in industries now delicensed were waived.

11. The system of endorsement of capacity expansion under modernisation/renovation was discontinued except in the case of industries which are still under compulsory licensing or are located in restricted areas.
12. The private sector allowed to invest in oil exploration and refining which is otherwise reserved for the public sector.
13. The power sector opened to both domestic and foreign private investment.
14. The sale of shares of some public enterprises has also brought a new dimension into their strategic thinking and made them more conscious of profitability and long term growth. The total shares disinvested during 1991-92 thus comprised of 8 per cent of the total Government shareholding in the 31 PSEs, and the total amount realised was Rs. 3038 Crores.

The process of industrial policy reforms initiated in July 1991 continued in 1993-94 and a number of measures were undertaken which are given below :

1. With effect from march 26, 1993, the 13 minerals earlier reserved for the public sector, have been opened for the private sector. Consequently, the number of industries reserved for the public sector is reduced to 6.
2. 'Motor Car' and 'White goods' industries were delicensed with effect from April 28, 1993. Raw hides and skins, leather and patent leather, excluding chamois leather also stand delicensed. Hence the number of items in respect of which industrial licensing is compulsory has been reduced to 15.
3. The manufacture of readymade garments opened to large scale undertakings subject to an export obligation of 50 per cent and investment in fixed assets in plant and machinery of the large unit not exceeding Rs. 3 Crores.
4. A five year tax holiday for new industries in industrially backward States and Union Territories and for power generation any where in India, introduced.
5. Export credit refinance limits were augmented.

6. The limit for compulsory consortium lending was raised from Rs. 5 Crores to Rs. 50 Crores.

7. Sick Industrial Companies (Special Provision) Act 1985 (SICA) amended in December 1993 to facilitate early detection of sickness in companies and speedy enforcement of remedial measures.

8. At the end of March 1993, a total amount of Rs 4950 Crores were disinvested to the public sector financial institutions, mutual funds and general public.

A Committee on Disinvestment of Shares in Public Sector Enterprises was reconstituted by the Government in November 1992 with Dr. C. Rangarajan as the Chairman. The major recommendations of the Committee are :

(i) The target level of disinvestment for the medium term should be consistent with the Industrial Policy. In general, the percentage of equity to be disinvested should be 49 percent in industries reserved for public sector and 74 percent in other cases.

(ii) Instead of year-wise targets of disinvestment, a clear action plan should be evolved.

(iii) A number of steps need to be undertaken which may include corporatisation of PSEs, restructuring of finances with a proper debt-equity gearing and an independent Regulatory Commission for the concerned sector, if necessary.

(iv) The choice of method of valuation of shares of a PSE needs to take into account the special circumstances affecting PSE's operations such as, the past focus on social responsibilities rather than pure commercial considerations.

(v) A scheme of preferential offer of shares to workers and employees in PSEs may be devised.

(vi) Ten percent of the proceeds of disinvestment may be set apart by the Government for lending to the PSEs on concessional terms to meet their expansion and rationalisation needs.

(vii) A Standing Committee on Public Enterprises Disinvestment may be constituted to oversee the action plan for reform, restructuring and disinvestment as well as monitoring and evaluation of progress made.

The year 1994-95 saw the fastest growth of the Indian economy in the last four years. The measures undertaken in 1994-95 are given below :

1. A New Drug Policy consistent with the liberalised industrial policy was announced. Industrial licensing was abolished for all bulk drugs and their formulations and intermediates except in few cases. Most basic drugs and formulations were also brought under the automatic approval policy for 51 percent foreign equity holding. The number of drugs under price control was reduced from 142 to 73 by defining transparent criteria for identifying drugs whose prices need to be controlled.

2. A National Mineral Policy was revised and the Mines and Mineral Act amended, to open up this sector to private and foreign investment. Thirteen minerals were deserved for exploitation by the private sector.

3. The RBI based automatic approval policy for foreign investment was made applicable to mining (except for atomic minerals and mineral fuels), subject to a limit of 50 percent on foreign equity.

4. The National Telecom Policy, 1994 allows private provision of basic telecom services.

5. The new Air Corporation Act 1994 enables private Air Taxi Companies to operate as regular domestic airlines.

6. Areas like development and maintenance of airport infrastructure and material handling at major airports have been opened up for private participation.

7. The National Highway Act has been amended to enable levy of tolls on national highway users. Government intends further amendment of the Act to allow private participation in construction, maintenance and operation of roads on Build-operate-Transfer (BOT) basis.

8. Private participation has been invited in leasing of port equipment, operation and maintenance of container terminals, cargo landing terminals, creating warehouse and storage facilities, transportation within ports, setting up of private berths by coast based industries, ship repairs and maintenance.

Besides the Central Government, the States have also started taking initiatives in the implementation in the new industrial policy.

References

1. Eight Five Year Plan (1992-97), Planning Commission, Govt. of India, New Delhi.
2. Economic Survey 1992-93.
3. Economic Survey 1993-94.
4. Economic Survey 1994-95.

11

Industrial Sickness

A strong industrial sector is the backbone of the economy. The growing incidence of industrial sickness both in the small-scale and large industries during the last few years has drawn the attention of planners and economists as it leads to a colossal wastage of scarce resources available in the country. It greatly effects the owners, creditors and employees and generates social unrest in the system. Therefore, it is the need of the hour to devise such measures in dealing with sick units and simultaneously making suitable arrangements for detecting symptoms of industrial sickness at an early stage so that a unit may not fall sick.

Definition

Various definitions have been given for industrial sickness.

The Report of the study Team of the State Bank of India on the "Role of the Bank in the effective growth of small Scale Industries" defines a sick unit as "one which falls to generate internal surplus on a continuing basis and depends for its survival on frequent infusion of external funds".

The Reserve Bank of India defines a sick unit as "one which has incurred losses for the current year as well as the following year and the unit has an imbalance in its financial structure, such as, current ratio being less than 1:1 and there is worsoning trend in debt-equity ratio."

The Sick Industrial Companies (Special Provisions) Act, 1985, defines a sick industrial company as "an industrial company (being a company registered for not less than seven years) which has at the end of any financial year accumulated losses equal to or exceeding its entire networth and has also suffered cash losses in such financial year and the financial year immediately preceding it."

Actual Sickness

(i) Erosion of net worth by 50 per cent and more.

(ii) Units being closed for a total period of six months and more during the last year; and

(iii) Default in payment of loan instalments.

Incipient Sickness

Capacity utilisation is less than 50 percent of the highest achieved during the preceding five years.

According to the State Financial corporations (SFCs), any unit which fails to pay 3 consecutive instalments (half-yearly) of interest and/ or principal is sick.

The government responded to the growing incidence of industrial sickness by establishing the Industrial Reconstruction Corporation of India (IRCI) for rendering assistance to sick units. The name of this Corporation was changed into Industrial Reconstruction Bank of India (IRBI) with enlarged powers to deal with the growing number of sick industrial units.

In 1937, the government established one more institutional viz. the Bureau of Industrial and Financial Reconstruction (BIFR) with statutory powers to determine the ameliorative, remedial and other measures required for the benefit of the sick units.

In order to examine the bottlenecks in industrial and corporate restructuring and to suggest suitable measure for early closure of unviable units and quick revival of viable units, the Government appointed a committee on Industrial Sickness and Corporate Restructuring in May 1993. The Committee submitted its Report in July 1993. The Committee submitted its report in July 1993. The recommendations of the Committee were as given below :

- *The Definition of Sickness Should be Changed to :*

(i) Default of 180 days or more on repayment to term lending institutions; and

(ii) Irregularities in cash credits or working capital for 180 days or more.

- A sick company's own reference to BIFR should be voluntary, not mandatory.
- The only operationally significant basis for BIFR should be that of being a fast track facilitating and ocassionaly an arbitrator.
- To reduce the problem of delays in winding up there must be five fast track winding up tribunals.
- The Industrial Disputes Act (IDA) should be amended to effect the following :

(i) Section 25(N) and 25(0) of IDA may be amended so that there is no need for seeking prior approval of the Government for lay off and retrenchment of workers and for permanent closure. Chapter V B of the Industrial Disputes Act (which governs lay-off, retrenchment and closure) applies to undertaking having 100 or more workers. This should be raised to 300 or more; and

(ii) Compensation for retrenchment and closure may be increased from 15 days wages to one month wages per year of the completed service.

Magnitude of Industrial Sickness

Industrial sickness has been attracting lot of attention from the Central and the State Governments. The Reason is that only the number of sick units are rising rapidly but that the amount of the capital involved in these sick units has also risen substantially. Thus the scarce capital resources of the banking system are locked up in these units and on the other hand the financial needs of the viable and running units cannot be made available.

At the end of September 1992, there were 2.36 lakh sick or weak units. Of these 2.33 lakh units were in the small-scale sector. The amount outstanding has increased from Rs. 11, 533 Crores at the end of March 1992 to Rs. 12,586 Crores at the end of September 1992, showing an increase of 9.1 per cent. Although small-scale industries accounted for 98.7 per cent of the total sick or weak units at the end of September 1992, their share in aggregate locked in bank credit was only 26.6 percent (Table 1).

TABLE 1
Industrial Sickness

	Number of Units				Amount Outstanding (Rs. Crores)			
	End December 1988	End March 1990	End March 1991*	End March 1992*	End December 1988	End March 1990	End March 1991*	End March 1992*
1	2	3	4	5	6	7	8	9
1. SSI Sick Units	240573	218828	221472	245575	2141.00	2426.94	2792.04	3100.67
2. Non-SSI Sick Units	1241	1455	1461	1336	3387.30	4538.82	5105.57	5786.55
3. Non-SSI Weak Units	770	814	876	813	2177.00	2386.77	2870.21	2646.08
Total	242584	221097	223809	247724	7705.30	9352.53	10767.82	11533.30
Change over previous year - percent.								
1. SSI Sick Units	17.80	-9.04	1.21	10.88	19.10	13.36	15.04	11.05
2. Non-SSI Sick Units	10.90	17.24	0.41	-8.56	20.90	34.00	12.49	13.34
3. Non-SSI Weak Units	3.90	5.71	7.62	-7.19	31.40	9.64	20.25	-7.81
Total	17.78	-8.86	1.23	10.69	23.20	21.38	15.13	7.11

* The figures for March 1991 and Mrach 1992 do not include sick SSI Units which are either not traceable or non-existent.

Source : Economic Survey 1993-94.

Since inception, upto the end of September 1994, Bureau of Industrial and Financial Reconstruction (BIFR) received 2207 references Under Section 15 of Sick Industrial companies Act (SICA). Of these, 1602 references were registered for further action under the provisions of the Act. Of the 1602 references, 334 were dismissed as not maintainable, revival schemes were sanctioned or approved in respect of 463 cases and 343 cases were recommended to the concerned High Courts for winding up under the provisions of the Companies Act. 10 references were dropped as the networth of the company became positive during the course of the enquiry. A recent study of the revival schemes under the implementation, reveals that about 20 percent cases are on the road to revival, in about 20 per cent cases it is too early to form an opinion and the progress is not satisfactory in the remaining 36 percent.

As a result of the steps taken by BIFR to streamline internal procedures, it was possible to reduce the time taken between registration of a case and its first hearing. Barring cases held up due to stay by High Courts, all references registered in BIFR during 1987 stand disposed. The pending cases of 1988, 1989 and 1990 (barring those stayed by courts) have either reached the penultimate stage, or are in an advanced stage of processing.

Causes for Industrial Sickness

An industrial unit becomes sick due to numerous reasons. The factors responsible for industrial sickness can broadly be classified into two viz., external and internal. The external factors are those over which the industry has no direct control, while internal factors are those which are directly under the control of the management.

External Factors

- Non-availability of raw materials.
- change in Government Policy regarding import-export of raw materials, finished products, plant and machinery etc.
- Recession in the economy may lead to a shortfall in demand.
- Decline in demand because of obsolete product due to technological advancement.
- Creation of surplus capacity but product not in much demand due

to substitute quality product in the market.

- Power cuts and water shortage.
- Nature calamities like Floods, fire etc.
- Transport Bottlenecks.
- Political upheaval affecting industrial environment in the region.
- Inter-union rivalry.
- Problem of over-staffing/surplus labour.
- Cost escalation in project due to delay in import or installation of machinery as per schedule. It effects the amount of interest on funds already invested.
- Decline in Government Investment.
- Increase in production cost when the product is under price control.
- Rapid turnover of key personnel of the organisation.
- Death of an important person in a small unit.
- Credit restriction especially when a unit is under expansion/ diversification.
- Non-availability of working capital when commercial production is to commence.
- Change in government priorities/investment pattern in the developmental plans.

Internal Factors

(A) *Management*

- Poor talent of the management.
- Weak organisational set-up.
- Lack of vision and control.
- Deliberate diversion of funds for personal gains.
- Unplanned diversification.
- Manipulation of accounts and siphoning of funds.

- Infringement of law and non-compliance of legal procedures.
- Differences among partners/directors.

(B) *Production*

- Improper location and layout.
- Frequent breakdown of machinery, lack of maintenance and deferment of essential replacements.
- Lack of production Planning.
- Low capacity utilisation
- Wastage of materials.
- Deterioration of quality leading to high rejections.
- Lack of skilled labourers or supervision
- Deterioration of Industrial relations.

(C) *Marketing*

- No proper study of Market.
- Lack of orders due to poor marketing efforts, low quality of products, technical obsolescence, irregular delivery and thereby loss of market and goodwill.
- Improper distribution channel.
- Inadequate margin in pricing.

(D) *Finance*

- High and uneconomic inventory build-up.
- Poor collection and high receivables.
- Distress selling at heavy discount.
- Disproportionate borrowing and high incidence of interest.
- High overheads not covered by sales realisation.
- Diversion of short-term funds to long-term needs and vice-versa.[1]

The most important aspect that needs to be studied is that it is very rare that only one factor be held responsible for a unit becoming sick. It is usually the sum total of all the factors given above — the difference perhaps being in the weightage assigned to each factor.

Rehabilitation of Sick Units

Putting the sick units on the right track is of vital importance. The revival of these units will help in the productive use of the capital already invested, facilitate in increasing production and provide employment. Following are the measure suggested for rehabilitation of sick units.

(1) There should be a proper co-ordination between commercial banks and term-lending instructions in formulating, implementation and rehabilitation packages.

(2) There should be effective co-ordination among all government agencies (both at the Central and State level) including regulatory and promotional to restore sick units.

(3) Arrears like sales tax, rent, electricity charges may be deferred until the sick unit becomes a running concern.

(4) Working capital provided by the banks should charge less rate of Interest.

(5) Healthy Industrial Units should be encouraged to takeover sick units by providing proper incentives.

(6) Workers should be encouraged to run such units on a co-operative basis.

In our country, the problem of industrial sickness has assumed alarming proportions. Measures should be undertaken to prevent it by creation of a monitoring system by the lending institutions. This will help in the long run and solve a number of problems.

Reference

1. Mukerjee S. "Industrial Sickness, Reasons and Remedies" Economic Times, April 7, 1982.

12

Location of Industries

One of the major problems faced by the planners is regarding the selection of a suitable for locating the business enterprise. If due importance is not given to this problem, the business unit may be located at such a place where it may not be possible to manage it economically in spite of the availability of adequate capital and managerial skill. In view of this, due attention is to be given on this factor. In deciding about the location of an enterprise, the study of pure theories of location are of immense value.

Location Localisation and Planned Location of Industries

Before studying the theories of location, it is necessary to distinguish the above terms. Industrialists locate their industries in those places where the cost of production is minimum at the time of their establishment. This is known as Location of industries. The industry in a specified area is termed as Localisation of Industries, for instance Jute Industry in Calcutta, Textile Industry in Bombay, etc. Planned Location of Industry means that the location of industry is planned to give each industrial area a variety of industry, large industries being dispersed and not localised. Planned location of industries helps in developing the country in all the regions and checks expansion of industrial cities and areas only in certain regions.

Weber's Deductive Theory of Location

This theory was first enunciated by Prof. Alfred Weber of Germany in 1909. It was originally published in German language but it became popular in 1929 when it was translated into English. Weber's deductive theory is based on general principles which have a direct bearing on the locating of industries.

Weber discovered by investigation the factors which effect location. Making a thorough cost analysis, Weber classified the causes which influence the location into two main categories : (i) Primary causes of regional distribution of industry (regional factors); and (ii) Secondary causes (agglomerative and deglomerative factors) that are redistribution of industry.

Primary Causes (Regional Factors)

To make out the important regional factors, Weber states the elements of cost as follows : "(a) the cost of grounds; (b) the cost of buildings, machines and other fixed costs; (c) the cost of securing materials, power and fuel; (d) the cost of labour; (e) the cost of transportation; (f) the interest rates; and (g) the rate of depreciation of fixed capital".

Transportation costs and labour costs are the two regional factors on which Weber's pure theory is based. The main factors which determine the transportation are (i) the weight to be transported; (ii) the distance to be covered; (iii) the type of transportation system and the extent of its use; (iv) the nature of the region and kinds of roads; and (v) the nature of the goods themselves.

The location of the factory mainly depends on the transport relation with regard to the place of consumption and the location of raw materials. Weber classifies and calls those raw materials which are practically available everywhere as 'ubiquities' (like brick, clay, water etc.) and 'localised' (like iron-ore, limestone, minerals, wood etc.) which are available only in certain regions. He further states that localised materials play an important role on the location of an enterprise than the ubiquities. He further classifies raw materials are pure" and "weight loosing". The examples of pure raw materials are cotton, jute or wool and examples of weight loosing raw materials are located towards their deposits. For instance Iron and Steel Industry is located near iron-ore and coal mines.

Weber formulates the "laws of transportation" based on these simple deductions. He says that the proportion of the weight localised materials to that of final product is the governing factor on location of industry. He calls it as material index which can be written as :

$$\text{Material Index} = \frac{\text{Weight of localised materials}}{\text{Weight of finished product}}$$

He further examines the causes of deviation from the centres of least transportation costs. When differences exists in labour costs the industry may deviate from the optimal point of transport orientation. The transport oriented location of an industry is attracted towards the cheap labour centres. Such migration of an industry from a point of minimum transport costs to a cheap labour centre may be likely to occur only when the savings in the labour cost are larger than the additional transport cost which it is likely to occur.

The attracting power of labour location depends on two important factors (i) Locational Weight (total weight per unit to be transported during the stages of production); and (ii) Labour Cost Index (the proportion of labour cost to the weight of the product). The extent of deviation caused by varying labour costs is determined by the ratio of the labour cost to the locational weight and is termed as 'Labour Coefficient". The higher the coefficient the greater is the tendency for labour locations.

Secondary Causes (Agglomerative and Deglomerative Factors)

The deviation from the minimum transport cost point takes place also because of the secondary causes for agalomerative and deglomerative factors. Agglomeration means concentration of an industry in a particular area. At such centres several facilities like banking, insurance and marketing facilities as well as chances of securing external economies are available. On the other hand deglomeration refers to decentralisation. Industries are located away from the industrial areas, as it way be advantageous due to deglomerating factors because of the rise of land values, taxes etc. due to concentration. These two factors act in the opposite directions.

Split Location

Weber considers the location for an industry at more than one place. He says, "single location of production will be the exception and a split of production into several locations will be the rule for productive process which can technically be split". In other words if a production consists of two or more processes and each one is carried independently it is possible to have a split in location of plant. In the paper industry, pulp is manufactured near the forests which is the source of raw materials. The manufacture of paper from pulp is taken up near the centres of consumption.

Locational Coupling

Weber considers that establishing different type of industries on a particular area is feasible. If a by-product of an industry is the raw material of another industry, then, the two industries can be located at a single place. It is termed as 'Locational Coupling'. For instance molasses are the by-product of sugar industry whereas molasses are raw materials for the distilleries. Also market connections between two units bring about locational coupling.

Criticism of Weber's Theory

Weber's theory has been criticised by Sargant Florence, Andreas Predohl, S.R. Dennison and A Robinson etc. on various points which are given below :

1. Weber has been criticised for unrealistic approach and deductive reasoning. Sargant Florence says that this theory fails to explain locations resulting from historical and social forces.
2. Andreas Predohl criticises this theory while saying that this theory is more selective than deductive while referring to his classification of primary and secondary causes that influence locational trend. The very difference between the primary and secondary is itself artificial and arbitrary.
3. Regarding labour orientation Weber assumes two aspects: firstly fixed labour centres and secondary unlimited supplies of labour. But it is argued and that rise in industry may create new labour and it cannot be assumed unlimited labour supplies at any particular centre.
4. The assumption of fixed points of consumption does not work well in a competitive market structure. Austin Robinson points out that in reality the markets are wide spread and are widening further everyday.
5. Weber deals only with transportation and labour costs and excludes

important factors like climate, governmental attitude towards business etc.

6. According to Dennison, Weber has given more importance to technical aspects. Costs and prices, which must form the basis of any such theory are given message treatment and the theory is full of technical coefficients. Investigations of all economist must be based on cost price considerations.

Inspite of all these limitations Weber's theory of location of industry in an important development in the economic history as it gave a field to the economists which was totally univestigated.

Sargant Florence's Inductive Analysis

This theory has gained wide popularity in the recent years. He did not agree about Weber's geographical aspect of location. He observed that "the relation of an industry to an area is not so important as the relation of industry to the distribution of the occupied population as whole".

Sargant Florence introduced two new concepts in his theory of location. They are "Location Factor" and "Coefficient of Localisation".

Location Factor : It is an index of the degree of concentration of an industry in a particular region. It is calculated by the ratio of the percentage of all workers in a particular industry found in a certain region to the percentage of all workers in that industry in the whole country. If the quotient is one the location factor is unity which means that the industry is evenly distributed over the whole country. If the location factor is more than one the region is supposed to have a higher share of the industry in that region. If the location factor is less than one it means that the region does not have a sufficient share of the industry.

$$\text{Location Factor} = \frac{\dfrac{\text{Total Industrial Population of the region in the industry concerned}}{\text{Total Industrial population of the country in the same industry concerned}}}{\dfrac{\text{Total industrial population of the region}}{\text{Total industrial population of the country.}}}$$

Co-efficient of Localisation : It refers to a particular industry and not to a particular region. It is in relation to an industry's tendency for localisation anywhere in the country. The coefficient of localisation is calculated as follows :

(i) Firstly the percentage of all workers found in each region is determined.

(ii) Secondly the percentage of the workers of the particular industry in each region is determined.

(iii) Thirdly the positive deviations of the above two are added up.

(iv) Fourthly the sum of the positive deviations are to be divided by 100. The figure arrived at, will be the coefficient of localisation.

The basic aim of finding the coefficient of localisation is to make a classification of industries according to their qualities of dispersion or concentration. Industries having high co-efficient show very little tendency to disperse whereas industries with low co-efficient can be developed in any region.

Criticism of Sargant Florence Analysis

The theory of Florence has been criticised on the following grounds :

1. Florence's analysis measures the degree of industrial concentration more accurately but does not explain the reasons for such concentration.
2. It uses work force as a parameter to measure concentration which is not satisfactory. Capital investment, techniques of production, climate conditions, output etc. can be other parameters.

In spite of these shortcomings Florence's indices are of great use in studying the locational aspects in any country.

Factors Influencing Location

The decision regarding the location of any business enterprises is very important. Firstly because it effects the cost structure and profitability of the plant and secondly once the plant is erected at one place, it is difficult to shift at any other place subsequently. Besides there are many factors which influence the location of the plant and some are discussed below :

Easy Proximity to Markets : Marketing goods quickly can be ensured by being close to the markets. Perishable goods and bulky commodities which cannot be transported for long distances should be produced near the consuming centres. Accessibility of markets is more important in the case of consumer goods industries rather than capital goods industries because the former require adjustments constantly with the changes in the consumer behaviour.

Easy Access to Raw Materials : In determining the location of an industry, closeness to the source of raw materials is an important consideration. For instance sugar industry is concentrated where sugarcane is cultivated; steel industry is located near iron-ore and coal mines. This factor needs careful consideration as the raw material cost forms bulk of the cost of finished product.

Transport and Communication Facilities : It is one of the major factors which influences the location of an industry. Transport network of roads and railways should be well developed and communication facilities like mail, telephone, telegraph etc. must be adequate. Cement industry is located at a point where the transport cost is minimum in relation to raw materials, markets and power. Bombay enjoyed excellent transportation and communication network and this led to the heavy concentration of cotton textile industry in the city.

Labour : The manufacturing companies in their process require labour with different skills. The availability of such kind of labour in a region has favourable impact on the location of the industry. The availability of skilled workers in the interior parts of Bombay was one of the reasons responsible for the initial concentration of textile mills. The labour played a vital role in the beginning of the establishment of Iron and Steel industry at Jamshedpur.

Power, Fuel and Water : Availability of cheap power, fuel and water is one of the main factors in the choice of location of the industry. Coal as a source of industrial power led to the concentration of industries near coal mines. But with the advent of electricity with high tension lines, it has helped in the dispersal of industries. But still many industries which use coal as one of its raw materials prefer to be located near coal mines. In the case of industries which use water for cooling purpose on a large scale prefer to be located where water resources are available throughout the year.

Climate Factors : Climate plays an important part in the location of industries. Watch industry is always located in dust-free atmosphere, cotton textile industries require humid climate whereas potteries require dry climate. But if a industry does not place any climate demand, a moderate climate with low temperature variations is suited.

Apart from the factors discussed above certain non-economic reasons often influence the location of the industry like being the entrepreneur's home town, some historical reasons, strategic reasons etc.

State and Industrial Location

In the recent years the Government has started paying attention to the problems associated with industrial location. Concentration of industrial units producing similar products have led to many problems. The only solution to solve these problems is to regulate industrial location. Concentration of industries in a few selected regions have led to a number of problems as given below :

(i) Unbalanced regional growth;
(ii) Increasing fixed and operating costs;
(iii) Congestion, traffic jams etc. in urban industrial areas;
(iv) Severe housing shortage and growth of slum areas;
(v) Acute air, water and noise pollution;
(vi) High mortality rates due to diseases, accidents and lack of provision of medical facilities;
(vii) Strikes, lock-outs, gheraos, dharnas, etc.;
(viii) Disparity in income;
(ix) Bad sanitary conditions; and
(x) High cost of living.

Importance of Balanced Regional Growth

There are numerous reasons for the geographical dispersal of industries. It helps in developing the local resources of the country. It provides employment opportunities on a wider scale and helps in reducing regional disparities in incomes and wealth.

The Government can control the location of industries in two ways : (i) By encouraging establishment of industries in certain areas, and (ii) By discouraging the establishment of industries in concentrated areas. The former constitutes the positive approach and the latter a negative approach.

Positive approach includes the following :

- By providing public utility services like electricity, transport, drinking water etc.;
- By providing education and health facilities;
- By making provision for economic facilities like establishing marketing institutions etc.;
- By establishing industrial estates in industrially backward areas;

The State should grant subsidies, tax concessions, loans on easier terms for establishing industries in backward regions;

The Negative Approach consists of

- By imposing taxes at enhanced rates to prevent concentration of industries in certain areas.

Industrial licensing system under the Industries (Development and Regulation) Act 1951 was introduced to prevent further concentration of industries in the developed regions.

Five Year Plans and Industrial Location

The importance of balanced regional development was also recognised by the planners. The Planning Commission observed that, "the balanced development of different parts of the country, extension of the benefits of economic progress to the less developed regions and widespread diffusion of industry are among the major aims of planned development. Successive five-year plans seek to realise these aims in large measures". The Second Plan made considerable effort to study and investigate the regional imbalance in industrial development. It stated that location for basic capital and producer goods industries proximity to raw materials and economic factors generally had to be decisive.

During the Third Plan, the measures taken in the Second Plan were continued. Some new measures were also taken which are : (a) Establishment of large number of industrial estates; (b) Expansion of technical training facilities in backward regions; (c) Encouragement for the mobility of labour force; and (d) Issuing of licences on a preferential basis who were establishing new units in backward regions.

The Fourth Plan observed that "the requirement of non-farm employment was so much and so widely spread throughout the country that a greater dispersal of development is a matter of necessity in Indian context. Even from the narrow and immediate economic viewpoint, the society stands to gain by dispersed development". This plan envisaged an important role for the State Government in the matter of development of industries in backward areas by providing infrastructural facilities; developing new growth centres through the setting up of industrial areas and promoting new industries with the help of Industrial Development Corporations.

In the Fifth Plan the Planning Commission viewed that industrial development of backward areas was an important means of raising the level of income and reducing regional disparities and this can be achieved through the development of small-scale industries.

During the Sixth Plan the Planning Commission stated that "a substantial part of the problem of poverty is due to the uneven levels of development in different parts of the country. Any attempt of redistribution on a national scale must imply a reduction in these inter-regional gaps in the levels of development, standard of living and quality of life. However to be successful such an attempt has to form part of the general development strategy". The approach during the Sixth Plan was to rely to a much greater extent on the development of agriculture, village and small industries and allied activities.

Plant Layout

After deciding the location for the industry, the entrepreneur has to decide about the selection of the site, regarding stability and loadbearing ability of the ground, availability of land for further expansion, drainage and sewage facilities, transport facilities, post and telegraph and banking facilities, availability of social amenities and facilities, for dumping waste material.

Once the site is selected, the management has to determine the plant layout. It is defined as, "the arrangement of the machines and equipment within a factory, the construction of which is designed to facilitate their placement. Ideal layout for a plant considers the type of industry, the quantity of production, the type of the product, the type of operation and the type of the worker". In other words it is a technique of locating machines, processes and plant services within the factory in order to secure greatest possible output of high quality at the minimum possible cost of production.

The various Objectives of a Good Plant Layout are :

(a) Minimizing the cost of production; (b) Better work environment so as to reduce accidents and health hazards; (c) Minimum capital investment; (d) Smooth flow of factory operations; (e) Economic use of available floor space; (f) Optimum use of available manufacturing facilities; (g) Efficient production control; (h) Adequate storage facilities; (i) Production of quality products; (j) Better customer services; and (k) Provision for further expansion.

For the purpose of plant layout factories are classified into two categories :

(i) Continuous Industries
(ii) Assembly Industries.

A continuous industry is one in which all the necessary material is received at one point and from which successive operations turn into a finished product. Some examples which come under this category are yarn spinning, paper and pottery manufacture. Continuous industries may be either synthetical or analytical. Under synthetical industry, raw materials are repeatedly operated from one process to another unit the final product is obtained. Under analytical industry the original raw material is separated into several parts in the production process. A refining plant comes under this category.

An assembly industry is one in which various parts and components are first manufactured and then put together for making the final product. For instance motor cars, trucks, typewriters, shoes etc.

Production System

It is mainly classified under three main headings :

(a) Job production; (b) Batch production; and (c) Mass production.

Job production is carried out to the customer's special requirements for specialisations. It is also known as 'special order' production. It is usually carried out by firms engaged on sub-contract work.

Batch production refers to production of goods in batches or fixed quantity on the basis of the requirements from the customers. In such case if a batch is required to fulfil a special order the items are produced in one run.

Mass production means production of huge quantity of products on a large scale. It is also termed as flow or continuous production. Production is standardised when the goods are produced on a large scale.

Type of Layout

There are basically two types of layout :

A. Product layout.
B. Process layout.

Product or line layout implies that the machines are arranged in order in which they are used in the production of a specific product. Under such type of layout, the raw materials are fed at one end and the finished product is received at the other end. It is suitable in continuous flow and mass production industries. The steel and aluminium industries, chemical industry, automobiles assembly line industry etc. use product layout.

Some of the Advantages of Product Layout are :

(i) Smooth flow of materials;
(ii) Facilities production control;
(iii) Reduced process time;
(iv) Reduction in inventories;
(v) Supervision is simplified; and
(vi) Savings of floor space.

Some of the Disadvantages of Product Layout are :

(i) Reduced flexibility
(ii) Greater investment in machines and equipment;
(iii) Problem of maintenance;

(iv) If there is a breakdown of any one machine, there is disruption of work in the entire plant; and
(v) Difficulty in securing specialisation in supervision.

In the process or functional layout similar machines are grouped together at one place according to the operations that they perform. Thus all types of lathes are placed together, all drilling machines; casting equipments etc. are grouped together. It is useful for job order production.

Some Advantages of the Process Layout are :

(i) Flexibility in the changes in operation;
(ii) Easy to change the volume of production;
(iii) Better utilization of skill of the workers by following the principles of specialization;
(iv) Breakdowns do not hold up the production process;
(v) Greater flexibility in use of machines.

Some Disadvantages of the Process Layout are :

(i) Backtracking and Sidetracking of the materials becomes costly;
(ii) Excessive hauling of the materials;
(iii) Production period is longer which leads to higher inventories; and
(iv) Production control becomes difficult and costly.

Plant Building

While constructing a building, proper planning should be undertaken. The structure of the building depends on the nature of the industry. According to James Lundy, "An ideal plant building is one which is built to house the most efficient layout that it can be devised for the process involved, yet which is architecturally attractive and of such a standard shape and on its construction". A well planned building helps in effective and efficient operation of the plant, reduces the production control costs; decreases plant maintenance costs; increases plant flexibility; reduces the manufacturing process time; reduce employee turnover and; increases their morale.

Advantages of Single Storeyed Plant Building

(i) Expansion is very simple; (ii) Flexibility in plant layout; (iii) Material handling and work supervision cost is less; (iv) Construction cost is economical and time required for its construction is also less; (v) It provides natural illumination and proper ventilation; and (vi) Greater manufacturing space is available due to the absence of many columns which are required to support in the case of multi-storeyed building.

Its main disadvantage is that the high cost of land means a high cost of manufacturing space. Such buildings are suited for steel plants, automobile and locomotive units etc.

Advantages of Multi-Storeyed Building

(i) Economic use of land space which means lower construction cost; (ii) It allows gravity flow of materials from upper to lower floors thus reducing the handling cost of materials; (iii) It is cleaner than the single storeyed factory buildings; and (iv) It is suitable for the manufacture of light type of goods.

The main limitation with such building is that the routing of materials becomes expensive and complicated. Such buildings are very well suited for drug industries, garment manufacturing etc.

References

1. Sargant Florence : Investment, Location and Size of Plant. Cambridge University Press, 1948, p. 34
2. First Five Year Plan 1951-56.

Part 2

General Management

13

Nature and Scope of Management

Management is universally present in the modern industrialised world. Every organisation, whether it is business firm, education and health services or a public enterprise, requires decision making, co-ordination of activities, handling of people and evaluating the performance individually as to how far the pre-determined objectives have been achieved.

The importance of management has increased because labour has become more educated and specialized, scale of operations have increased substantially, technological development in practically all the spheres of life has created new challenges; and the complex nature of human relationships at all levels.

Management experts agree that management is a specialised type of activity basically responsible to get things done through other people. According to James Lundy, " Management is principally a task of planning, co-ordinating, motivating and controlling the efforts of other towards a specific objective. It involves the combining of the traditional factors of production (land, labour and capital) in an optimum manner, paying due attention to the particular goals of the organisation". The definition makes management more comprehensive to include three major activities, viz (i) planning, (ii) implementing, and (iii) controlling. According to Henri Fayol, "To manage is to forecast and to plan, to organise to command, to co-ordinate and to control. To foresee and provide means examining the future and drawing up the plan of action. To organise means building up the dual structure, material and human of the undertaking. To command means maintaining activity among the personnel. To co-ordinate means binding together, unifying and harnessing all activity and effort. To control means seeing that everything occurs in conformity with the established rules and expressed command". In this definition he attempts to analyse the management with reference to the manager.

E.F.L. Brech states that " Management is a social process entailing responsibility for the effective and economical planning and regulation of the operations of an enterprise, in the fulfilment of a given purpose or task, such responsibility involving : (a) judgement and decision in determining plans and the development of procedures to assist control to performance and progress against plans; and (b) the guidance, integration, motivation and supervision of the personnel composing the enterprise, and carrying out its operation". Brech analyses the role of management as a social aspect involving the management of people and not only the management of machines or things.

Koontz and O'Donnel defined management as " the art of getting things done through and with people in formally organised groups. It is the art of creating an environment in which people can perform as individuals and yet cooperate towards attainment of group goals". This definition analyses the management as an art of creating an environment in which the group can achieve the pre-determined objectives.

Peter F. Drucker says that " Management is a multipurpose organ that manages a business and manages manager, and manages worker and work." Drucker emphasises three areas of management. If one is delinked there can be no business. It is the manager who has to create balance and carry out the three functions of the business.

Harbison and Myers offer three fold concept for emphasising a broader scope for the viewpoint of management. They observe management as (i) an economic resource, (ii) a system of authority, and (iii) a class or elite.

1. As viewed by the economist, management is one of the factors of production together with land, labour and capital. As the industrialisation of a nation increase, the need for management becomes greater as it is substituted for capital and labour. The managerial resources of a firm determine to a major extent is productivity and profitability. Management must be used more extensively in those industries which experience innovations.

2. As viewed by a specialist in administration and organization, management first developed an authoritarian philosophy with a small number of top individuals determining all actions of rank and file. Later humanitarian concepts caused some management to develop paternalistic approaches. Still later, constitutional management emerged having consistent policies and procedures for dealing with working group. Later with the expansion of education, the trend of management was towards a democratic and participative approach. Modern management can be viewed as a synthesis of these four approaches to authority.
3. As viewed by a sociologist management is a class and status system.

Administration and Management

There has been a lot debate regarding the difference between administration and management. Some experts view management having a wider connotation which includes administration. It includes administrative management and operative management. Administrative management (or administration) is basically concerned with policy framing, planning and if necessary changing the policies and controlling the entire business. Operative management is concerned with the execution of the policies, and plans and is directly responsible for the achievement of the stated objective.

Other management experts like Sheldon, Spriegel, Milward, etc. regard management as a lower level function and is chiefly concerned with the execution of policies framed by the top administration. These people restrict the meaning of the term " management ".

The difference between the two terms can be analysed from the definitions given. Oliver Sheldon says that " Administration is the function in industry concerned in the determination of the corporate policy, the co-ordination of finance, production and distribution, the settlement of the compass of the organisation and the ultimate control of the executive. Management proper is the function in industry concerned, in the execution of policy, within the limits set-up by the administration". According to J.N. Schultze, "Administration is the force which lays down the objects for which an organisation and its management are to strive and the broad policies under which they are to operate. Management is the force which leads, guides and directs an organisation in the accomplishment of a predetermined object". According to G.E. Milward

" Administration is primarily the process and the agency used to establish the object or purpose which an undertaking and its staff are to achieve; secondly administration has to plan and to stabilise the broad lines of principles which will govern action. These broad lines are in their turn usually called policies. Management is the process and the agency through which execution of policy is planned and supervised".

On analysing the above definitions we see that the manager performs both the functions at all the levels and no two groups of people are required to perform administrative and managerial functions. Every manager spends part of his time in administering and part of his time in managing. All managers at any levels of management perform the same functions. However if we go up at the higher level of management structure, the managers devote more time on administration and comparatively less time on operative management.

Activity Levels of Management

The management structure of a business firm can be divided into the following activity levels.

Top management : It consists of the Board of Directors, the Executive Director, Managing Directors, Secretary etc. primarily concerned, with the general operation of the business. They are the supreme level of authority and determine the objective, set the targets, frame the policies and see that the policies are executed efficiently and effectively.

Upper middle management : It consists of functional heads of production, finance, marketing, personnel, materials, R & D, and the like. They select proper staff to carry out the plans and policies of the top management. They design the operating policies and routines and assign specific duties to each department and each individual. They obtain the necessary finance to execute the target set forth.

Middle management : It consists of deputy heads of various sections, superintendents and the like or either line or staff functions. Mary C. Niles has summarised the functions of middle management in the following words :

(a) "To run the details of the organisation, leaving the top officers as free as possible of their other responsibilities.

(b) To co-operate in making a smoothly functioning organisation.
(c) To understand the interlocking of departments in major policies.
(d) To achieve the co-ordination between the different parts of organisation.
(e) To build up a contented and efficient staff.
(f) To develop leaders for the future by broad training and experience.
(g) To develop a company spirit".

Foremen : These persons directly supervise the working force in various areas of activity in the concern.

Operating force : It consists of those persons who themselves manage their assigned job and their equipments.

Management - Science or Art

Science is a systematised body of knowledge based upon certain observations, accurate measurement, experimentation and inferences obtained after analysing the data. Science gives the theory, principles and the laws of any branch. On the other hand art means a way of doing a particular thing. It is only through art that a person is able to reach concrete ends, effect results and produce favourable situations.

Management consists of both the elements of science and arts. The science of management provides certain principles or laws for guiding and solving the specific management problems and objective evaluation of results. The analysis of fundamental functions of management, has provided certain principles which can be universally applied as general guides for solving certain problems. Art reflects practical application of the knowledge acquired for achieving favourable results on situations in specific cases. Art does not depend only on knowledge but it derives its inspiration through institution and other subjective attributes.

Art and science are complementary to each other and art improves with the improvement in the knowledge of science. Both go together hand-in-hand and are mutually interdependant. Management is a science as it possesses a universally accepted principles but to implement those principles, it really needs art. Hence it is both science and art.

Management as a Profession

Louis A. Allen has said, " A professional manager is one who specialises in the work of planning, organising, leading and controlling the efforts of others and does so through systematic use of classified knowledge, a common vocabulary and principles and who subscribes to the standards of practice and code of ethics established by recognised body ".

Under the corporate structure there is a separation between the management and ownership and it was only after the World War II that the management assumed professional character consisting of the following features :

1. An organized and systematic body of knowledge.
2. A formal method of acquiring knowledge and skill through established institutions offering courses of business management.
3. Management tools have enhanced the practical utility of management science.
4. Growth of specialists in the field of management.
5. Formation of management associations.
6. Laying stress on code of conduct for management personnel.

Functions of Management

Management is defined as the guidance, leadership, co-ordination and control of a group of people towards some pre-determined objective. The manager is a person who gets the work done with the co-ordinated efforts of other people. Management is a ongoing social process. It is a process because it encompasses numerous actions that lead to the achievement of pre-determined objectives. It is regarded as a social process because it is basically concerned with manning the human resources so as to secure their co-operation. It is a ongoing process because cyclical operations of management never cease and it also indicates the dynamic nature of management.

In order to analyse the management process we have to study the functions of management which are given below :

Planning

It includes the determination of objectives i.e. what is to be done, formulation of plans, strategies, policies, procedures and similar things desired to achieve the goals. The process of planning includes : (a) determination of objectives of the organisation in each area of business;

(b) collection and classification of relevant information needed to achieve the objectives; (c) to select the alternative plans of action; (d) to establish policies, procedures, schedules, programmes budgets etc.

Planning can be defined as an integrated activity whose basic purpose is to achieve the pre-determined objectives efficiently and effectively.

Organising

It is a system which enables to achieve the pre-determined objectives. It is based on the principle of division of labour. It is a process of developing an organisation where people are given different activities to perform and these activities are so co-ordinated to achieve the given objectives. It includes the division of major tasks into smaller activities; assigning activities to the people; delegating the authority and assigning responsibilities; thus creating a authority responsibility relationship. The organisation set-up is a tool to accomplish the objectives. Efficient organisational set-up is a success to an enterprise.

Staffing

It is a process by which managers select, train and promote their subordinates. The staff carries out the work allotted to them. Staffing is done in such a way so as to meet the future manpower requirements.

Directing

Under this the manager directs his staff personnel to achieve the objectives. He sees that the staff is working in the right direction and they do not go out of track. It includes managing the workers by means of motivation, leadership, proper communication and providing a proper environment for the accomplishment of work.

Controlling

It is the process of evaluating the result, comparing the results with the standard of performance, determining the important deviations and rectifying whenever necessary. Rectification may lead to a change in the method of implementation of the plan or change in the objective.

Development of Management-Thought

The study of management as a separate field is a product of the

19th century. But it was only around 1900 A.D. that the management based on certain scientific principles gained impetus which was given by Taylor and his associates. The evolution of management thought may be classified into three broad stages.

Classical Theories of Management

A set of principles and concepts about management were developed around 1900 A.D., which is now termed as classical theory. This theory comprises of three areas (a) Bureaucracy; (b) Scientific Management, and (c) Process Management.

Bureaucratic Model : This model was enunciated by Max Weber. He thought that bureaucracy was the most efficient form of any complex organisation. His model has the following basic features; (i) Regular activities aimed at organisation, goals are distributed as fixed official duties; (ii) Organisation follows the principle of hierarchy; (iii) Operations are governed by a consistent system of abstract rules that are applied to individual cases; (iv) The ideal official operates as a formalistic impersonality without emotion; (v) Employment in the organisation is based on technical qualifications and is not subject to arbitrary termination; (vi) Bureaucracy attains the highest degree of efficiency.

Although Weber was criticised on being too autocratic, his concept of bureaucracy has had great impact on classical thinking about formal organisation.

Scientific Management : F.W. Taylor is known as " the Father of Scientific Management". Taylor, Frank and Lillian Gilbreth, Gantt and others are responsible for the movement of scientific management. The crux of scientific management was in four general areas. (a) Management through scientific method should try to determine the best way of accomplishing the task rather than to use, the rule of thumb approach. (b) The management should perform the planning function and the workers should follow the instructions given by the manager. (c) The management should select and train the workers and develop co-operation amongst them rather than encourage individualistic efforts by employees. (d) There should be a division of work between the management and workers. The management should analyse and plan the work in advance and the workers should execute the plan. Each one should be alloted those duties for which he is best suited so that there can be increase in efficiency.

Frank and Lillian Gilbreth worked on motion study and laid the foundations of job simplification, meaning work standards and incentive wage plans. Henry Gantt, an associate of Taylor emphasized the psychology of the worker and the importance of morale in production. Gantt developed a wage payment system which encouraged foremen and workers to strive for improvement in work practices. He developed a charting system for scheduling production. H. Emerson developed twelve principles for efficiency, five relating to employer employee relations and seven relating to systems in management.

Process Management : The process management approach was first enunciated by Henri Fayol in Europe. He concluded that all industrial activities could be categorized into six groups : (1) Technical activities (2) Commercial Activities (3) Financial activities (4) Security Activities (5) Accounting activities (6) Managerial activities.

Fayol in his book "*General and Industrial Management*" described fourteen management principles which are given below :

(a) Division of work; (b) Authority and responsibility; (c) Discipline ; (d) Unity of command; (e) Unity of direction; (f) Subordination of individual interest to general interest; (g) Remuneration of Personnel; (h) Centralisation; (i) Scalar chain; (j) Order; (k) Equity; (1) Stability of tenure of personnel; (m) Initiative; and (n) Esprit decorps.

J . Mooney and Alan Reiley supported the process management approach. These two experts identified and elaborated principles of organisation such as co-ordination, scalar principle, line and staff duties etc. Upwick and Gullick have also emphasised the need for process management approach.

Neo-Classical Theory of Management

This theory lays emphasis on the person manning the machine and gives importance to individual as well as group relationships in the plant of working place. It is categorized into two parts (a) Human Relations approach; and (b) Behvioural Science approach.

Human Relations Approach : It is an interdisciplinary activity in the study of management. Elton Mayo and a team of social scientists conducted studies in the Hawthorne plant of western electric company in U.S.A between 1927 and 1932. They made an attempt to explain the variations of productivity in the factory. They explained that the employee morale, both individually and in groups has an effect on productivity.

Management should have more people-oriented approach rather than machine oriented approach. They said that psychological factors were very important in increasing the overall productivity. They also emphasised the importance of physical factors, lighting and working conditions.

Behavioural Science Approach : This approach was a further development of human relations approach and it covered a much wider àrea in interpersonal roles and relationships. A. Maslow developed a need hierarchy to explain human behaviour within and organisation. F. Herzberg and V. Vroom studied the causes of human behaviour and motivation in business. D. McGregor gave certain basic assumption about the human element.

From the above we can conclude that there are three elements of the neo-classical theory.

The Individual : The neo-classical theory laid stress on the individual differences. It suggests that an individual has feelings, motions, attitudes and perception. In the determination of productivity the inner part of the worker is more important than reality, and inter-personal relations determine the rise or fall in productivity.

Work Groups : When an Individual is in group he develops certain social desires. Management should treat the workers as social beings. This theory has discussed the important effects of group psychology and behaviour on motivation and productivity.

Participative Management : The participative management emerged when due emphasis was given on the individual and groups. The supporters of this theory want workers participation in management. It is their thinking that if workers are allowed to participate in decision making, there can be an increase in productivity.

Modern Management Theories

The modern management theories have further refined and extended the classical and non-classical approaches to management.

Quantitative Approach : It is also known as operations research (OR). New mathematical and statistical techniques are applied in the decision making of commonly used are linear programming, game theory;

simulation, probability etc. The help of computers is taken to solve the complex management problems. Operations research, computer and management information system (MIS) are modern techniques of management regarding decision making programmes.

Quantitative approach to management can only suggest the best alternatives based on quantitative data. The final analysis and decision has to be taken by the management. This approach is a good supplement than a substitute for managerial decisions.

System Approach : This is an entirely new approach in the modern management. It lays emphasis on the inter-relatedness and interdependence of all activities within an organisation. The modern thinkers consider an organisation as an adaptive system which can adjust itself to the changing environment.

A system is a set or group of interrelated elements to achieve certain predetermined objectives. Thus we see that every system is goal oriented and the elements should be arranged in such a manner so that maximum productivity and satisfaction can be achieved. The systems approach gives management a view of looking organisations as a whole and a part of larger external environment. Systems approach suggests that activity of any part of an organisation affects the activity of every other part.

The systems approach to management encompasses a number of concepts :

Subsystems : The parts that make up the whole of a system are called "Subsystems". And each system in turn may be a subsystem of a still larger whole called supersystem. Thus a department is a subsystem of a unit which may be subsystem of a company, which in turn may be a subsystem of an industry which is the subsystem of the national economy.

Synergy : It means that whole is greater than the sum of its parts. In organisational terms, synergy means that within an organisation the separate departments co-operate with each other and they become more productive than if each department has acted in isolation.

Open and Closed Systems : A System is said to be open if it interacts with its environment and considered closed if it does not.

System Boundary : Each System has a boundary that separates it from its environment. In the open system the boundary is flexible whereas in the closed system the boundary is rigid.

Flow : A System has flows of various things. These enter the system from the environment as inputs, undergo transformation process within the system, and leave the system as outputs.

Feedback : It is very important aspect of systems control. As the operations of the system proceed, information is fed back to the appropriate people so that the work done can be assessed and if necessary, rectified.

Contingency Approach : The contingency approach developed when different concepts of management were applied in real life situations. Therefore we cannot have universal principles or oganisation and management which can be applied in all situations and in all environments. Thus under the contingency approach the task of the management is to identify which technique will, in a particular situation, under specific circumstances and at a given time, best contribute to the attainment of management objectives. The contingency approach means that we must be aware of the complexity in every situation and that we must take an active role in trying to determine what would work best in each case.

Thus we see that different schools of management thought have contributed to manager's understanding of organisations and to their ability to manage them. Each has given a different perspective for defining management problems and ways and means to encounter them. But it is only on the management to select the appropriate method for each situation.

Reference

1. Frederick Harbison and Charles Myers : Management in the Industrial World, New York : Mcgraw-Hill book Company, 1959.

14

The Process of Planning

Planning is the primary task of every management. It is performed at every level of management. Planning is the determination of line of action to achieve the desired goals. Planning is deciding in advance what should be done, how should be done, what at a certain time and who will do it. Planning encompasses (a) assessment of the future; (b) determination of the objectives; (c) development of alternative course of action; and (d) selecting the most appropriate course of action among these alternatives.

Various definitions have been given by different experts. Alford and Beatty define it as "Planning is the thinking process, the organised foresight; the vision based on fact and experience that is required for intelligent action". Louis A. Allen says," Management planning involves the development of forecasts, objectives, policies, programmes, procedure, schedules and budgets". In the words of Koontz and O'Donnel, " Planning is an intellectual process, the conscious determination of courses of action, the basing of decision on purpose, facts and considered estimates".

The Nature of Planning

The Following points describe the nature of planning.

Objectives

The Plan must aim at achieving certain objectives. It frames how to achieve them.

Primacy of Planning

Planning is the basic requirement of all managerial functions whether it is organising, staffing, directing or controlling.

Pervasiveness of Planning

Planning is such a function which is present at all levels of management, though the scope of planning varies with the authority of managers.

Efficiency and Economy

Efficiency of a plan is measure by its contribution to the objectives as economically as possible. It also concentrates on accurate forecasts.

Co-ordination

Planning co-ordinates the activities of the organisation like what, who, how, where and why of planning.

Limitation

Planning recognizes the shortcomings and limitations and frames and plan taking these aspects into consideration.

Flexibility

The planning process should be flexible so as to adjust in the changing conditions.

Importance of Planning

1. Planning concentrates on the feature with some basic purpose. Managerial planning emphasizes the accomplishments of pre-determined objectives in a specified period of time.
2. Planning makes provisions for decision making in a unified manner. There are various functional departments in the organisation and if they work according to their own wish, they shall not be able to achieve the corporate goals. It is only planning which makes possible for a unified decision process.
3. Plan helps in the identification of potential opportunities and uncertainties. The environmental conditions are constantly changing and the opportunities and uncertainties are common steps in the process of planning. Objectives are framed on the

basis of environmental conditions prevailing in the economy.

4. Planning provides specified standards for the targets to be achieved. The performance of the organisation is measured on the basis of such a specified performance standard.
5. Planning is the only instrument which assures the survival and continuity of the organisation.

Advantages of Planning

1. Integrated purposeful action is easily accomplished. There is optimum utilisation of resources and unproductive work is eliminated or minimised.
2. It enables an organisation to exist and survive and remain competitive in the market.
3. It helps in avoiding delays and rectifying mistakes. Anticipating uncertainitites, planning helps the management to be prepared to meet such situations.
4. Planning provides a sound basis for effective control.
5. Planning provides effective delegation of authority, removes communication gaps, helps in co-ordination and integration of all functions.

Limitations of Planning

Some of the limitations of business planning are as follows :

1. As the social, economic, political and technological environment has become very unpredictable, the accuracy and reliability of most of the forecasts diminishes and the plan framed goes useless.
2. Planning is time consuming and expensive process. It involves a lot of time, energy and money without any assurance as to the realisation of objectives. Small units cannot afford comprehensive planning.
3. Once the plans are framed, there is a reluctance to change, even though change is desirable.
4. The effectiveness of planning is limited because of the external factors which are not under the control of the planners.
5. It is difficult to assure the correctness of planning since it takes time to get results in the form of feedback data.

These limitations of planning can be overcome by taking suitable measure. In reality, no organisation can exist without some planning.

Types of Planning

According to the nature of planning some of the important types may be discussed as below :

Strategic Planning

It is the process of selecting the objectives of the organisation and the methods to achieve them within the resources available and likely to be available in future. It includes strategies, programmes, policies, procedures and standards that will determine the procurement, use and disposition of these resources.

Tactical Planning

Such type of plans cover short periods not exceeding one year. They usually support the overall strategic panning and specific plans for the functional areas of the organisation. Examples of tactical planning are marketing, production finance, personnel etc.

Long-Range and Short-Range Planning

Long-range planning sets long-term targets for the organisation and formulates specific planning for the accomplishments of these targets. On the other hand short-range planning is concerned with the determination of short-term activities to attain the long term objectives. It usually covers a period of one year and is co-ordinated with the long-range planning.

Standing Planning

These plans are framed to be used over and over again. They include policy formulation in different areas, standard procedures, standard methods and rules.

Single-Use Planning

They are developed for a certain purpose. Once the purpose is achieved the plans cease to exist. These plans are framed to meet a particular situation and once the objective is achieved they have no other value.

Administrative and Operational Planning

Administrative planning is done by the middle level management and it provides guidelines for operational planning. Operational planning is concerned with the planning structures and repetitive activities in the departments. For instance planning of routing, scheduling and despatch in production, planning to accelerate research projects, cash flow budgets etc.

Components of Planning

Objectives

Before taking any line of action, the objectives must be clearly stated and understood. The determination of objectives has a direct impact on the organisation, planning and control. Objectives are the ends towards which the activities of an organisation are directed. If an organisation has well defined objectives and goals it can grow and develop in an orderly and progressive manner.

Features

There are Certain Basic Feature of Objectives :

(a) They must be determined much in advance; (b) They must be realistic; (c) It should be in such a manner so that the performance can be easily measured; (d) The objectives must be framed in a descending order i.e. total divisional, regional etc; (e) There are generally multiple objectives; and (f) There are time bound objectives like Short-range, medium-range and long-range objectives.

Advantages

(a) Overall Objectives provide direction for the organisational efforts. Departmental objectives provide direction for departmental efforts; (b) They help in motivating the personnel of the organisation; (c) They facilitate in integrated planning; (d) They help in developing a control system; (e) The objectives guide to co-ordinate between the various departments and individuals; and (f) The objectives reflect the management by objective (MBO) which is the modern management philosophy.

Types of Objectives

Every organisation has a number of objectives which may be

included under two categories.

External Objectives

The first and foremost objective of any organisation is to provide service to its customers. Secondly it has certain responsibilities towards the society also. It should give help in educational, health and other programmes which will benefit the entire community.

Internal Objectives

The first internal objective is the position of the company in the competitive market economy. It may try to achieve a major share of the market. The second one is to provide maximum satisfaction to its employees. The third one is to give fair return to the shareholder's investment.

Management by Objectives (MBO)

MBO is a participative process activity involving managers and staff members at every organisational level. MBO helps in building up link between the planning and controlling functions which overcome many of the barriers to planning. Under the MBO system managers and their subordinates act together in framing the objectives. Each person's major areas of responsibility are clearly defined in terms of measurable expected results or objectives. These objectives are used by subordinates in planning their work. Performance appraisal are conducted jointly on a continuing basis, with provisions for regular periodic reviews.

MBO lays emphasis on participation by directly involving sub-ordinates in framing objectives for their work. It encourages innovation as it lays stress on results and less on the method employed in achieving the targets.

Policies

They are broad guidelines which determine the course of action. They are the guiding plans for the management to conduct the operations of the organisation so as to accomplish the given objective. Policies deal with these problems which are recurring in nature. It is a means to achieve a given objective.

There are three types of policies based on the area and level of management :

Basic Policy

It is a more specific in nature and is mainly used by the middle management. For instance giving top priority to local dealers in the matters of purchasing.

General Policy

It is a more specific in nature and is mainly used by the middle management. For instance giving top priority to local dealers in the matters of purchasing.

Departmental Policy

It is very specific in nature and applies to the routine activities in the department. It is used by low level managers. For instance the employees will sign the register twice a day.

Besides, the policies may be framed in the important areas of management like marketing, personnel, finance, production and so on.

Though the responsibility of laying down the policies rests with the Board of Directors, the middle level management should be consulted and due weightage should be given to their views. So that there may not be any problem at the time of implementation. There are certain basic features which should be taken into consideration while laying down the policies.

(a) The policies should be in writing and express the intentions of the management.
(b) There should be uniformity in formulation of the policy.
(c) There should be uniformity in the applicability of the policies also.
(d) There should be an appraisal of policies after a specified period to know their effectiveness.

Once the policies are finalised, they should be communicated to the persons who are going to use it in the organisation. Every policy must have effective communication.

Procedures

The procedures are sequence of steps in implementing various plans. Procedure gives a sequence of actions which are uniformity and consistently performed e.g. placing an order, selection of employees etc. A procedure statement is very specific in nature as it elaborates the steps to be taken in sequence in order to accomplish a given objective.

Procedures can be differentiated from policies. A policy is a guide for thinking whereas procedure is guide for action and performance. Policy is always superior to procedure. Policies are specified guidelines framed by the top management. Procedures are systematic ways of performing certain tasks which are executed by the subordinates.

Methods

A method is highly specific in nature. Every procedure consists of various methods to perform each phase of work. A method is a working plan which enumerates in detail the manner and sequence by which each operation is performed. The scope of methods is very limited because it deals with only one step of procedure.

Rules

They are the most specific type of plans chosen from various alternatives. It is rigid in nature and allows no liberty. It clearly states whether a particular action has to be taken or not, with respect to a situation. ' No smoking ' or ' It is not a throughway ' are examples of a rule.

Programmes

A programme is a sequence of activities designed to achieve a specific objective. It lays down the principal steps for accomplishing the given task. A programme involves a complex of activities, resources to be employed and other elements necessary to carry the given line of action. They require systematic thinking and auction. For instance we may have production programme, expansion programme etc.

Schedules

Schedules are action plans. They are fixing the time sequence or completing the programmed operations. It formulates the time limit when each of the series of action should take place. It helps in avoiding delays and ensures in the continuity of the activities to be performed.

Budget

Budgets are statements of expected results expressed in numerical terms-in monetary units. Budgets is a means of planning as well as it is used as a control device. Usually there are departmental budgets and a master budget for the entire organisation. The budget covers a specified periods usually 12 months. Budgets for capital expenditure may be a longer duration. Budgets should be flexible and have a structural form. Budgets are means of better planning improved co-ordination and basis for control. For instance there may be sales budgets, advertising budgets, production budget and so on. Budgets are the best device for evaluating the performance of the company.

Strategy

It is a wide programme for achieving the organisation's objective. The term programme means that mangers shall perform an active and rational role in formulating the strategy of the organisation. Strategy guides in the deployment of resources so as to achieve the objectives of the organisation. Strategy creates a relationship between human and other resources of the organisation and the environment.

Strategic Planning

It is defined as the long-range planning process analysing the overall corporate objectives, policies and strategies that will govern the utilisation of resources to achieve the organisational goals. Strategic planning includes all important areas of business activities such as anticipated profits, capital expenditure for growth, diversification programmes, technological capabilities, management development, social responsibilities and so on.

Strategic planning has gained importance in the recent years because mangers can adjust with the fast changing environment on which their organisation operate. The importance of strategic planning has increased because of the following reasons:

(a) To increasing rate of technological developments have made the procedures to seek new opportunities actively.

(b) The nature of job of the manager has become complex because of the changing factors-inflation, social responsibility, the shift from urban marketing to rural marketing, government regulations etc., have created new challenges.

(c) Management decisions depend upon long term profit expectation rather than on immediate sales prospects.

(d) The growing awareness regarding environment has compelled the management to change their production techniques so that pollution can be minimised to a major extent.

15

Organising Process

Once the policies and objectives are framed the process of organising starts. Organisations is the division of work between the people whose efforts should be co-ordinated to achieve the predetermined objectives. The basic features of the organising process are (a) Span of Supervision (b) Departmentation (c) Delegation and Decentralisation (d) Authority; and (e) Line, Staff, Functional and Committee Organisation.

Span of Supervision or Control

The term span of supervision means the number of subordinates to be supervised and controlled by a manger. It is a very important principle of organisation. This principle is based on the theory of relationships given by a French management consultant V.A. Graicunas. He gave a mathematical formula showing that as the number of subordinates increased arithmetically, the number of relationship among them increased almost geometrically. But he was unable to give reasons which actually govern the span of supervision.

The modern management system believes that there cannot be any rigid formula regarding span of supervision. It usually depends on the number important activities at the next lower level of the organisation. Proper span of supervision is considered a necessity for efficient and effective co-ordination.

Factors Affecting Span of Supervision

The factors which effect the span of supervision are given

below :

Ability of The Manager : Individuals differ in various qualities like intelligence, expression, leadership, decision making etc. A manger who has more capacity as compared to others, can supervise more people.

Availability of Time For Supervision : The span of supervision should be narrow at the higher level because the higher level managers cannot devote full time in supervising their subordinates. They have to perform other managerial functions like planning, organising, directing and controlling.

Nature and Importance of Activities : The lower level managers deal with simple and routine problems and therefore they can supervise the activities of a greater number of subordinates. Whereas the top level management supervise the activities of lesser number of subordinates because they have to deal with complex problems which require serious attention.

Ability of Subordinates : Subordinates who are trained in managerial work can discharge their duties in a better way than untrained personnel who will require more time. Supervision needs less time or those subordinates who have judgement, initiative and a sense of devotion towards their organisation.

Degree of Decentralisation : If there is a higher degree of decentralisation then the manager can supervise a large number of subordinates. On the other hand if he has to take a number of decisions he cannot successfully supervise his subordinates.

Assistance of Staff : When staff personnel provide guidance to subordinates regarding methods, procedures and other managerial work, then supervisions take more time and they cannot supervise more subordinates.

In the end we can say that the span of supervision should be determined by the position of the manager. Secondly it should be flexible in nature so that adjustments can be easily made. With the changing environment, it should be seen to what type of activities the manager is performing. A practical approach should be taken rather than following a set pattern. It should be taken care that there should not be any communication gap which leads to many problems.

16

Departmentation

When similar or homogenous activities are grouped together on the basis of special nature of activities, it is known as departmentation. Departmentation may be further explained as the process of forming departments or sections by grouping similar activities of an organisation to achieve efficient and effective functioning.

Aims of Departmentation

The following are the aims of departmentation.

(a) Grouping of similar activities into separate departments so that there can be efficient management.
(b) To bring specialisation in the performance of different activities.
(c) To fix responsibility on the departmental or section heads for the achievement of pre-determined objectives.

Advantages of Departmentation

Specialisation

Since different activities are grouped according to their relation with specified functions, every sectional head specialises in the duties and tasks assigned to him.

Control

It helps in effective and efficient administrative and managerial control of each and every department.

Fixation of Responsibility

Since the organisational duties are divided into various units, authority and responsibility are delegated to different personnels, the task of fixing the responsibility to different managers for assessing their performance becomes very easy.

Freedom to Work

Once the departments are assigned their job, the department head is free to get the work done. This helps in increasing the efficiency of the departments.

Management Development

The departmental or sectional heads are able to develop their managerial skill as they have to take certain decisions and initiative alone, so as to get the work done.

Basis of Departmentation

The basis of departmentation of any business organisation is discussed below :

Function

Creating departments on the basis of function is the most common form of grouping activities in any organisation. Here the word function means the major activities of an organisation. Production, marketing, finance, personnel, materials, etc. are the typical functions of an industrial organisation and departments are created on the basis of such functions. The importance of these functions depends on the type of business organisation. Secondly the size, nature and volume of business has an important bearing in the creation of various departments. The departments created on the basis of various functions is known as functionalization.

Advantage : The advantages of functional departmentation are as follows : (i) It is the natural form of departmentation based on certain logic; (ii) It brings specialisation which leads to maximum utilisation of human and material resources; (iii) It lays stress on each activity making each department to contribute towards the organisational objectives; (iv) It provides suitable delegation of authority, thus giving more time for planning to the higher management executives; (v) Services of the executives can be obtained to perform certain specific activities.

Disadvantages : The disadvantages of functional

departmentation are as follows : (i) With too much emphasis on specialisation, the generalists feel ignored which leads to certain personnel problems in the organisation, (ii) Lack of co-ordination and understanding amongst the departmental heads may lead to certain managerial and organizational problems; (iii) At times it becomes difficult to control various specified activities on the organization; (iv) Some times the functional departmentation leads to increase in expenses.

Product

In the case of product departmentation, departments are created on the basis of products. Organisations which manufactures many products prefer to group their activities on the basis of products or product classes. Under the product departmentation all activities pertaining to a particular product line or class may be grouped together under the direction of a product manager who is delegated the authority of operating the product according to the nature of demand in the market.

Advantages : The following are the advantages of product departmentation : (i) The performance of each product or a product line can be assessed and distinction between profitable and unprofitable products can be easily made; (ii) The strategy of marketing becomes more realistic; (iii) The top management is able to concentrate on important areas such as planning, research and development etc; (iv) It helps in product expansion and diversification; (v) Due to decentralisation, each division encourages initiative and efficiency.

Disadvantages : The following are the disadvantages of product departmentation : (i) There is duplication of physical facilities and service functions; (ii) The operating cost is high and the small and medium sized concerns are unable to adopt such pattern; (iii) The capacity of the plant may remain unutilised if a product does not find place in the market.

Territory

Departmentation by territory takes place when the company is organised into a number of regions located in different areas. Also known as geographical departmentation, it is useful or banks, insurance companies, petroleum companies etc. They usually divide their activities into regions, zones, divisions and branches.

Advantages : The following are the advantages of territorial departmentation. (i) Since they are near the market and fully aware of the local conditions, they can adopt and respond to the local situation with speed and accuracy; (ii) The cost of production is lower because of the economy in transportation and favourable raw material prices; (iii) Better co-ordination and control is achieved by establishing regional offices; and (iv) It helps in expanding business at the local level effectively.

Disadvantages : The following are the disadvantages of territorial departmentation : (i) There is duplication of physical facilities; (ii) At times there may be problem of co-ordination among the various regions; and (iii) Centralized services to various departments becomes difficult.

Customers

Departmentation by customers takes place when the company is offering specialised services and to give special emphasis to the various groups of buyers, the marketing activities are divided into various parts.

Advantages : The following are the advantages of departmentation by customers : (i) Its chief aim is to satisfy the customers; and (ii) It supplies goods according to the specific needs of the customers.

Disadvantages : The following are the disadvantages of departmentation by customers : (i) It creates the problem of co-ordination among the different departments as it is exclusively applied to the marketing department; and (ii) The specialised sales staff becomes idle when the sales of any particular group of buyers decline.

Process

A manufacturing company may departmentalise its activities on the basis of production process. Similar machines are grouped into separate sections that are used for a specific operation on the job. For instance lathe, drilling machines and so on are located in specified units.

The justification for a separate unit for similar machines is that it is difficult to instal a costly equipment in every department which needs its use.

THE FUNCTIONAL DEPARTMENTATION

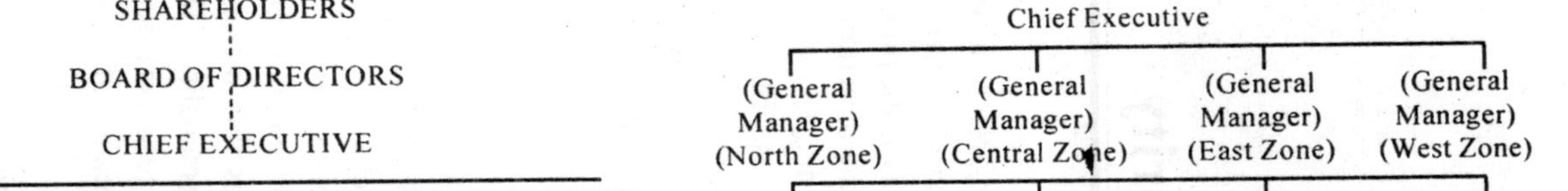

THE TERRITORIAL DEPARTMENTATION

DEPARTMENTATION BY PRODUCT

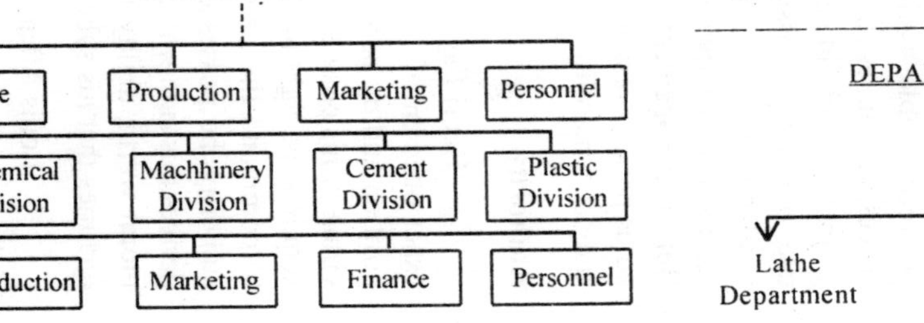

DEPARTMENTATION BY CUSTOMERS

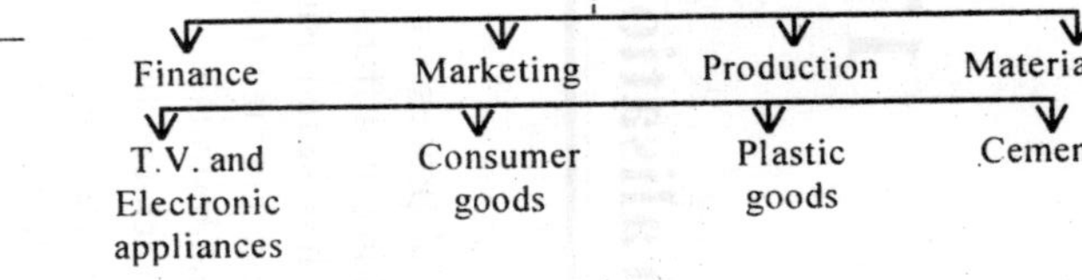

DEPARTMENTATION BY PROCESS

Production Division

Lathe Department | Grinding Department | Milling Department | Assembly Department

17

Decentralisation of Authority

Organisational process is the establishment of relationship between people working at different levels. No person can manage successfully unless he has the requisite authority. Authority is the power given to an individual to get the work done. It includes the direction to take decisions, to issue instructions to the subordinates and to use the available resources to achieve the organisational objectives. But there can be no authority without responsibility. Both of them go side by side. But in management, accountability is also an important aspect which holds persons responsible for their acts. Hence authority, responsibility and accountability exist more or less simultaneously.

Authority

Henri Fayol defined authority as "the right to give orders and exact obedience". He has distinguished the authority of manager by position and by personality. The manager derives formal authority by virtue of his position in the organisation. By virtue of this authority he acquires the right to take decisions, to act according to the situation and to command the persons working under him. Besides this official authority, he possesses the authority by virtue of his personality. He derives this authority by way of his intelligence, knowledge, experience, moral worth, ability to provide leadership etc. It is because of these qualities that his subordinates accept his authority.

Louis Allen has defined authority as the sum of the powers and rights entrusted to make possible the performance of the work delegated. According to Theo-Haimann " Authority is the rightful legal power to request subordinates to do a certain thing or to retain from doing so, and if he does not follow these instructions the manger is in a position, if need be, to take disciplinary action, even to discharge the subordinate".

Louis Allen has classified authority into three categories namely: (i) Authority of knowledge; (ii) Authority of position; and (iii) Legal authority.

Authority of knowledge is possessed by these persons appointed by the company as consultants and they influence the staff by the knowledge they possess. Some persons acquire authority by way of their position. Legal authority is the authority which is entrusted to him by the law of the nation.

Sources of authority : There are three different schools of thought regarding the sources of authority.

Formal Authority Theory

According to this theory, the entire authority originates in the formal structure of the organisation. The ultimate authority in the company form of organisation rests with the shareholders. The shareholders entrust their authority and management to the Board of Directors who in turn delegate some of their authority to the chief executive who entrusts authority to the departmental mangers and so on. Every departmental manager possesses authority by virtue of the organisation position and such authority is known as formal authority. Legal authority is also regarded as formal authority. The formal authority of the manager is accepted by the subordinates because of his organisational position. This theory also states that the managers have the right to delegate their authority to their subordinates. Formal authority flows from top to the bottom.

Acceptance theory of authority : According to this theory authority is that is accepted by others. Formal authority becomes nominal authority if it is not accepted by the subordinates. A manger has authority if his subordinates obey him. According to this theory, authority flows from top bottom to the top. This theory lays stress on the financial incentives that a manager can use and overlooks the influence of various social institutions. Subordinates obey their managers because they fear of losing financial incentives.

Competence theory : According to this theory the authority is derived by the personal qualities of the individual may not possess any kind of authority but because of his academic knowledge and technical competence people may go to him to seek guidance in certain matters.

Responsibility

Responsibility is usually stated as the activity, duty, task, assignment which a person is expected to perform. Alvin Brown has stated that " responsibility is capable of being understood in two senses. In one it denotes the definition of a part to be performed in administration. In the other, it denotes the obligation for the performance of that part ". But this definition is inappropriate because it says that responsibility cannot be delegated. It is better to separate responsibility with accountability, the former can be delegated within framework of authority whereas the latter cannot.

Viewed in this context, responsibility may be defined as the obligation of a subordinate to whom a duty has been assigned, to perform the duty. Responsibility arises from the superior subordinate relationship, from the fact that some one has the authority to expect specific services of another person. Responsibility may be a continuing obligation or it may be discharged by a single action.

One of the fundamental principles of management is the ' parity of authority and responsibility '. This principle states that while delegating the superiors must match the responsibility of subordinate with the grant of commensurate authority.

Accountability

Louis Allen has defined accountability as, " the obligation to carry out responsibility and exercise authority in terms of performance standards established". Accountability is the obligation of an individual to render an account of the fulfilment of his responsibilities to the superior to whom he reports.

The basic features of accountability are :

(i) Accountability cannot be delegated;
(ii) Accountability flows upwards;
(iii) The scope of accountability cannot be extended beyond the limit of authority and responsibility;
(iv) The subordinate may be held accountable only when the delegated authority and responsibility is judged objectively.

Power

Before we define the word power we shall define 'influence'. Influence is defined as the actions which directly or indirectly cause a change in the behaviour or attitude of another person or a group of persons. For instance a hard working person may influence others to increase productivity. Such type of influence may bring about a change in the attitude.

We can define 'power as the ability to exert influence'. To have power is to be able to change the behaviour or attitudes of other people.

Authority is usually adorned with power to secure obedience. The power may be positive or negative. The positive power is characterized by group achievements. Managers who exercise their power positively encourage their subordinates to develop strength and competence they need to succeed. Positive power includes giving incentives, awarding promotions, granting more facilities and so on to subordinates. Negative power includes inflicting penalties such as fines, demotions etc. Negative power is self-defeating because people either resist leadership or become passive.

Authority without sufficient power is weak and ineffective whereas excess power leads to dictatorship and corruption. The authority should be given adequate powers but there should be certain checks to prevent its misuse. Good managers exercise power with restraint, thereby encouraging team spirit and raising morale of their subordinates.

Duty

Duty is a work or a part of it, specified by the superior and assigned to a person usually subordinate to discharge it. Duties may be expressed either on terms of functions or in terms of achievements. If the duties are clearly expressed by the superior and well understood by the subordinate, they can discharged efficiently and effectively.

Delegation of Authority

Delegation of authority is the most important process in organising. The managerial task is divided into manageable units. It means assigning work to subordinates and vest them with authority to do it. It enables the managers to distribute their load of work to their subordinates and devote time on other organisational work.

The shareholders elect the Board of Directors who after framing the plan and policies entrust the chief executive cannot carry on the entire work. So he passes a part of his authority to his departmental managers to get the plans and policies executed. Similarly they also pass, part of their authority to their subordinates to get the work done. This process is known as delegation of authority.

According to E.F.L. Brech, " delegation means, in brief, the passing on to others of a share in the decision for determining specific objectives, plans and targets, for directing given operations and in the control of the activities of persons performing these activities". Louis Allen defines delegation as, " the process a manager follows in during the work assigned to him so that he performs that part which only he, because of his unique organisational placement, can perform effectively, and so that he can get others to help with what remains". He further says, " delegation is the instrument of responsibility and authority to another and the creation of accountability for performance".

Need for Delegation

With the growth of industries the volume of work has increased tremendously. The manager cannot do all the work and he has to delegate his authority to his subordinates. Delegation relieves the manager of some of his work and he can develop the abilities and skills of the subordinates. The work can be done faster.

Delegation helps in generating a sense of responsibility among the subordinates. It creates interest and enthusiasm on the part of subordinates because they have greater participation on decision making. The process of delegation develops managerial development training. It helps in self-advancement, self-expression and self-assessment. Delegation of authority helps in creating a second line of defence and there can be continuation of management and organisation stability.

Benefit of Delegation

Some of the advantages of delegation of authority are given below :

(i) Delegation of authority is an important process in the organisation set-up. Without this it is only a one man show;

(ii) Delegation helps in developing managerial talent;

(iii) It helps the subordinates in showing initiative and taking decisions;

(iv) Duties which are delegated get constant attention; and

(v) Delegation makes the decision making process more effective.

Barriers on Delegation

Though delegation seems to be a simple process but delegation of authority is retarded due to certain problems which may be from the part of superiors or subordinates.

Due to Superiors

There are managers who are reluctant to delegate authority. The reasons are given below :

(a) Some managers think that "I can do it better myself" and they are unable to delegate the authority;
(b) Some manager do not have the ability to plan judiciously and issue guidelines, thus creating problems for effective delegation;
(c) When manager do not have faith in their subordinates, they do not delegate authority; and
(d) Sometimes the managers think that their subordinates will outshine them, hampers in delegating authority.

Due to Subordinates

Many times the superiors are ready to delegate authority but the subordinates are reluctant in accepting it. The reasons are given below :

(i) The subordinate thinks that if he makes any mistakes he will be criticised;
(ii) Sometimes the subordinates want to play safe and they depend on all the decisions taken by the superiors;
(iii) Lack of self-confidence;
(iv) The subordinate desires certain incentives to take up additional responsibilities; and
(v) If the subordinate is overloaded with work he may resist in taking up any other work.

Decentralisation

Centralisation

Centralisation of authority means withholding the authority by few persons at control points. It means that most of the decisions are not done by those who execute the work but by high ups. According to Louis Allen, "Centralisation is the systematic and consistent reservation of authority at central points in the organisation".

The factors which favour centralisation are given below :

(i) The success of a small company depends on the personal leadership. In small enterprises the operations are small and the chief executive can control the entire authority which results in quick decisions and high flexibility;

(ii) It helps in unifying and integrating the total decisions of the organisation; and

(iii) It helps in taking rational decisions if emergency conditions develop to endanger the very existence of the organisation.

Decentralisation

Decentralisation of authority implies the decision making power to the lower organisational units. When the organisation is large and has a number of divisions it cannot control by taking decisions at the central level. Therefore the management decentralises the organisation with widespread decision making power. According to Louis Allen, " decentralisation refers to the systematic effort to delegate to the lowest levels all authority except that which can only exercised at central points". In other words the top management reserves some authority while it delegates authority to take decisions at places where the activities or actions take place.

There is a close relationship between decentralisation and delegation. Decentralisation is the delegation of authority to all the divisions or departments in the organisation in the broader context. Delegation basically means the transfer of authority from one individual to another. Delegation in the process whereas decentralisation the superior controls the subordinate to whom he delegates the authority whereas under decentralisation, top management exercises broad and minimum control and delegates the authority to the divisional or departmental managers. Delegation is very much necessary for the efficiency and effective functioning of an organisation. On the other hand decentralisation is optional as the top management may or may not delegate the authority. It becomes necessary only when the organisation grows big.

Factors Determining Decentralisation

The following factors in an organisation determine the policy of decentralisation :

Decisions

The management reserves decisions in cases where policy matters are involved and delegates those decision making powers where routine type of work or other than policy matters are involved.

Large Organisation

When the company grows big and its activities spread to distant places it becomes necessary for the top management to decentralise.

Control Techniques

If the control techniques are effective and efficient then decentralisation works very well.

Nature of Products

The nature of products and the variations in marketing markets, require decentralisation of decision making. Sometimes technological changes also create conditions to decentralise.

Diversification of Activities

When the company undergoes diversification there is a need for decentralisation in order to get quick results.

Advantages of Decentralisation

The advantages of decentralisation are given below :

(a) It reduces the burden of the top management from taking decisions on routine matters.

(b) When the organisation goes for diversification decentralisation helps the top management, as it an devote more time in planning, organising and controlling the major activities of the company.

(c) It helps in developing managerial skill and talent amongst the junior executives.

(d) Research studies have shown that decentralisation helps, in the motivation of junior executives or to the staff whom the authority is delegated.

(e) The morale of the staff increases which helps in higher productivity.

(f) It helps in effective span of control, effective supervision of officers, of the lower level workers, because it helps in taking quick decisions.

Extreme of anything is not good. There should be a balance between centralisation and decentralisation. The administration should be decentralised whereas the top management should centralise co-ordination. By doing this the organisation can be more flexible and become more thrustful.

18

Authority Relationships

Another important aspect of the organising process is the formation of a suitable organisational structure. An organisational structure is a framework of position which is used by the management to achieve the objectives of the enterprise. It is a classification and grouping of activities, assignment of activities to individuals and also giving them authority and responsibility. It lays down the management policy regarding centralisation and decentralisation, co-ordination and control.

There is no best organisational structure which is suited to all the organisations. The form of organisational structure basically depends on the activities and specific needs of the business unit. The following three types of organisation structure are usually found in business, these are :

Line Organisation

Line organisation is the oldest and simplest form of internal organisation. The line of authority is straight and vertical and flows from top to the bottom According to James Lundy, " such a type of organisation is characterised by direct lines of authority flowing from top to the bottom of the organisational hierarchy and the lines of responsibility flowing in an opposite but equally direct manner ". The maximum authority is at the top and reduces at each successive level down the hierarchy.

Line authority is an essential and important relationship between superior and subordinate level. It has full powers to issue commands, to exact accountability and to take disciplinary actions for any violations.

Line authority is always vertical in character and never crosses departmental lines horizontally.

Basic Features

(i) The lines of authority are vertical.
(ii) There is a command relationship between the superior and the subordinate.
(iii) The line of authority is the chain of communication, co-ordination and delegation.
(iv) It provides the channel of accountability in the organisation.

Advantages of Line Organisation

The following are the advantages of line organisation :

(i) It is simple and can be easily understood by everyone working in the organisation;
(ii) The authority and responsibility are clearly defined;
(iii) It facilitates quick decisions and prompt action;
(iv) It is easy to maintain discipline; and
(v) Communication is easy and quick.

Disadvantages of Line Organisation

The following are the disadvantages of line organisation.

(i) There is concentration of authority at the top level management which creates problems for the success of the organisation; (ii) If there are too many levels of management, the flow of communication becomes difficult; (iii) In big organisations the line authority cannot operate satisfactorily, and (iv) The line officers get overloaded with work and they cannot devote sufficient time for planning.

Despite these limitations the line organisation structure is accepted in small organisations where few people are working and the levels of authority are small.

Functional Organisation

Functional organisation which is also called functional foremanship was developed by F.W. Taylor to bring specialisation of management. His plan of functional control went down to the lowest level in the organisation. Taylor felt that a foreman cannot be a specialist in all the fields. So he advised substitution of line organisation by functional foremanship at the lower levels of the organisational structure. Under this system the office work is separated from the shop or the plant work.

Taylor suggested eight specialists instead of one foreman and responsibility of each specialists were clearly defined. The eight staff specialists to guide the workers in different functional area are :

(i) Route clerk
(ii) Instruction cards clerk
(iii) Time and cost clerk
(iv) Shop disciplinarian
(v) Gang boss
(vi) Speed boss
(vii) Repair boss
(viii) Inspector.

There is functional relationship in the structure because every worker is responsible to gang boss regarding setting up the machine and moving jobs from machine to machine, to time and cost clerk regarding routing, and scheduling of work and so on. Thus having one boss the worker had to serve eight bosses. This is totally unrealistic as it violated the basic principle of unity of command and it created divided responsibility due to many bosses.

Functional Authority

In a big organisation there may be functional authority when a person has to take decisions outside the chain of command. A superior person having a functional authority is a specialist in his own field but the he may also be a line of staff manager. But functional authority is only for particular activities and is granted when it is necessary. Thus functional authority can be defined as " the power of one department or section to give directives to any department or departments in the organisation with the right of accoutability from the department to whom the directive has been issued ".

It should clear that unnecessary grant of functional authority erodes the basis of line authority. Functional authority is binding on line authority but disciplinary action for violating it can only be enforces unless there is a rule framed by the management.

Advantages of Functional Organisation

The following are the advantages of functional organisation :

(i) It helps in achieving the benefits of specialiasation which helps in increasing the efficiency; (ii) The workers are able to perfect their skills as they get the expertise of specialists; (iii) It reduces the burden on the top managers as the specialist has to supervise his specified area; (iv) The business can be expanded without effecting the efficiency and control; and (v) It helps in developing trained executives in shortest possible time.

Disadvantages of Functional Organisation

The following are the disadvantages of functional organisation :

(i) It violates the principle of unity of command as the workers have to report to a number of bosses; (ii) Since there is overlapping of authority and division responsibility it becomes difficult to locate responsibility for unsatisfactory performance; (iii) There is lack of co-ordination among the functional executives which results in delay in decisions; and (iv) This type of organisation is not suited for non-manufacturing concerns.

Line and Staff Organisation

Due to limitations of the line and functional organisation they were rarely used in their pure forms. Hence to eleminate their disadvantages and secure their merits a new type of organisation called the ' line and staff organisation ' was developed. In brief, the line portion of line, and staff organisation helps in maintaining stability and discipline whereas the staff or functional part brings expertise on specific problems.

Though there are divergent views on the concept of ' staff ' it has been accepted that staff functions are auxiliary functions. The line managers are responsible for execution whereas the staff is a supporting activity. Staff members give expert opinion to the line managers.

Line and Staff Authority

According to Louis Allen, "Line refers to those positions and elements of the organisation, which have the responsibility and authority and are accountable for the accomplishment of primary objectives. Staff elements are those which have responsibility and authority for providing advice and service to the line in the attainment of objectives. " Henri Fayol observes, "Staff is a group of men who have the strength, knowledge and time which the line manger may lack. It is a help or reinforcement, a sort of extension of the manager's personality".

From the above we can analyse that line managers have the executive power, and the authority flows from top to the bottom. The staff managers have to assist and advice the line managers.

Need for Staff

The need for staff to provide auxiliary services to the line managers has been growing with the expansion of business. The reasons for the requirement and importance of staff is given below :

(i) With the expansion of business at the national and international level;
(ii) With the increase in knowledge and advancement of technology;
(iii) With the increasing use of specialised services;
(iv) With the growing complexities in the business environment; and
(v) Business planning and policy framing, demand a large number of specialists.

Conflict between Line and Staff

There are various causes for line and staff conflicts. Some of them are discussed below :

(i) Sometimes the staff managers interfere in the affairs of the line authority;
(ii) Staff managers are specialists in their area and they are not well versed with the practical problems of the organisation;
(iii) As staff managers are not directly accountable for the results they suggest such measures which are practically not feasible;
(iv) Communication gap creates misunderstanding;
(v) Sometimes the line managers do not like to share with staff officers the credit of achievements. They do not consult the staff men except when emergency arises and that is of no use; and
(vi) The line and staff men are not familiar with the work of each other.

Improving Line and Staff Relationships

In order to maintain good relationship between the line and staff people the following measures should be undertaken : (i) The top management should clearly lay down the authority responsibility relationship in the organisation. This can be done by better and more communication, clearly defining the channels of authority and the limitations of line and staff managers, (ii) Line managers and staff men should work in spirit of co-operation. Line managers should work in spirit of co-operation. Line managers should give due consideration to the staff advice and give reasons for not accepting it. (iii) The line and staff men should try to understand the problems of each other and strive hard to achieve the organisational goals in an organised manner.

Now it is being argued that the difference between line and staff authority is an obsolete concept. It is further said that to differentiate organisational activities on the basis of the contribution to the achievement of objectives, is no more considered. In the recent years the work flow and the horizontal and diagonal relationship among the officers is gaining more ground that the vertical relationship as given in line authority.

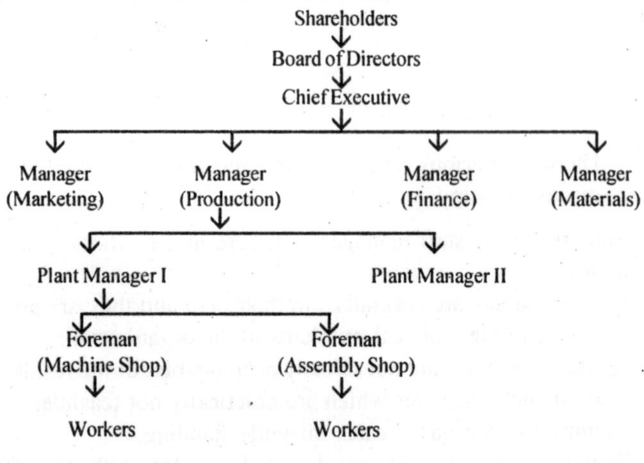

19

Co-ordination

Co-ordination is the systematic arrangement of group efforts to provide integration, in order to achieve the given objectives. Various views have been expressed by different experts on co-ordination. Henri Fayol considers co-ordination as one of the functions of management. Similar views have also been expressed by Louis Allen. Jamey Mooney defines it as " the orderly arrangement of group effort, to provide unity of action in the pursuit of a common purpose ". Ralph Davis considers it as an important aspect of controlling. According to Theo Haimann, "Co-ordination is the orderly synchronisation of efforts of the subordinates to provide the proper amount, timing and quality of execution, so that their unified efforts lead to the stated objective, namely the common purpose of the enterprise ".

Thus we can define co-ordination as the continuing process under which the manager develops an integrated, systematic and synchronised pattern of group effort among his subordinates in an unified manner so as to accomplish the organisational goals.

Basic Features of Co-ordination

The above definition gives the following features of co-ordination : (i) It is an important function of management; (ii) It is a continuing process; (iii) It is applicable to group effort and not to individual effort; (iv) It lays emphasis on unified action; (v) It is directed towards the accomplishment of common objectives; and (vi) It consists of three main dimensions namely time, quantity and direction.

Need of Co-ordination.

When a number of people are working together to accomplish a particular task, it is only co-ordination which can help in synchronisation. It helps in avoiding conflicts between various personnel in the organisation. The factors which necessitate co-ordination are given below :

Specialised Activities : In the modern world of management the activities are divided on the basis of product specialisation or function specialisation or regional specialisation or in some other kind of specialisation. Thus there are persons of various skills and abilities who tend to concentrate on the activities and objectives of their own department. This situation needs special attention of co-ordination.

Growth in Size : When the organisation expands it generates more employment which makes the work of synchronising regular activities more difficult. The communication gap between various personnel makes the situation more complex. Such factors demand co-ordination.

Personal Differences : With the growth of organisations, individual differences among the managers also develop leading to personal revalries and jealousies. The line and staff conflict or differences between the various departments speak for the need of co-ordination.

Clash of Interests : When the individual interest becomes more important than the organisational interest it demands co-ordination of efforts for achieving common goals.

Importance of Co-ordination

The importance of co-ordination in any organisation is discussed below :

Essence of Management : Co-ordination is the most important problem of any organisation. It is the end result of the management process. It is important and encompasses the entire concept in management. Management is basically, concerned with co-ordinating the entire activities and resources to achieve the objectives of the enterprise.

Greater Output : Management helps in generating creativity, Group action when co-ordinated creates a result greater than the sum total of individual efforts. Group effort under team spirit and integration provides creative force.

Unity of Direction and Objective : Co-ordination generates a feeling among the managers to see the organisation as a whole from different angles. It ensures unity of direction by developing a sense of co-operation among the various departments. All departments are duly knitted into one united and integrated whole, working to achieve common objectives.

Morale and Job Satisfaction : Co-ordination helps in developing general level of employee moral and provides job satisfaction. Because of job satisfaction the organisation can get better services of their managers with steady growth in their capacity.

Principles of Co-ordination

Mary Parker Follet has laid down certain principles of co-ordination. Some of them are discussed below :

Direct Personal Contact : It is suggested that co-ordination can be effectively achieved by direct personal contact among the responsible persons concerned. This principle states that co-ordination can be achieved through interpersonal relationships of people in an organisation, which can be achieved through personal communication. On the other hand written communication may result in the misinterpretation of language and create misunderstanding among the persons concerned.

Early Stage : Co-ordination can be had more easily in the initial stages of planning and policy framing. Once the policy is framed without consulting other departments, it becomes difficult to secure co-ordination at the execution stage.

Reciprocal Relationships : This principle states that all factors in a situation are reciprocally related. For instance when two people work together, each of them finds influenced by the other and both are influenced by other persons and environment in the total situation. Thus this principle demands integration of all efforts, actions and interests towards some common purpose.

Continuity : According to this principle co-ordination is a continuing process and permeates through each managerial function. Constant efforts should be made to secure co-ordination in the management process and some machinery of co-ordination must always be there to give continued services.

Techniques of Co-ordination

Proper division of work is an important factor in the organising process. But it is equally important to make adequate arrangement for co-ordination. Co-ordination can be secured in a better way if managerial functions are designed properly. Planning, departmentation, delegation of authority, leadership and control are some managerial functions which effect co-ordination. Techniques for achieving co-ordination can be had by the following means :

Grouping

Formation of departments on the basis of important functions having similar activities not only promotes co-ordination but also reduces co-ordination problems.

Committees

Committees help in co-ordinating the activities of various departments. They cover a wide area and have a greater acceptance of their decisions.

Group Meetings

The manager may call staff meetings of his subordinates at specified periods to promote co-ordination by making direct contacts and communicating with them regarding problems, their solutions and their point of view.

Conferences

It is another method of co-ordination and taking collective decisions. A conference provides a platform for free and frank discussion and helps in understanding the problems of the organisation in a better way.

Communications

Effective and good system of oral and written communication helps in co-ordinating the activities of various departments, as well as outside agencies also.

Cross Functioning among Departments

Mary Follet suggested cross functioning departments at the same level in the organisation. It is also termed as lateral communication.

Two managers of different departments of the same level can resolve their issues and bring about co-ordination without taking up the matter at the higher level.

Types of Co-ordination

Co-ordination is usually categorised into two broad classes. Firstly on the basis of its shape in the organisation set up and secondly on the basis of scope and coverage. The former is termed as vertical and horizontal co-ordination and latter one as internal and external co-ordination.

Vertical and Horizontal Co-ordination

Vertical co-ordination is used when co-ordination is to be secured between various levels of the organisation. It is needed in order to bring harmony at all levels of organisation so that the policies and programmes may be executed accordingly. Vertical co-ordination can be achieved through delegation of authority and authority relationships. Horizontal co-ordination is used when co-ordination has to be secured between various departments on the same level in the managerial hierarchy.

Internal and External Co-ordination

Internal co-ordination is a term used when co-ordination is to be secured various departments, sections and units within the organisation. It includes both vertical and horizontal co-ordination and is desired with the objectives and policies of other organisations, rules and regulations of the government, with technological advances and so on. Co-ordinating the activities with the outside forces and influence is termed as external co-ordination.

20

Controlling

Control is an important function of management. It is a continuous proces on the part of managers. It is a process of determining whether the plans are being implemented properly and if there are deviations, corrective measure are to be undertaken.

According to Henri Fayol, "control consists in verifying whether everything occurs in conformity with the plan adopted, the instruction issued and principles established. It has for object to point out weaknesses and errors in order to rectify them and prevent recurrence. It operates on everything, things, people, actions". According to Ernest Dale, "The modern concept of control envisages a system that not only provides a historical record of what has happened to the business as a whole but pinpoints the reasons why it has happened, and provides data that enable the chief executive or the departmental head to take corrective steps if he finds he is on the wrong track". And according to George R. Terry, "controlling is determining what is being accomplished, that is the performance, evaluating the performance, and if necessary applying corrective measures to that performance takes place according to plans."

Thus from the above definitions we can conclude that control is concerned with measuring actual performance and then comparing it with the standards set by plans, and taking corrective actions for deviations to assure accomplishment of objectives according to plans.

Nature of Control

The nature of controlling can be better understood by classifying its basic features.

Managerial Function

Controlling is the function and responsibility of all managers at different levels. He has to see that the operations occur in conformity with the established standards. The function of controlling is to be performed at every level of management.

Elements

Controlling consists of three elements namely (i) setting of standards that represent desired performance; (ii) determining the actual performance and comparing it with the desired performance to find out the variations; and (iii) taking corrective measures to rectify the errors committed and prevent them from occurring in future.

Extensive Activity

Controlling is a very extensive activity covering every sphere of activity in the organisation. It operates on every person, every action, every process and procedures etc.

Continuous Activity

It is a continuous activity as the manager has to continuously see that the operations are taking place in the right direction.

Forward-Looking

It is related to the future as the past events cannot be controlled. The manager analyses the past performance and tries to see that the errors committed in the past may not be repeated in future.

Inter-Relationship

Controlling cannot be exercised exclusively. It has a close relationship with planning, co-ordination and organisation. Controlling reveals the deficiences of planning, attempts to rectify them, leads to setting up of new goals if necessary and assists in changing the techniques of directing.

Advantages of Control

The advantages of effective control system are given below :

(a) Control helps in providing a base for the future action. It points out errors so that same mistakes may not be repeated in future and also suggests corrective action.

(b) It helps in decision making. The process of control is complete when corrective actions are undertaken.

(c) Controlling helps in taking decisions regarding decentralisation of authority.

(d) Controlling and planning go simultaneously. It is only through control through which the management knows that the plans are being implemented efficiently and effectively.

(e) It facilitates the co-ordination of activities of the various departments of the organisation.

Limitations of Control

Following are the limitations of Control :

(a) The external environment, such as government policies, technological changes are beyond the control of the organisation.

(b) The expenditure incurred on controlling the subordinate staff is usually very high. Besides it requires a lot of time and effort.

(c) Sometimes the subordinates resists control because it reduces their freedom. Thus the effectiveness of control is reduced.

Steps in the Control Process

In the process of control mechanism there are three basic steps, namely establishment of standards, comparing it with established standards and taking corrective actions.

Establishment of Standards

A standard acts as a basis of comparison of actual performance. Setting standards is a part of planning and also an essential component for controlling. Without performance standards, actual performance cannot be measured and control becomes unrealistic and ineffective. Different performance standards are set up for various operations at the planning stage which serve as the basis of any control system. Performance standards are expressed in terms of quality, quantity, time and cost because it is necessary to determine how the performance is going to be measured. Standards should be accurate, precise and workable. Standards should be flexible.

Various types of standards are used to measure the different phases of corporate operations. Standards may be tangible or intangible, and specific or vague. Tangible standards are capable of physical measurement and can be easily established and precisely measured. Intangible standards cannot be precisely expressed and directly measured. They are indirectly measured by relating them to some other units which can be measured. Vague standards are not accurately expressed, but they are usually decided by conventions or traditions.

There are numerous standards, but the manager should select certain standards which may best reflect the objectives of the department and which can show him whether these objectives are being achieved or not.

Measuring Performance

This is the second step in the control process. This step involves measuring of actual performance of the various individuals and departments and then comparing it with the standards which have already been set up at the planning stage. Since there are various standards, the measurement has also to be done in different ways, according to the nature of standards.

Under the process of performances appraisal, the deviations from the standards are revealed. The manager should try to analyse the deviations and try to determine the reasons. The manager should concentrate on those areas where the performance significantly deviates from the established standards and control is very much necessary when such deviations take place. This is known as management by exception.

Corrective Actions

This is the third and final step on the control process. Under this corrective action is taken to that the deviations may not occur again because there is no control over the past events. A corrective action is only possible when the cause of deviation is clearly identified. For instance there is fall in production than the established standards due to many reasons, such as power cut, labour absenteeism, breakdown of machines, delay in supply of raw materials and so on. This may involve taking certain decisions by the management like replanning of goals, redesigning of duties, resheduling of production and so fourth. It may also require reforming the selection process, mode of training and developing new skills. Corrective action may relate to correction of men, machine, materials, method or standards or other managerial functions.

Requirements of an Effective Control System

An effective control system should possess the following qualities :

Objectives

The control system should be laid only after knowing the objectives of the organisation. The basic aim of a control system is to achieve the objectives.

Suitability

The nature of the activity determines the type of control system. Control system of a production department will be entirely different from those used in sales or finance department. Each specific area will have its own control system to serve its specific demands.

Quick Information of Deviations

Since the control is forward looking the deviations should be quickly reported to the management in order to take corrective action and safeguard the future. Delayed reporting may result in losses.

Flexibility

A good control system must keep pace with the continuously changing business environment. It should be flexible enough so as to adopt to the latest developments and changed circumstances. According to Geotz "the control system should report such failures and should contain sufficient element of flexibility to maintain managerial control of operations despite such failures".

Economical

The benefits derived from the control system should be more than the expenditure incurred on the control system. Costly control system is not required for a small organisation. A control system should be developed according to the needs and size of the organisation.

Objectivity

An effective control system should have objectivity, accuracy and suitable standards to that they can be easily verified by the managers at various levels.

Strategic Point Control

Effective control can be exercised if critical and strategic points can be identified and attention may be directed to adjustment at these points. It is also termed as control by exception.

Management Control Techniques

A number of control techniques have been developed to help the business in controlling their operations. They have been classified under the following categories :

(a) Budgetary Controls
(b) Non-Budgetary Controls
(c) Network Techniques.

Budgetary Control

It is one of the traditional control techniques still used in business. But before discussing the nature, advantages and disadvantages of budgetary control we should discuss the nature of budgets and different types of budget.

Nature of Budget

A budget is an instrument whereby the management plans the future course of activities and the ways and means to achieve them. According to G.R. Terry, "Budget is an estimate of future needs arranged according to an orderly basis, covering some or all of the activities of an enterprise for a definite period of time". According to the Institute of Cost and Works Accountants, England, "A Budget is a financial and/or quantitative statement prepared to a defined period of time, of the policy to be pursued during the period for the purpose of attaining a given objective". Budgets cover all phases of operations for a definite period in future by giving formal expression to policies, objectives and goals laid down in advance by top management for the undertaking as a whole and for each subdivision thereof.

Characteristics

From the above definitions we can visualise certain

characteristics of a budget. (a) It is a device whereby management determines the future course of activities. (b) It is essentially for a specified period. (c) It is expressed in quantitative terms. (d) It is flexible in nature and can be modified whenever necessary. (e) It is based on certain concrete expectations. (f) It is the yardstick for measuring the success, deviations and for providing corrective actions.

Types of Budgets

There are various types of budgets and some of them are discussed in brief :

Fixed Budget

It consists of single plan only and does not permit any changes during the budget period. The basic objective of fixed budget is to co-ordinate the activities of different departments to achieve the pre-determined objectives. It is prepared for a given level of production, sales, income, costs and other important activities concerning business.

Flexible Budget

Also termed as variable budget is prepared in such a way that it gives budgeted cost for varying levels of activity. It is prepared after taking into account the fixed and variable elements of cost and over which the organisation has control.

Master Budget

It consists of all departmental and supporting budgets in a summarized form. The basic idea behind such a budget is to secure an overall coordination in the budgetary programme. It is an effective tools for the top management to exercise control over various departments.

Sales Budget

It is the basic activity of business. It includes sales forecast during a specified period expressed in money or quantities. The forecast incorporates the total volume of sales and splits down product-wise and area-wise. The budget is prepared by the sales manager. Sales budget is of great important in an organisation because other budgets are based upon it.

The following factors are necessary for preparing the sales budget : (a) Market information and statistics (b) Population and its composition (c) General economic condition (d) Extent of competition (e) Production capacity (f) Government regulations (g) Orders in hand (h) Reports from staff.

Production Budget

It is the planning and controlling of the production activities during the specified period of time. It is usually related to the sales requirements as it is the responsibility of the production department to schedule its activities according to sales forecast.

Materials Budget

It deals with the purchasing and maintaining adequate stock inventories for a specified period so that the production schedule may not be disturbed. Materials budget takes into account the purchase policies, inventory policies, storage facilities, cost of carrying inventory, availability of goods or their substitutes, economy in purchases and so on.

Labour Budget

It depends upon the estimates of production budget. It gives the labour required for a given period of time and the financial requirements of the wages of workers. It helps the finance department in ascertaining the cost of labour.

Capital Expenditure Budget

It is prepared to carry out expenditure on capital items in a planned manner. It includes construction of huge buildings, purchase and installation of big machines etc. which involve heavy financial resources. A long term budget is prepared which is broken down into yearly budgets. It is prepared very carefully so that the normal functions of the business are not disturbed.

Budgetory Control

G.R. Terry defines budgetary control as "a process of finding out what is being done and comparing actual results with the corresponding budget date in order to approve accomplishments or to remedy differences by either adjusting the budget estimates or correcting the cause of differences". The Institute of Cost and Works Accountants, England defines it as "the establishment of budget relating to the responsibilities of executives to the requirements of a policy and the continuous comparison of actual with budgeted results either to secure by individual action the objective of that policy or provide a basis for its revision".

Objectives

The main objective of budgetary control is to enable the management to carry its business operations efficiently and effectively. Budgetary control includes the whole activity of management right from the stage of planning to its implementation. It serves the following objectives :

Planning

Budgeting is planning by an organisation regarding the future activities to be undertaken within a specified period in order to attain the predetermined objectives. The budgets are framed on the basis of forecasts about market conditions and are prepared for different fields of business activities.

Control

Another objective of budgeting is managerial control. It helps in comparing the performance of different sections and departments with the standards already laid down in various budgets. It helps in determining the variation from the budgets.

Co-Ordination

Budgeting helps in co-ordinating the various activities of an organisation. It is only through the budget that the sales, production, materials and such activities are co-related. It forces the management to develops plans in a group.

Requisites for Effective Budgetary Control

The following are the requisites for effective budgetary control :

Objectives

The objectives and policies of the organisation should be clearly stated so that the budget can be framed accordingly.

Manual

A budget manual is prepared so that the staff engaged in budget preparation of various departments know about the rules and regulations for budgetary control and reporting methods.

Preparation

The responsibility of budget preparation and execution is clearly stated.

Co-ordination and Cooperation

Budgets cannot be prepared in isolation. They require effective coordination at all levels of management and cooperation from various groups in the organisation for their effective implementation.

Period

It usually depends on the type of budget. Short-term budget like cash, revenue and expenses are usually for one year. Long term budget like capital expenditure are for more than one year. Budget period should be appropriate to the nature of business.

Flexibility

It should be flexible in nature because if need arises changes can be brought about in the budget.

Accounting System

An integrated accounting system should be considered while framing the budget.

Advantages of Budgetary Control

Following are some of the benefits of budgetary control :

(a) It is an effective tool of controlling various operations of a business organisation.

(b) It provides standards against which actual performance can be measured. It helps in taking necessary action in time.

(c) It co-ordinates the various activities of the business.

(d) It helps in reducing waste of resources.

(e) It helps in financial planning and proper use of scarce financial resources.

(f) It facilitates 'management by exception'. It helps the management in concentrating in those areas which are of most important in business.

(g) It is an important tool for fixing the responsibility on managers occupying different positions.

Limitations of Budgetary Control

Following are some of the limitations of budgetary control :

(a) Too much emphasis on budgeting leads to rigidity rather than flexibility.

(b) Budgets are usually framed on the prices of a particular period. If there is inflation or depression in the economy the estimates become redundant.

(c) The success of such a system depends upon the cooperation among the workers and manages and any resistance leads to failure.

(d) Defective budgetary standards may lead to a loss to the business organisation.

Non Budgetary Control

Besides, budgetary control there are many other control techniques available to the management. The techniques are discussed below :

Cost Control

It is being used extensively and today it is the most effective technique of managerial control. Cost information has assumed to be a very important criteria for all managerial decisions. The basic aim of cost control is to reduce the cost of products or services and to minimise wastage. According to D.E. Ewans Hemming, "an effective system of cost control is necessary to enable the management of a business to attain its objectives". Cost control gives an idea about where and how the costs can be reduced. It involves the optimum utilisation of men, materials, machines and capital so as to give maximum output.

Cost control is effective only when actual cost is compared with standard cost. Standard cost is defined as, "the predetermined cost of an operation or a unit of finished product intended to represent the value of direct material, direct labour and manufacturing burden normally required under efficient conditions and normal capacity to process a unit of product". The standard cost is never static and is adjusted periodically with the changing situations. Once both the costs are compared and if actual cost deviates from the standard one, the management takes corrective actions.

Advantages of Cost Control

Following are the advantages of cost control :

(a) Costing helps the management in determining the activities which are profitable and unprofitable and accordingly take measures to reduce or eliminate unprofitable activities.

(b) It helps in developing budgets more precisely and accurately.

(c) It facilitates price fixation thereby enabling the management to quote competitive estimates of the tenders.

(d) It facilitates on controlling various inventories and expenses.

(e) Periodical analysis of cost figures reveal the sources of inefficiency, wastages, pilferages and losses.

Internal Audit Control

Also termed as Operation audit is one of the important tools of management control. Internal audit was basically concerned with accounting and financial matters, but today its activity is enlarged and it deals with matters of operating nature. According to Koontz and O'Donnell, "Operation auditing in its broadest sense is the regular and independent appraisal by a staff of internal auditors of the accounting, financial and other operations of the business. Although, often limited to the auditing of accounts in its most useful aspect, operational auditing involves appraisal of operations generally, weighing actual results in the light of planned results".

Advantages of Internal Audit

Following are the advantages of internal audit control device.

(a) It is an important tool in measuring performances, evaluating results and suggesting remedial measures for their improvement.

(b) Defective and outdated plans and procedures are detected and recommended for alternation.

(c) It helps in developing efficiency and minimising omissions and frauds.

External Audit Control

It is imposed by the Government by law on all companies so that the interests of the investors may be protected against the unscrupulous activities of the management. It may be defined as "the verification of accounting records and transactions as per the financial position disclosed by the books of accounts and balance sheet of the company. This task is performed by an independent auditor not related to the organisation. This auditor is a chartered accountant. The basic idea behind external audit control is to verify whether the accounting records and transactions are in conformity with the company rules and other legal provisions.

Advantages of External Audit

Following are the benefits of external audit control device :

It reveals mistakes and errors which can be rectified.

It brings into notice the irregularities and frauds of the management before the investors.

It also helps in bringing about efficiency throughout the organisation because everyone is afraid of the adverse remarks of the auditor.

Break-Even Point Analysis

It is one of the important tools available to the management to check the operations of the business. It shows the relationship of different volumes, costs, rules, prices and profits. This analysis helps in determining the volume of sale at which total costs are fully covered and beyond which profits will be earned.

The break-even point is defined as that level of volume of sale at which total revenue equals total cost. It is that point where operation pass from being profitable to a less or vice-versa as shown in the figure. This facilitates the management in deciding the levels of production, cost and sales. *(See* Break Even Chart).

The break-even chart shows the level of costs and revenue for each level of sales and indicates that at 40,000 units the organisation would break-even showing neither profit nor loss. The chart depicts the cost-volume profit analysis.

BREAK - EVEN CHART

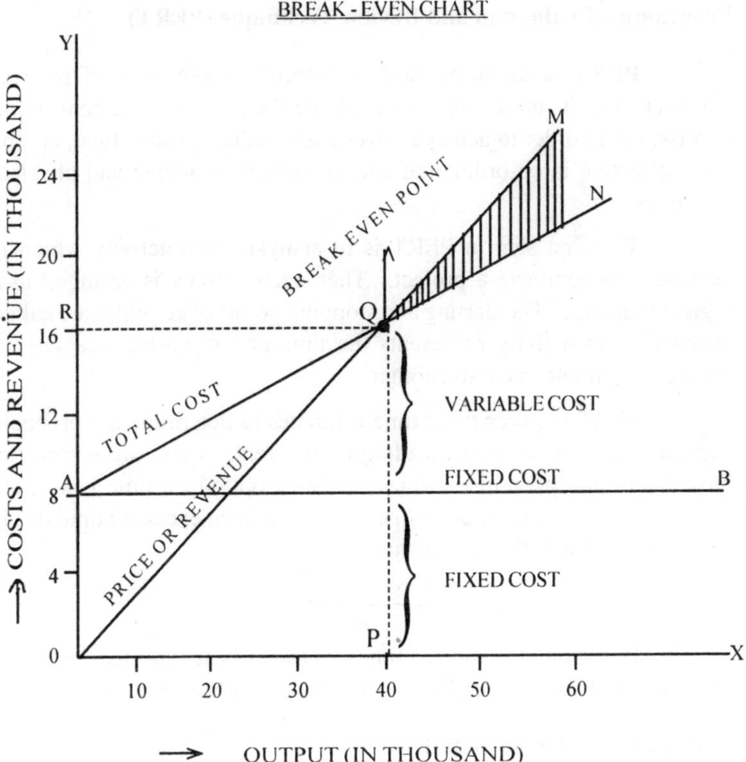

Advantages of Break-Even Analysis

(a) It is useful in planning and control because it emphasises the marginal concept.

(b) On its basis estimates of profit at different levels of activity can be ascertained.

Network Techniques

They are means of planning and controlling the project implementation economically and efficiently. There are many techniques of which PERT and CPM have assumed importance. They are discussd below :

Programme Evaluation and Review Technique (PERT)

PERT is an important technique in the area of project management. Its basic aim is to facilitate the planning and controlling of a project in order to achieve lower costs, reduce project time, and be more effective in co-ordination and utilization of human and physical resources.

The first step in PERT is to analysis each activity which is necessary to complete a project. Then each activity is arranged in a logical sequence. The starting and stopping points of activities are called "events". An activity represents the time and resource necessary to progress from one event to another.

PERT requires three time estimates to determine the probable expected time for activities leading to an event. These are optimistic, most likely and pessimistic times. If most optimistic time is x, most likely time is y and most pessimistic time is z, then expected time (te) is calculated by the following formula.

$$te = \frac{(X + 4Y + Z)}{6}$$

Based on the expected time (te) the earliest expected time (TE) and latest allowable time (TL) are developed for the network.

Critical Path Method (CPM)

This was developed to reduce time in project implementation. There is vitually no difference between PERT and CPM. PERT lays emphasis on time whereas CPM emphasized cost as well as time. Critical path is considered to be utmost importance because any delay in completion of the project will disturb the entire schedule. Once the management knows the critical path it will lay greater stress in those areas which will help speed up the completion of the project.

Application of PERT and CPM

These techniques can be applied in the following areas.

(a) Construction of a huge building, roads and highways.

(b) launching of a new product.

(c) Manufacturing ships, aeroplanes and other heavy machinery.

(d) Maintenance of oil refineries and other petro-chemical projects.

(e) Installation of a computer.

(f) Maintaining financial records.

Advantages of Network Techniques

Following are the advantages of Network techniques to the organisation.

(a) Research studies have shown that the application of these techniques reduces time by 30% and cost by about 20 percent as compared to similar projects not using these techniques.

(b) As it can be depicted in a chart, it facilitates communication to the management.

(c) Since all the activities and events have to be put in a logical sequence the chances of avoiding any activity is reduced or minimised.

(d) There are number of checks and if there is deviation it can be restored.

(e) It is highly flexible in nature.

(f) Planning, implementation and performance are closely associated.

21

Motivation

In any organisation the basic aim of management is to co-ordinate all the factors of production in such a manner so as to achieve the pre-determined objectives. It depends on two factors, viz., human factors and non-human factors. The efficiency of non-human factor depends on the level of technology whereas the human factor depends on the performance level. Thus to make both the factors effective and efficient the most important task of management is to improve the performance level of the human resources. This performance mainly depend on two elements : (a) level of ability to perform a particular function; and (b) level of motivation. If both the elements are high then the performance would be high. If any of the elements is at a low level the performance will be at a low level.

Motivation can be defined as the complexities of forces which inspire a person to enhance his willingness to use his capabilities for the achievements of certain goals. To a major extent the behaviour of a person is determined by motivation. According to Mc Farland, "Motivation refers to the way in which urges, drives, desires, aspirations, strivings or needs direct control or explain the behaviour of human beings".

The term motivation is derived from the term motive. Motives are the expression of needs, wants, drives and impulses within an individual. According to Keith Davis, " Motives are expressions of a person's needs; hence they are personal and internal ". The word 'needs' means something within an individual which stimulates him to act. Motives give direction to human behaviour because they are directed towards certain goals.

Human needs can be broadly classified into two categories viz; (a) Basic and primary or physiological needs; and (b) Secondary or social or psychological or Acquired needs. The former are natural to all human beings, their intensity may differ from person to person. It includes, food, water, sleep, shelter and other bodily needs. The latter are needs of the mind and soul. It includes honour, self-respect, status, sense of duty, ambitions, self-assertion and so on.

Theories of Motivation

From time to time lot of material has been developed regarding how to motivate people. The approaches of social scientists have different resulting in a number of theories concerning motivations. These theories differ considerably and can be grouped into three categories; (a) theories associated with human needs; (b) theories associated with basic nature of human beings; and (c) theories associated with expectancy of individuals. Some of the theories are discussed in brief.

Maslow's Need Hierarchy Theory

Maslow's theory is based on the needs of the people. He believed that needs have a certain priority and once the basic needs are met he tends to satisfy higher needs. Maslow proposed a hierarchy of five types of needs :

Physiological needs, i.e., food, clothing, shelter, thirst and other bodily needs.

Safety needs, i.e., protection against danger, security and protection, need for job security.

Social needs, i.e., love and affection, sense of belongingness, friendship, acceptance.

Esteem needs, i.e., self-respect, freedom and achievement which are internal esteem factors and status, recognition and knowledge are external esteem factors.

Self-actualisation needs, i.e., to maximise one's potential whatever it may be. It includes self-development, self-fulfilment, to be creative.

(5th)	Self-actualisation	
(4th)	Esteem needs	Higher Order Needs
(3rd)	Social needs	

(2nd) Safety needs

(1st) Physiological needs Lower Order Needs

(Maslow's Need Hierarchy)

According to Maslow an individual seeks to fulfil the needs in a sequence. The first to be fulfilled by him are physiological or basic needs. Once it is fulfilled he moves to satisfy his safety, social, esteem and self-actualisation needs in that order. The 1 and 2 need levels are called Lower Order Needs and 3, 4, and 5 are called Higher Order Needs.

Maslow distinguishes the two by saying that lower order needs are fulfilled by extrinsic factors such as monetary and non-monetary compensation whereas the higher order needs are fulfilled by intrinsic factors such as participation in decision making, greater responsibilities, opportunities for advancement and so on.

Herzberg's Motivation-Hygiene Theory

On the basis of research with engineers and accountants, Herzberg developed a two factor model of motivation. He concluded that there are two sets of needs independent of each other affecting behaviour in different ways. His findings were that some job conditions operate primarily to dissatisfy employees when they are absent but their presence does not operate in a strong way. These job conditions are referred as maintenance factors or hygiene factors. Another set of job conditions operate primarily to build strong motivation but their absence rarely proves strongly dissatisfying. These job conditions are referred as motivational factors.

According to Herzberg there are ten maintenance or hygiene factors. They are (a) Company policy and administration. (b) Technical supervision. (c) Interpersonal relations with supervisions. (d) Inter-personal relations with peers. (e) Inter-personal relations with subordinates. (f) Salary. (g) Job security. (h) Personal life. (i) Work conditions and (j) Status. These maintenance factors are necessary to maintain a reasonable level of satisfaction among employees. These are not intrinsic factors of a job, but they are related to conditions under which a job is performed. Any increase beyond a certain level will not provide any satisfaction to the employees, but any decline below a certain level will dissatisfy them. Because of this they are also called dissatisfiers.

On the other hand motivational factors have a positive effect on job satisfaction. Herzberg includes six motivational factors. They are

(a) Achievement (b) Recognition (c) Advancement (d) The Work Itself (e) The Possibility of Growth and (f) Responsibility. An increase in these factors will satisfy the employees but any decrease will not effect their level of satisfaction.

Herzberg is of the view that potency of various factors is not completely a function of the function themselves. It is also influenced by the personality trials of the individuals. Therefore individuals can also be categorised in two classes, viz., motivation seekers and maintenance seekers.

McGregor's Theory X and Theory Y

According to Douglas McGregor the management's action of motivating human beings in the organisation are based on certain assumptions and generalisations which predict the human behaviour. McGregor has stated these assumptions into two sets - Theory X and Theory Y.

Theory X : This is the traditional theory of human behaviour. He has certain assumptions about human behaviour which are as follows:

(a) Management is responsible for organising the elements of productive enterprise money, materials equipment, people - in the interest of economic ends.

(b) With respect to people, this is a process of directing their efforts, motivating them controlling their actions, modifying their behaviour to fit the needs of the organisation.

(c) Without this active intervention by management, people would be passive - even resistant - to organisational needs. They must be persuaded, rewarded, punished, controlled, their activities must be directed. This is management's task.

(d) The average man is by nature indolent-he works as little as possible.

(e) He lacks ambition, dislikes responsibility, prefers to be led.

(f) He is inherently self-centered, indifferent to organisational needs.

(g) He is by nature resistant to change.

(h) He is gullible, not very bright, and the demagogue.

Of these assumptions the first three deal with managerial actions and the last five deal with the human nature. This theory regards that the workers would work only when forced to do so. There is no place for worker's co-operation. It also regards unrestrained authority as the only effective means to supervise and control workers.

Theory Y : This theory implies a more human and supportive approach to managing people. According to McGregor the assumption of Theory Y are as follow :

(a) The expenditure of physical and mental efforts is as natural as play or rest. The average human being does not inherently dislike work. Depending upon controllable conditions, work may be a source of satisfaction or a source of punishment.

(b) External control and the threat of punishment are not the only means for bringing about efforts towards organisational objectives. Man will exercise self-direction and self-control in the services of objectives to which he is committed.

(c) Commitment to objectives is a function of the reward associated with their achievement. The most significant of such award, e.g. the satisfaction of ego, and self actualisation needs can be direct product of effort directed towards organisational objectives.

(d) The average human being learns under proper conditions not only to accept, but to seek responsibility. Avoidance of responsibility lack of ambition and emphasis on security are generally consequences of inherent human characteristics.

(e) The capacity to exercise a relatively high degree of imagination, ingenuity and creativity on the solution of organisational problems is widely, not narrowly, distributes in the population.

(f) Under the conditions of modern industrial life, the intellectual potentialities of the average human being are only partially utilised.

The assumption give a new direction in management. It attempts on the co-operative endeavour of management and workers. McGregor's assumption are based on the Maslow's need hierarchy model.

Vroom's Expectancy Theory

According to Vroom, motivation is a product of three factors viz., valence, expectancy and instrumentally. This relationship is shown in the following manner :

Valence X Expectancy X Instrumentally = Motivation.

Valence refers to the strength of an individual's preference to achieve a specified Goal. If a person strongly desires promotion, then promotion has high valence for him. Valence may vary over a period of time as old needs become satisfied and new one emerge. The relative valence which an individual attaches towards the achievement of goals in influenced conditions like age, education and type of work. With the change in economic conditions and individual may also change his preference for various goals.

Expectancy is the strength of belief that work related efforts will lead in the achievement of goal. It is an association between efforts and performance.

Instrumentality represents an individual's belief that the goal will be achieved, once the task is completed.

This theory recognises individual difference in work motivation. It also clarifies the relationship between individual and organisational goals. This theory suggests that the management develop an environment for performance, taking into account the difference in various situations.

Theory Z : Developed by William Ouchi, it has attracted a lot of attention of managers as well as researchers.

There are four postulates of this theory : (a) strong linkage between organisation and employees; (b) Employee involvement (c) No formal organisational structure and (d) Co-ordination of staff personnel.

Strong Linkage Between orOrganisation and Employee : This theory suggests that there should be a strong linkage the organisation and employees. This can be achieved by various ways. There can be life time employment in the organisation as followed by Japanese companies. This stability can be made by developing work culture and environment and allowing to participate in decision making process. There should be no layoffs and the shareholders should bear the loss by accepting less profits or moderate losses for a short period. Another method of providing stability in employment is by giving more emphasis on horizontal movement of employees rather than vertical. Career planning for every employee should be developed. Slowing down of promotion and financial incentives can be compensated by non-financial forms.

Employee Involvement : Employee's participation in the decision making process is an important factor of this theory. It is not necessary that all decisions should be taken after consulting the employees. Only those decisions which affect them should be taken after consultation. However certain decisions which the management takes solely, the employees should be informed about this, so that they do not feel sidetracked. The basic idea is to give due recognition to the employee.

No Formal Organisation Structure : This theory suggests that there should be no formal organisation structure but a perfect teamwork which should share the information regarding policies, plans and resources. It suggests to develop group spirit rather than individualistic approach. He lays stress on rotational aspect of employee placement so that he can understand how his work affects others or is affected by others.

Co-ordination of Staff Personnel : This theory further suggests that the main aim of management is to co-ordinate people to achieve higher productivity rather than developing or bringing high technology. It involves the commitment of employees through collective approach. For this the leader must win the confidence of his fellow workers and must be trustworthy so as to develop an effective working relationship.

From the above we can analyse that this theory is not only a motivational technique, but includes the entire transformation of management actions and various management techniques.

Job Enrichment

There should be a high degree of flexibility regarding incentive policy of the organisation. The incentive policy should be able to adjust with the human factor and the situation. Job enrichment, developed by Herzberg was based on his research with motivation and maintenance factors. It is an extension of job enlargement technique. Job enrichment emphasis on satisfying higher order needs. Job enlargement concentrates on horizontal loading by adding additional tasks to the worker's job for greater variety. Job enrichment encourages growth and self-actualisation. Intrinsic motivation is encouraged which helps in improving the performance. Job enrichment takes place when the work itself is more challenging when achievement is encouraged, when there is opportunity for growth and when responsibility, advancement and recognition are provided.

Morale

Morale has been recognised as one of the important factors in increasing the production of a business organisation. It has been defined by various authors in different ways. According to Edwin Flippo, " morale is a mental condition or attitudes of individuals and groups which determines their willingness to co-operate. Good morale, as defined by management is evidenced by employee enthusiasm, voluntary conformance with regulations and orders and a willingness to co-operate with others, in the accomplishment of organisation objectives. Poor morale is evidenced by surliness, cases of insubordination, discouragement and dislike of job, company and associates". According to Leighton. " Morale is a capacity of a group of people to pull together persistently and consistently in pursuit of a common purpose ".

Morale is the enthusiasm and willingness with which the individual members of a group set out to achieve the task given to them. Morale depends upon the mental condition like zeal, spirit, enthusiasm, satisfaction and develops the individual's behaviour, attitude, feeling and willingness to work. Individual morale relates to an individual's mental attitude towards his job, working conditions, his superiors and subordinates, satisfaction, willingness to work and acceptance of organisational policies and objectives. Group morale refers to the total feelings, attitudes, opinions, etc., Job morale refers to the mental condition of an individual or a group towards a specific job.

The morale of the employees may be high or low can be easily determined. According to Ralph C. Davis high morale leads to the following advantages; (a) Willing co-operation towards organisation objectives (b) Loyalty to the organisation and its leadership (c) Good discipline or the voluntary conformance to rules, regulations and orders (d) Strong organisational stamina or the ability of the organisation to "take it" during times of difficulty. (e) High degree of employee's interest in the job and the organisation (f) Pride in the organisation. If the morale of the employees is high, they identify themselves as part and parcel of the organisation, work willingly and co-operate in work with their superiors.

On the other hand if the morale of the employees is low it has many disadvantages and some of them are given below : (a) The employees will disrespect and disobey their superiors. (b) There are industrial disputes and the whole atmosphere is vitiated. (c) It develops mental tension, frustration, dissatisfaction and whole energy is directed towards destructive activities rather than constructive ones. (d) It effects the quality, quantity and productivity of the goods.

Factors Determining Morale

Morale of the employees is effected by numerous factors, some of them are discussed below :

Leadership : It influences the morale of the workers in the organisation. If the leader wins the confidence of the workers, the morale will be high. The leader should understand the problems and try to solve them. He should encourage efficient workers and inspire them to work unitedly.

Job Satisfaction : It is an important factor in keeping the morale of the workers high. If they are satisfied with their job, they will work with zeal and enthusiasm which will help in achieving organisational goals.

Confidence among Fellow Workers : If the worker is able to generate confidence among his fellow workers and expresses his views freely and frankly it will develop high morale. If he finds that his fellow workers have faith in him and give correct advice when problems emerge, it is bound to have a high morale on the worker.

Communication : The workers should be in a position to communicate their problems, their views and complaints to the higher authorities and similarly the management should convey its decision without any delay. This will make the workers feel that they are a part of the organisation and their views are also accepted.

Fair Remuneration : The workers expect adequate the fairwages for the work they perform, so that they can have decent standard of living. Besides, they should be given rewards for meritorious work and share in the profits of the organisation.

Job Security : It is very important factor. The employees should be made permanent as early as possible. The rules for termination should also be carefully evolved, so that there is a constant threat of loss of employment.

Fair Promotions : The workers should get chances for promotions and the promotions should be based on certain predetermined policies which should be honestly followed.

Environment : The working conditions should be proper where the workers perform their job. Proper seating arrangement, ventilation, lighting, machines, tools and equipment, medical aid, etc. have impact on worker's morale.

Other Welfare Measures : Proper housing facilities, recreation facilities, schools, hospitals and other psychological and social factors have a greater influence on worker's morale.

22

Communication

As we know, an organisation is a group of human beings, basically formed to achieve certain specified objectives. These objectives can be achieved only when the resources both human and material are properly co-ordinated. The human beings can be properly co-ordinated through communication which facilitates sharing of view and information. Communication is an essential element of management. Besides, it is an instrument of change in social behaviour either to develop harmony among the people or to motivate them to perform such actions as help in achieving social objectives. William Haney has said, " Communication is imminently essential in business, in government, military organisations, hospitals, schools, communities, homes any where people deal with one another. It is difficult in fact, to imagine any kind of interpersonal activity which does not depend on communication".

The term 'Communication' has a wide connotation. It incorporates the concepts of transfer, meaning and information. Koontz, O'Donnel and Weihrich have defined communication, " as the transfer of information from the sender to the receiver with the information being understood by both the sender and the receiver". On analysing the definition we find that firstly, there is something which is transmitted from the sender to the receiver, may be facts, feelings, ideas etc. Secondly, the definition emphasises the understanding element. Both the sender and the receiver would understand the facts, ideas or views which they are sending to one another. In managing the organisation understanding the message is of great importance as it gives direction for effective functioning.

Communication is an integral part of any business organisation. Today, when competition is rising, business concerns require information about prices, similar products of various companies, technology available, rules and regulations of the government, finances, etc. On the basis of this information, the business organisation decides the production and marketing strategy so as to adjust itself with the changing business environment. It is only because of communication that an organisation becomes an open system when it interacts with its environment.

The Communication Process

Communication is a dynamic process which affects and is affected by various variables. The communication process incorporates various elements as shown in the figure given below :

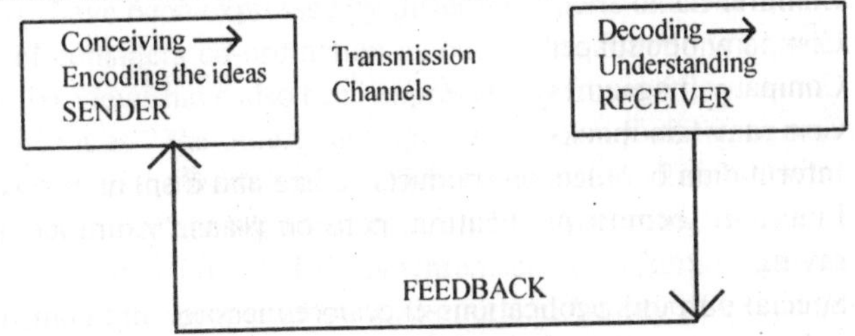

Communication process starts with the sender conceiving the idea which is encoded is such a manner that it can be understood both by the sender and the receiver. The subject matter of the idea, i.e., the information is transmitted through certain channels depending upon the situation of the sender and the receiver. The receiver is the person for whom the message is sent. The receiver converts or decodes the message from the sender. The communication process is complete only when the message is understood by the receiver. Feedback is important as it ensures that the receiver has received the message understands it in the same sense as the sender had desired. Further, the receiver may also suggest to the sender certain changes regarding the course of action in the communication process.

Classification of Communication

Communication can be classified on a number of bases. They can be :

(i) Formal and Informal Communication

(ii) Downward, Upward and Lateral Communication
(iii)Oral and Written Communication

Formal Communication

Formal communication is an officially created procedure for the flow of communication between the various positions on the organisational set-up. George Terry has given eighteen channels of formal communication :

(a) Special interviews
(b) Telephone Calls
(c) Departmental meetings
(d) Mass meetings
(e) Conferences
(f) Company newspapers
(g) Company magazines
(h) Company handbooks
(i) Information booklets on products selling and display materials
(j) Employee benefit publication, pension plans, insurance and savings
(k) Special purpose publications-executive message and company policies
(l) Pay roll inserts
(m) Plant bulletin boards
(n) Posters
(o) Annual report to employees
(p) Supervisory publications
(q) Direct mail letters
(r) Film strips, slides and motion pictures.

Informal Communication

Also termed as 'grapevine' is not due to any official reason but because of social relationship among the employees of the organisation. It is direct, quick and spontaneous. But sometimes information given through an informal system is erratic that any action taken based on such information may lead to a difficult situation in the organisation. The informal communication system is an integral part of the organisational process. The management can take suitable measure to minimise the negative effects of this system.

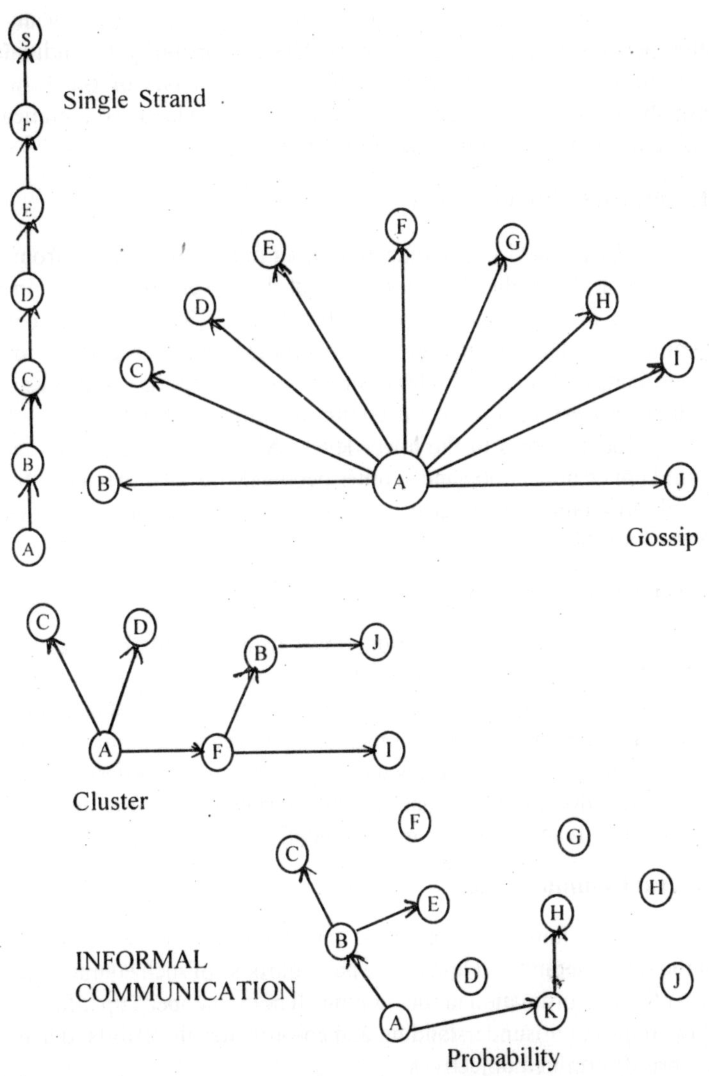

Source : Figures adopted from Keith Davis and Newstrom : Human Behaviour at work : Organisational Behaviour, International Student Edition. Mcgraw-Hill Book Company.

Four types of informal channels of communication have been indentified. They are (i) Single strand; (ii) Gossip; (iii) Probability; and (iv) Cluster.

In the single strand, an individual communicates with other individuals in a sequence. In gossip, the individual communicates to other persons on a non-selective basis. Under probability, the individual communicates with other individuals on the basis of the Law of Probability. Under the cluster network, the individual communicates with only those individuals whom he trusts.

Downward Communication

Downward Communication in an organisation flows from the superiors at the higher levels to those at the lower levels either in the same line of command or in a different one. The basic idea is to communicate the policies, procedures, programmes, orders etc. to the subordinates. It also includes instructions and reports. But these are certain barriers in downward communication. Information is often distorted as it comes to the lower level. Many directives, information would not be understood and at times people do not care to read it. Some people are against a message because they suspect their superiors motives. (See Chart P.243)

Upward Communication

Upward communication flows from the subordinates to the superiors. Such information is in the form of reports relating to the progress of performance specifically in the areas of production, marketing and finances, performance appraisal of the lower staff, opinion, attitude, feeling, suggestions and grievances, clarification of orders etc. This system has the limitation that certain information is often distorted or filtered as it reaches the top management.

Lateral Communication

Also known as horizontal communication, is between persons of the same hierarchical level. The basic purpose of such communication is to effect co-ordination in functioning. It helps the speed up information flow, removes misunderstanding and co-ordinates the efforts to achieve the pre-determined objectives.

Oral Communication

Oral communication is generally face-to-face communication between one person and another and between an individual and a group.

It can be either formal or informal. Oral communication is an effective method of conveying ideas, feelings, suggestions, information, etc. In oral communication, the response is immediate and the effect can be noted. Besides, it gives a feeling of importance and personal touch.

Oral communication can be classified under two heads : firstly, to individuals and secondly, to a group. Oral communication to individuals, becomes necessary under two conditions. Firstly, when specific instructions are to be given to individuals on different issues. On the other hand, oral communication to a group is given under the following situations :

(a) When the information is to be given within a short period to achieve the desired goals;
(b) When the same information is to be repeated to many persons at the same time; and
(c) When consensus has to be reached on a given issue.

Written Communication

It is the most important form of communication. Information, ideas, messages, orders, reports, bulletins etc. are communicated in written forms. A written communication is effective when it is clear, complete and can be easily understood by the other party. A written communication has the advantage of being more carefully thought of, it is better understood by the people, records for future references can be made and can also promote uniformity in policy and procedure. Its limitations are that written communication may create a lot of paper work which at times becomes difficult to maintain and it takes a long time to get the feedback.

Towards Effective Communication

Smooth and effective flow of information between various individuals is of utmost importance for efficient functioning of an organisation. The following points should be kept in mind in order to make communication effective.

Clarity : The communication should possess clarity in expression and transmission in order to avoid unnecessary seeking of clarification by the receiver. The fundamental idea of communication is to bring the communicator and receiver together and this is possible only when the sender's views are understood by the receiver in the same manner.

Adequate Coverage : The communication should ensure adequate coverage to various groups and individuals in the organisation, so that people can discharge their duties effectively.

Timing : The timing of communication messages is also very important. The allotment of duties, future plans regarding development and expansion and so on should be communicated at proper time so that the employees can prepare themselves mentally to perform various tasks. Any communication conveyed at the eleventh hour fails to achieve the desired objective and develops mental pressure on the employees.

Integrity : Integrity is an essential aspect of communication. Communication is not an end in itself, rather it is a means of getting a desired objectives achieve. This can happen only when the communication made by the superiors to their subordinates results in some action, only when the subordinates possess integrity in implementing the message conveyed to them both in letter and spirit. To develop integrity, the superiors should have faith in the subordinates and accept their viewpoints.

Frequency

How many times should the superiors communicate with their subordinates on the same topic is a point of debate. It depends on the individuals and on each case. In some cases repetition of instructions may produce better results but at times it has an adverse effect by arousing resistance in the receivers.

Barriers in Communication

The prime objective of communication is to bring about a change by influencing others to perform some kind of action. The communication may dissuade or encourage a person to act only when he is able to understand in proper perspective and is in a position to respond to action as desired by the communicator. Many a time there are various barriers which impede the smooth flow of communication. These are discussed below :

Semantic Barriers : These barriers are caused during the process of receiving and understanding the message. When the message is not clear and the words and phrases chosen are ambiguous, the receiver finds it difficult to put the words into action. Words communicate different meaning to different people. Everyone interprets various terms within his own experience, attitude and environment.

Inattention : At times, the receiver does not pay attention to certain communication due to heavy pressure of work. It is very common that certain people do not pay much attention to notices and reports.

Loss on Transmission : It is a common phenomenon that when a communication is transmitted through various levels in organisation, it loses its accuracy, especially in oral transmission. There is a possibility on a written communication also when it is interpreted and analysed at various levels. Secondly, the personnel at various levels retain only a part of the information which is passed to the lower level. Retention of information is one of the barriers in different organisations.

Under Stress on Written Information : It is the tendency of most of the people to accept the viewpoint through written communication only. Face to face discussion and communication is much better than a written document. Any organisation can function only when there is mutual trust amongst its employees. Written communication lacks the persuasive quality. Therefore written communication must be considered as supplementary to the fact-to-face communication.

Failure to Communicate : It is sometimes seen that superiors fail to communicate the required message to their subordinate, due to laziness or on the assumption that everybody knows or to deliberately embrass their subordinates.

Rules and Regulations : Sometimes the rules and regulations of the organisation affect the flow of messages. The communication given through the proper channels delays the message to be communicated. The barrier is very common in our Government organisations.

Interpersonal Relationships : The relationship between the sender and the receiver influences the entire communication process. Superiors play a vital role in this process. If their attitude towards their subordinates is unfavourable, the messages would not flow adequately from and towards them. Secondly, sometimes they withhold some information so that their subordinates may not know their weaknesses and administrative secrets, at times, the superiors are not aware of the importance of communication flowing downwards and as such the information is withheld.

Similarly, the subordinates have a major role to play in the communication channel. Sometimes they do not communicate certain information to their superiors because they feel that it may adversely affect their career prospects and performance. Secondly, they do not give any suggestions to their superiors because of lack of motivation.

Methods of Removing the Barriers

As we have already seen, communication is an integral part of management and plays a significant role in the organisational process. It is necessary, that the management should try to remove these barriers or try to reduce them to the bare minimum so that there can be smooth flow of communication in all directions. The following methods are suggested in order to remove these barriers :

(a) The organisational policy pertaining to the flow of communication should be clear and encourage the flow of message on all directions.

(b) The policy should clearly spell out the subject matter of the communication so that there is no ambiguity in transmission of the message.

(c) Though it is necessary that the information should flow through the proper channels as far as the routine job is concerned, but too much emphasis should not be put on it. If the situation demands so it can be bypassed and the concerned persons may be informed that the channel is not necessary in all cases.

(d) Superiors play a more important role in transmitting communication rather than their subordinates. It is the managerial personnel at the higher level that can set examples for a smooth flow of communication.

(e) Adequate facilities and their proper use can facilitate communication. Senior managers should encourage and keep a check on the use of the facilities provided.

(f) Senior managers should create an atmosphere of mutual trust and confidence which is conductive for the smooth flow of informations on all directions. A distinct change in the organisation is necessary for promoting communication.

(g) The flow of communication and policy should be evaluated periodically so that problems affecting the flow of informations may be identified and corrective measures taken.

Reference

1. George Terry : 'Principle of Management', Richard D. Irwin Inc., Homewood, Illinois, 1968.

23

Leadership

With the growth of complexities in the human behaviour, leadership has become indispensable for the effective functioning of the family or a group of persons or the society or business or the government. The concept of leadership has undergone a change in the last few decades.

Leadership has been defined in various ways. According to Keith Davis, "Leadership is the ability to persuade others to seek defined objectives enthusiastically. It is the human factor which binds a group together and motivates it towards goals". In the words of Robert Tannenbaum" "Leadership is interpersonal influence exercised in a situation and directed through communication process, towards the attainment of a specialised goal or goals". George Terry defines it as, "the activity of influencing people to strive willingly for mutual objectives".

From the above definitions we can ascertain the basic features of leadership. They are :

(a) Leadership is usually a personal quality and it is this quality which motivates people to join such leaders.
(b) Leadership influences the individual behaviour to attain the pre-determined objectives in the desired manner.
(c) Leadership is a continuous process of influencing behaviour and is exercised in a specific situation.

Need for Leadership

The success of any organisation depends on effective leadership. Without a good leader an organisation can neither grow nor can it function in an efficient and effective manner. The importance of good leadership is discussed below :

(a) The persons working in an organisation come from different backgrounds having different values, interests, attitudes and beliefs. A competent leadership organizes the entire groups and directs them in order to achieve the organisational goals.

(b) Leadership generates perfection in the formal organisational structure.

(c) With the fast changing socio-economic structure and the technological advancement taking place, an organisation can only exist when it has an effective leader who can foresee the likely changes taking place and initiate steps to meet them intelligently.

(d) Good leadership motivates employees for high performance. Besides, it helps in raising the morale of the employees which leads to higher productivity in the organisation.

Characteristic of Effective Leaders

Numerous research studies have taken place to identify the basic characteristics of effective leaders. Keith Davis has identified four characteristics that leaders tend to have. They are :

Intelligence : Leaders tend to have somewhat higher intelligence than their followers.

Social Maturity and Breadth : Leaders have a tendency to be emotionally mature and to have a broad range of interests.

Inner Motivation and Achievement Drives : Leaders want to accomplish things, when they achieve one goal, they seek out another. They are not primarily dependent on outside forces for their motivation.

Human Relations Attitude : Leaders are able to work effectively with other persons. They respect individuals and realize that to accomplish tasks they must be considerable to others.

Leadership Theories

Various research studies have been conducted by behavioral scientists as to how leaders are made. They have not been able to give satisfactory answers but these researches have resulted in the development of various theories or approaches which help in understanding how a leader emerges.

Trait Theory

The theory of Trait represents the earliest notions of leadership. It considers traits or features of the individual as the basis of leadership concept. These traits were classified as honesty, loyalty, sincerity, ambition, initiative, imagination etc. This theory held the view that these traits were inborn which are usually inherited. The various traits can be categorised into innate and acquirable traits.

Innate Traits

These are inborn qualities and are known as 'God gifted'. These cannot be acquired by the individuals. Some of the innate qualities of a successful leader are given below :

Physical Qualities : These are determined by the heredity characters. Physical features lead to personality formation which is an important factor in determining leadership success.

Intelligence : Leadership requires a higher level of intelligence, which is basically a natural quality. However in certain cases environment plays a major role in developing intelligence.

Acquirable Traits

These qualities of leadership can be acquired through various processes. Some of them are discussed below :

Emotional and Mental Stability

A leader should be emotionally stable and consistent in action and should refrain from anger. He should adjust himself in different situations and should be self confident in meeting various situations successfully.

Human Relations

Successful leadership requires adequate knowledge to human relations. Leadership requires voluntary co-operation from the people so as to achieve organisational goals. Adequate knowledge of individual and group behaviour facilities leadership in facing different situations.

Objectivity

Leadership depends on the objective attitude of the leader. Whatever step or action a leader takes should be based on relevant facts and information, without being prejudiced or biased towards anybody.

Motivating Skills

Leadership requires skill which motivate people to help in achieving the desired goals. An effective leader activates his followers and inspires them to become good citizens of the country.

Other Skills

Besides motivating skills, a good leader should possess communicative and social skills also. Communicative skills are a powerful tool in persuading and activating the people. Similarly, social skills help in understanding the strength and weakness of the people.

The above mentioned qualities can be acquired and they contribute to the success of leadership.

But this theory has several limitations. Firstly it lays emphasis on personal qualities without considering the environment in which they are to operate. Secondly, there are problems in measuring the traits. Thirdly, there have been many people with the traits specified for a leader, but they have not been good leaders.

Behavioural Approach

Under this approach due emphasis is placed on the behaviour of the leader. Leadership is exhibited more by the acts of the leader rather than his traits. Though traits have an influence on the acts of the leader, yet the activities of the leader are also affected by the followers, objectives and the environment which these acts take place. Thus, leadership depends on four elements, (a) leaders, (b) followers, (c) objectives, and (d) environment. On classifying environment it can be found stable or instable. Under stable environment, the behaviour of the leader is calm. But under unstable environment, the leaders have to be active, take risks and have to initiate future course of action. Determining objectives, motivating the followers for achieving the objectives, increasing their morale, cultivating team work, effective communication are some of the elements of functional behaviour for an effective leader.

Situational Approach

Under this approach, emphasis is not on the individual characteristics of the leader but on the situation under which he operates and on the existence of a group, because the leadership concept is more applicable to the group rather than on an individual. Researches conducted by behavioural scientists have given four situational variables which affect the performance of leadership. They are : (a) cultural environment, (b) individual differences; (c) variation in jobs; and (d) variation in organisations.

This theory helps in analysing how leadership behaviour varies with situational variables. In other words, this theory facilitates the analysis of why a leader is successful in a particular situation whereas he is unsuccessful in another situation.

Leadership Styles

Leadership style is somewhat different from the personality trait of the leader. Though his behaviour is affected by his personality trait, he is more influenced by the conditions prevailing around him. It may be termed as external environment. Thus, all the situational variables, the external environment and his personality trait determine the style of functioning, known as leadership style.

Leadership styles may be classified under three heads :

Autocratic Leadership

Under this style of leadership, the authority is centralised by the leader regarding decision making. The leader takes a decision and announced it. In some cases, the leader gives a detailed explanation regarding his decision, whereas, in other case, the leaders do not feel the necessity of giving such explanation. There are three categories of autocratic leaders viz. (a) Strict autocrat, (b) Benevolent autocrat, and (c) Incompetent autocrat. A strict autocrat deals his subordinates very strictly by criticising subordinates and by imposing penalty if they slightly go wrong. A benevolent autocrat possesses decision making power but his motivation style is positive. An incompetent autocrat adapts autocratic style so as to hide his weakness. But this does not last long as he is exposed after sometime.

Though this style has the based advantage to quick decisions, still there are many limitations. The subordinates lack motivation, develop frustration thereby developing conflict in the organisation. Individuality is suppressed and thus future leaders in the organisation do not developed.

Democratic Leadership

This style of leadership is based on the principle of participation of subordinates in the decision making process. It is also termed as participative style. When the subordinates are involved in the decision making process, they are encouraged to contribute to the organisational objectives and share responsibility.

There are numerous advantages of this style of leadership. Firstly, subordinates are highly motivated when their ideas are incorporated in the decision making process. Secondly it enhances productivity. Thirdly, it provides stability in the organisation as it raises the morale of the subordinates. It has been said that "democratic leadership produced less aggressive behaviour, less dependence on the leader, more group initiative and more productive behaviour than the other two types of leadership".

Free-Rein Leadership

Under this style of leadership, complete freedom is given to the subordinates. The superior frames the policy and gives full freedom to the subordinates to implement it. This style is usually not practicable. It is used in a small group of highly intelligent and experienced people.

Leadership as a Continuum

There are various styles of leadership behaviour between two extremes of autocratic leadership and free-rein leadership. Tannenbaum and Schmidt have developed a continum moving from autocratic leadership behaviour at one end to free-rein leadership bahaviour at the other end.

To select the most effective leadership style for a given situation Tannenbaum and Schmidt have suggested that three variables should be analyzed. These are, forces within the leader, forces in the followers and forces in the situation.

Forces in the Leader : This refers to the personal traits, his value system, his confidence and faith in his subordinates, leadership

Inclinations and feeling of security in an uncertain situation.

Forces in the Subordinates : This refers to their high needs for independence, their readiness to assume reasonability for decision making, high tolerance for ambiguity, understanding and identifying organisational goals, interest in the problem, knowledge and experience to deal with the problems and learning to expect to share in decision making.

Forces in the Situation : This refers to the environmental factors, the type of organisation, effectiveness of the work group, the type of problem and the pressure of time.

Later Tannenbaum and Schmidt updated their view on leadership and republished their original article. They acknowledged that the organisations were affected by external environment leading to an increase of factors in situational variables, thereby affecting the leadership pattern.

Likert Management System

Rensis Likert, with his associates, studied the patterns and styles of managers and developed certain concepts and approaches important in understanding leadership behaviour. He has given a continum of four systems of management in terms of leadership styles, viz. Exploratative autocratic (System 1), Benevolent autocratic (System 2), Participative (System 3), and Democratic (System 4). Likert has also isolated three variables which are representative of his total concept of system 4. These are : (i) the use of supportive relationships by managers; (ii) the use of group decision making and group methods of supervision; and (iii) his high performance goals.

Managerial Grid

One of the most widely known approaches of leadership styles is the managerial grid developed by Robert and Jane Mouton.[2] The grid has two dimensions, concern for people and concern for production. Their 'concern for' purchase has been used to convey how managers are concerned for people or production, rather than 'how much', production is getting out of a group. 'Concern for production' incorporates attitudes of a supervisor towards a number of things such as the quality of policy decisions, procedures and processes, creativeness of research etc. 'Concern for people' includes degree of personal commitment towards goal achievement, maintaining the self-esteem of workers, provision of good working conditions, satisfying inter-personal relations. The managerial grid identifies five leadership styles based upon these two factor found in organisations are shown in the Figure below.

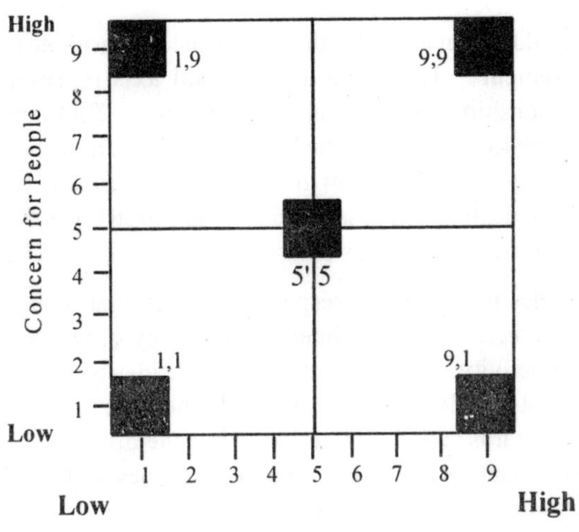

Concern for Production

THE MANAGEMENT GRID

Blake and Mouton have described the five styles as follows :

Style 1, 1 under this style (also termed as 'Impoverished Management') the exertion of minimum effort is required to get work done and sustain organisation's morale.

Style 1, 9 Under this (also termed as Country Club Management) thoughtful attention to the needs of people leads to friendly and comfortable organisation atmosphere and work tempo;

Style 9, 1 Under this (also termed as 'Autocratic Task Managers') adequate performance is encouraged through balance of work requirements and maintaining satisfactory morale.

Style 9, 9 Under this (also termed as Team Managers) work accomplished is from committed people with independence through a common stake in organisation purpose and with trust and respect.

The managerial grid is useful device for identifying and classifying managerial styles. It is widely used throughout the world as a means of managerial training and of identifying various combinations of leadership styles.

Tridimensional Grid

W.J. Reddin[3] developed a three dimensional grid, also known as '3-D Management'. The three dimensional axis represents task orientation, relationship orientation and effectiveness. *Task orientation* (TO) may be defined as an effort by the manager to direct his subordinates' efforts towards the achievement of objectives. It includes planning, organising and controlling. *Relationship orientation* (RO) is defined as the extent to which a manager has personal relationship with his staff.

It includes mutual trust, respect for subordinates suggestions and views etc. Effectiveness is defined as the ability of the manager to obtain high productivity. When the style of the leader is appropriate in a given situation, it is called effective and when the style is inappropriate in a given situation it is called ineffective. Thus the difference between the two is not the actual behaviour but the appropriateness of the behaviour in the given situation when it is used.

R.O		
	Related,	Integrated
	Separated	Dedicated
	T.O	

TASK AND RELATIONSHIP ORIENTATION

These four styles represent four types of behaviour. Separated manager is primarily concerned with correcting deviations. A related manager views the organisation as a social system, likes to work with others and set examples. A Dedicated manager is dominating in nature, cannot work without power and is only interested in production. An Integrated manager gets involved with his staff and organisation, identifies with the organisation and lays stress on team work. Any of these styles can be effective in one situation and ineffective in other. None are more or less effective in themselves. Their effectiveness depends on the situation in which they are used.

In other words, each one of the four basic styles has a less effective equivalent resulting in eight managerial styles.

Basic Style	*Less Effective Managerial Style*	*More Effective Managerial Style*
Integrated	Compromiser	Executive
Dedicated	Autocrat	Benovolent Autocrat
Related	Missionary	Developer
Separated	Deserter	Bureaucrat

According to this, the less effective managerial styles are discussed below :

Compromiser : He is both task and relationship oriented but is capable or unwilling to integrate and take decisions. He is weak and yielding and his decisions are influenced by pressures.

Autocrat : he is concerned with only the immediate task and has no concern for others. His decisions are centralised. He believes in suppressing, disagreement and thinks that everyone should obey his authority.

Missionary : He believes in maintaining good relationship with everyone and tries to avoid conflicts. He believes in a warm, pleasant, social atmosphere where an easy going work tempo may be maintained.

Deserter : He shows lack of interest in both task and relationships. He is ineffective, does not work and hinders the performance of others. He avoids responsibility, gives minimum output and works to rule.

The four more effective managerial styles are discussed below :

Executive : He view his job as getting the best out of others. He sets high standards for production and performance. He believes in teak work, considers task as independent and integrated. He welcomes disagreement and does not avoid conflict as he believes that they can be sorted out mutually. He believes in a democratic leadership style.

Benevolent Autocrat : he is a hard task master who knows what he wants and gets things done without resentment. He is highly ambitious but less people oriented. He is fully committed and adopts positive economic motivation for getting things done.

Developer : He places implicit trust in people. He is effective in working with and motivating people. He is basically concerned with developing the talents of others. He relies on high relationship orientation and less task orientation.

Bureaucrat : He is highly oriented towards organisation rules, maintains an air of interest and gets personally involved with problems. He produces few ideas and is less task and relationship oriented.

Fielder's Contingency Model

As already discussed, a particular style of leadership cannot be applicable under all environments. Fiedler[4] developed a contingency model of leadership under the assumption that the effectiveness of leadership is based on the leader's ability to act in terms of situational requirements. Fiedler gave two major styles of leadership : Firstly, task oriented style which is primarily concerned with achieving the task performed. Secondly, human relations style which is oriented towards achieving good interpersonal relations and toward attaining a position of personal prominence.

Fiedler identified three dimensions of the leadership situation that help determine what style of leadership will be most effective.

(a) Leader-member relationship.
(b) Task structure.
(c) Position power.

The leader's position obtained through formal authority enables him to obtain good followership than one without power. If the tasks are clear, the quality of performance will be good. The leader-member relationship is the most important dimension in determining the situation's favourableness because it is the group member's willingness to follow and trust the leader or not. Fiedler defined favourableness of the situation as the degree to which a given situation enables a leader to exert influence over a group.

A leader is responsible for meeting the needs of an organisation. The success of leadership depends on the response of the organisation. A number of approaches have been developed. Various styles have been identified. But in order to develop and be successful a leader has to lead by performing activities by himself in accordance with the norms laid down. He has to solve the problems which emerge. He has to maintain cohesiveness among his group members so that he can accomplish his objectives through teamwork and forge ahead.

Reference

1. Robert Tannenbaum and Warren H. Schmidt. "How to choose a Leadership Pattern" Harvard Business Review, March-April, 1958 pp. 95-101.

2. R.R. Blake and J.S. Mouton : The Managerial Grid, Houston, Texas : Gulf Publishing Company, 1964.

3. W.J. Reddin : Effective Management, Tata-McGraw Hill Pub. Co. Ltd., New Delhi, 1987 pp. 71-75.

4. F.E. Fiedler : A theory of Leadership Effectiveness (New York : McGraw-Hill Book Company, 1967).

Part 3

Production Management

24

Production Planning and Control

One of the major functions of management is to develop a systematic programme of production to achieve qualitative, quantitative and economical manufacture of goods. When a product is to be manufactured, the production must be carefully planned in order that the manufacturing departments are loaded efficiently and within their capacities. During the manufacturing process the production must be controlled to ensure that the programmed output is maintained constantly. These functions are known as production Planning and Production Control respectively.

Alford and Beatty have defined it as, "Production Planning and control comprise the planning, routing, scheduling, despatching and follow-up function in the productive process, so organized that the movements of material, performance of machines and operations of labour, however sub-divided are directed and co-ordinated as to quantity, quality, time and place. It is adopting as a business principle the old adage of 'plan your work and work your plan'. Charles A. Koepke has defined it as "the co-operation of a series of functions according to a plan which will economically utilize the plant facilities and regulates the orderly movement of goods through their entire manufacturing cycle, from the procurement of all materials to the shipping of finished goods at a predetermined rate".

Production Planning

Planning function seeks to determine as to what type of production is to be performed, anticipate difficulties and take measures to remove the causes before they take place. According to Lawrence,

Bethel and others, 'Production planning takes a given product or line of products and organises in advance the manpower, materials, machines and money required for a predetermined output in a given period of time. It starts with a product concept capable of being manufactured, a general idea of the process by which it can be made and a sales forecast for the discernible future".

The principal aims and objectives of production planning are :

(i) To determine the quantum and quality of men, materials and machines required to fulfil the production target in the most economical way;

(ii) To determine as to when these things would be required and to procure them in advance;

(iii) To make all arrangement regarding the manufacturing processes which are necessary to achieve the production target;

(iv) To operate the plant at a predetermined efficiency;

(v) To capture a desired share of the market; and

(vi) To achieve a prescribed level of profit.

The production planning results in increased production with reduced cost, reduction in manufacturing time and the orders are executed in time.

Production Control

Just by planning the production, it is not necessary that the actual production would conform to the planned activities. It is production Control that regulates the flow of production so that the goods of desired quantity and quality are produced at the right time most economically. The basic aim of production control is to facilitate the task of manufacturing and to co-ordinate all the necessary production activities so that the manufacturing is done strictly according to the pre-planned schedule. Spriegal and Lansburgh define production control as "the process of planning production in advance of operations, establishing the exact route of each individual item, part or assembly, setting, starting and finishing dates for each important item, assembly and the finished products, and releasing the necessary orders as well as initiating the required follow-up to effectuate the smooth functioning of the enterprise." According to James L. Lundy, "Basically the production control function involves the co-ordination and integration of the factors of production for optimum efficiency. Overall sales orders or plans must be translated in specific schedules and assigned so as to occupy all work centres but overload none. Thus the principal objective of production control is to facilitate the task of manufacturing and see that everything is being done strictly in accordance with the plan".

Steps in Production Control

The following steps are taken under production control :

Routing : It is concerned with the determination of the process in which the products are to be manufactured and lay down the route over which the raw materials are to be transformed into finished products. "Routing determines what work will be done on a product or part as well as where and how it will be done. It establishes the operations, their path and sequence and the proper class of machines and personnel required for these operations. It is also connected with the field of product development in designing a product that can be readily manufactured. It is closely allied with plant and industrial engineering in setting up the most efficient operating methods and handling and back-tracking. In the case of continuous production or mass production plan, Routing becomes automatic for standardized production with standardized operations. But the problem acquires certain dimensions in the case of job production or batch production, because the products are different and there may be several ways of routing materials. Through experience the most economical routing may be prepared by the planning section.

The routing procedure for a new product or part consists of the following activities :

(a) Analyzing the product as what to make and what to purchase;

(b) Analyzing the article to determine what materials are required;

(c) Determining the manufacturing operations and their flow of path;

(d) Determining the lot sizes;

(e) Determining the scrap factors;

(f) Estimating the cost of article; and

(g) Complete collection of various control forms.

Scheduling : It shows the time required for each production. It involves the scheduling of all items required for production. It is an important aspect of production control as all the future process of production is based on it. 'Scheduling involves establishing the amount of work to be done and the time each element of the work will start, or the order of work. This includes allocating the quality and the rate of output of the plant or department and also the date or order or starting of each unit of work at each station along the rute prescribed. In other words developing a programme schedule helps in knowing what items or parts are to be produced, what shall be their sequence of production and what shall be the time limit to complete the work.

Scheduling is classified into three categories. Master scheduling helps to assign dates on which the production is to complete. Operation scheduling helps to assign the time necessary to complete a piece of work with a given machine. Detail operation scheduling helps to assign the time necessary to do each detail operation of a given work with a given machine.

Despatching : It is concerned with starting the production operation on the basis of route sheets and schedule charts. It gives necessary authority to commence work as per route sheets and schedule charts. "Despatching involves meeting the schedules by proper utilization of machines, work places, materials and workers as designated by the routing. The despatching unit of the planning department thus includes all persons whose duty it is to see that orders are issued to the shop, that materials are at the work-place, that tools are provided, that job cards are issued and in general, all necessary steps are taken to insure that the schedules will be properly carried out".

The main functions of despatching are as follows :

- To issue the necessary items from stores to machines;
- To issue the right tools, fixtures and gauges;
- Allocating proper labour force and machines for the execution of production orders;
- To issue necessary production orders to perform the work in accordance with the pre-determined dates and time;
- To issue inspection orders needed at different states of production; and
- Keeping record of the various subsidiary orders for reference.

The despatching system may be centralised or decentralised. Decentralised despatching consists of issuing manufacturing schedules or work orders in blanket fashion to the foreman or despatch clerk within each department who must then determine the relative sequence in which those orders will be started within that departments. The Centrallised system involves the despatching of orders from the central despatching division directly to the machine or work.

Follow-up or Expediting : It is concerned with the evaluation of the results achieved through the production process. It takes into account the deficiencies encountered during the production process and take necessary steps to rectify them. It also includes expediting the movement of materials though it may involves a little cost. This function also involves the maintenance of proper records and the delays and bottlenecks. According to Bethel and others, "Follow-up or expediting is that branch of production control procedure which regulates the progress of materials and parts through the production process. Follow-up serves as a catalytic agent to fuse the various separate and unrelated production activities into the unified whole that means progress. It endeavours to see that the promise is backed up by the performance".

Inspection : Production control system not only ensures that the goods are produced as per programme but also tries to see that the goods produced are of standard quality. Inspection is done from the stage of procurement of raw materials to that of the actual completion of the final product. It involves the inspection of tools and machines being used in the process of production. Inspection differs from product to product and from company to company. According to Alfred and Beatty, "Inspection is the art of applying tests preferably by the aid of measuring appliances, to observe whether a given item of product is within the specified limits of variability".

Requirements for Efficient working of Production Control.

For the efficient functioning of the production control department, it should possess complete information relating to the following :

1. Information regarding production materials required for sub-assemblies and final assembly.
2. Information regarding the standard of quality for each item.

3. Information regarding machine output or equipment capacity.
4. Information regarding operation technique.
5. Information regarding the sequence of operations and acurate knowledge of machine layout.
6. Information regarding work to be done, conditions under which it is to be done and the type of skilled personnel required.
7. Information regarding completion times of all previous operations and their actual costs.
8. Information regarding orders booked and their delivery dates.

Statistical Quality Control (SQC)

It refers to the application of statistical techniques for the purpose of checking the quality of the products. It is based on sampling probability and statistical inference. According to alfred and Beatty, "It is the mechanism by which products are made to measure up to specifications determined from the customer's demands and transformed into sales, engineering and manufacturing requirements. It is concerned with making things right rather than discovering and rejecting those made wrong". The statistical quality control has two main functions, viz., prevention and assurance. Firstly it prevents variations from the standard quality and secondly it assures the maintenance of quality within the prescribed limits of errors.

However, the goods produced may not conform to the standards developed mathematically because many factors are not controllable and they effect the quality of the product, as desired. In actual practice there is no such thing as exact standard as it is very difficult to attain perfection. Therefore, some deviation from the standard set is tolerated or allowed. It is termed as tolerance. This tolerance defines by means of limits the zone of acceptability - a zone of variation that may be permitted without altering the functional fitness of the article involved".

The scope of quality control varies from industry to industry. In industries manufacturing arms and aeroplanes a rigid quality control is necessary whereas industries manufacturing agricultural machinery, a much less rigid inspection in required. In chemical industries a different type of inspection takes place where the product manufactured should strictly conform the standardised quality.

Control charts and Acceptance sampling are the two major techniques of statistical quality control widely used by the industrial concerns.

Benefits of Statistical Quality Control

Statistical quality control enables production at the most economic level consistent with full consumer satisfaction. It ensures production of standardised goods. It helps in reducing the cost of production by reduction of variations in products, reduction of waste and scrap and by improving efficiency effectively. According to Alfred and Beatty the advantages are summarised as follows :

1. Improvement in the quality level.
2. Greater uniformity in the finished product.
3. Greater sales volume at the same price.
4. Reduction in inspection costs.
5. Reduction in rejections, scrap and rework.
6. Improvement in the quality consciousness on the part of those concerned with quality control.
7. Improvement in the designs and processes leading to reduced production costs for given product standard.
8. Improvement in producer-customer relations.
9. Improvement in technical knowledge.

References

1. Spriegel and Lansburgh, Industrial Management, p. 361.
2. James L. Lundy, Effective Industrial Management, p. 302.
3. Spriegel and Lansburgh, op cit, p. 371.
4. Spriegel and Lansburgh, op cit, p. 382.
5. Alfred and Beatty, Principles of Industrial Management, p. 451.

25

Purchasing

The production process in an economy depends upon the conversion of raw materials into forms which have higher utility and satisfaction to the consumers. Creation of utility is termed as production function. Purchasing and storekeeping are two basic functions of production.

Purchasing

In order to keep the wheels of an industry moving, constant supplies of necessary materials is of utmost importance. Such materials have to be procured in a systematic manner. Earlier it was referred as an act of buying but today with the growth of business activities it is termed as purchasing which encompasses a much broader sense. Today it implies as "a managerial activity that goes beyond the simple act of buying and includes the planning and policy activities covering a wide range of related and complementary activities". In other words the purchasing department not only performs the buying function but also the control and advisory functions.

Purchasing involves the procurement of materials of right quality because if the materials is of low quality it can effect the quality of the finished product; of right price because higher price increase the cost of production, which can effect the sale; on the right quality so that there may be no bottlenecks at the production level at the same time the inventory level may not be too high; and at the right time so that the goods produced can be sold in the market in right time.

Objectives of Scientific Purchasing : Some of major objectives of scientific purchasing are given below :

1. Procurement of given quantity and quality of materials at the price commesurate with the policy of the organisation.
2. Procurement of materials which best suit the product and for the purpose for which they are procured.
3. Purchasing sufficiently in advance so that there may be no delay in production plans.
4. Purchasing should aim in avoiding waste, duplication and obsolescence;
5. Purchasing should try to create a better image of the enterprise in the minds of the supplies by making prompt payment to them.
6. It should aim at the "development of internal relationship that lead to understanding and harmony among the various organisational units within the company".

Functions of Purchasing Department

The purchasing department performs a number of functions. Some of them are given below :

1. To locate and select sources of supply or material or services required as per established schedule.
2. To maintain records of purchases made from time to time from various suppliers.
3. To secure quotations and conducting negotiations with the prospective suppliers.
4. To verify the quality and quantity of goods.
5. To approve invoices, before payment is made.
6. To study the markets so that necessary purchases can be made at appropriate time.
7. To dispose off the obsolete or excess material or equipment.
8. To collect information regarding the development of new products so that necessary items can be substituted with the new ones.

Factors in Buying

Purchasing has assumed an important function of the

management and to a major extent the success of the business concern depends upon the working of the purchasing department. The purchase personnel should bear in mind the following factors while making purchases.

Quality : Due importance should be given to this factor at the time of making purchases because the quality of the finished product depends on the quality of the raw material used. If the quality of the product is good it captures the market and the company does not have any difficulty in facing competition. At the same time it can fetch a good price. Quality of a produce enhances the image of the good company also.

Quantity : The basic aim of any purchasing department is to keep a regular flow of materials for the production activity. At the same time the company cannot purchase in bulk to lock up its capital, it has to follow the policy laid down by the company. The decision regarding right quantity is related to the period for which it is purchased and also the minimum total cost which may obviate shortages.

In this case order quantity concept has to be taken into account. It means "the quantity that is ordered at a given time". "This is calculated by dividing the total periodical requirements by the number of orders to be placed during that period. It is of three types viz., Economic order Quantity, Bulk Order Quantity and Arbitrary Order Quantity.

Price : This is also an important factor which is considered by the purchasing department. If the price is too high the cost of the finished product will go up. Besides there are number of factors which effect pricing. Therefore, the purchasing department has to consider various factors which determine the optimum price of the materials.

Suppliers : Purchasing department should select those suppliers who can supply the required materials as per schedule. If the supplies are irregular, it will have adverse effect on production plans. If there is a rush order for the materials then higher price has to be paid. Therefore, the purchasing department should well in advance anticipate the needs and fix with the suppliers.

Purchasing Methods

There are many ways of buying and one of the method is followed by the business concern. They are given below :

Concentration of Purchases : Under this method all the purchases are made from a single supplier or only a limited number of suppliers. The main advantages of such purchasing are that the company can maintain continuous relations and it helps in getting better services; large orders help in high discount rates and lower prices; cost of contact is reduced; and the cost per unit of freight and other charges is reduced. There are certain disadvantages as it is very risky to depend on a single or limited number of suppliers because if he fails to supply in time there shall be dislocation in production and secondly once the buyer contracts with a single supplier he is tied down and cannot choose from a wide range of items.

Diversified Purchasing : When the purchases are made from a large number of suppliers it is termed as diversified purchasing or scattered buying. The main advantage of such buying are that there is a certain amount of flexibility in the buying plan; there is no risk of the supplies being stopped; due to completion the buyers may get better terms and lower prices; and the buyer is free to choose from a number of items. There are some limitations also as the buyer may not be able to get quantity discount and secondly freight and handling charges are on the higher side.

Reciprocal Buying : Under this method the producers may agree to purchase their requirements from those suppliers who agree to purchase in turn their finished products. This is also termed as buy back agreement. For instance a steel company may use the services of railways only if the latter agrees to make purchases from the steel company. The main advantages regarding such buying is that both the parties establish good relationship because of mutual dependence, and secondly both the parties can secure reasonable prices with better quality. There are some limitations also such as the selling department will lose its incentive and there is no choice of various items.

Current Market Purchasing : This method involves purchase of goods according to the current requirements of the producing concern or of the immediate future. It avoids the purchase of material in large quantities. The basic advantage of this method is that the company can derive the benefits of price fluctuations. But there are certain limitations also. The company does not get quantity discounts as the purchased amount is small. Secondly in lean period the company may not be able to get materials of desired quantity and thirdly purchase being made in small lots, numerous formalities have to be done, a number of times.

Speculative Purchasing : This is done with the hope of profiteering from price changes in the future. Under this method materials are purchased when the prices are low and are resold when the prices rise. No purchasing manager, howsoever may be good in forecasting he will never go for speculative purchasing because it can land him and his organisation into trouble and earn a bad name.

Purchasing for Future : When a company used some materials regularly it may buy those materials in excess of the minimum requirement. It is also termed as forward purchasing. According to Westing, Fine and Zenz, "Forward purchasing includes all purchasing in excess of the minimum stock required to keep plant to operating on a basis of normal output and average delivery times. It excludes a advance purchases made with the object of realising speculative profits". Under future purchasing the period covered should not be very long as certain changes might occur in the market. This method of purchasing if used helps the company to beat its competitors in a market which is subjected to inflationary price trends, scarcity and profiteering.

Group Purchasing : Under this method the purchasing department places one order for a number of small items required by the company instead of placing a large number of orders. Experience has shown that group purchasing lowers the cost and thus it is a benefit to the company.

Scheduled Buying : When purchasing is closely related to controlled production then scheduled buying is resorted to. This helps the manufacture in reducing his inventories and unnecessary blocking his capital.

Thus we see that there are a number of methods of purchasing. Different companies resort to different methods of purchasing as their policies vary. The purchasing should be done to keep the wheels of the industry moving without dislocating the production plans.

Buyer-Supplier Relationship

The relationship between the two has an important effect on the quality and price of the materials and on the after sales services rendered by the supplier. If the supplies are of right quality and quantity and at the right time then the relations between the two are very cordial.

The efficiency of the purchasing department is also responsible for good relationship.

At times the buyers are tempted to purchase from such suppliers whose terms and conditions are not favourable. To avoid such a situation the buyer should check the price conditions prevailing in the market. Buyers should only enter into long-term agreements with the suppliers when they are fully satisfied with price, quality, quantity, delivery schedule and other terms and conditions. They should also see their past performance.

If there is a mutual understanding between the buyer and the seller then their relationship can be rewarding for the manufacturing concern. Because the seller can render some valuable services also. These include giving advice to the buyer, providing materials at the time of crisis without charging extra rates etc. Another point which the buyer should keep in his mind is that by changing the suppliers from time to time, it may be difficult for him to get suppliers during periods of shortage. Suppliers usually favour those buyers who have been maintaining a cordial relationship for a fairly long time.

Centralised and Decentralised Purchasing

It all the departments of an organisation are situated at one place centralised purchasing of goods, suits best. But if an organisation has its factories situated in different places then the mode of purchasing becomes controversial. Below we discuss regarding centralised purchasing for an organisation having units operating at different places.

Advantages of Centralised Purchasing

1. Materials purchased being in large quantities, the benefits of large-scale economies is achieved by the company; 2. Uniformity of policies relating to different matters can be followed; 3. Specialists in purchasing can be appointed which can be useful to the concern; 4. It helps in better financial control and the quality of the materials purchased can be checked easily; 5. It avoids duplicating of purchases; and 6. Advantages of competitive bidding are more useful in such cases.

Disadvantages

1. It cause considerable delay which may effect the production plants; 2. At times misunderstanding between the branch office and the

central office results in the purchase of defective and wrong materials; 3. Perishable goods are not suited; 4. It ignores the various local conditions where the units are situated.

In the end we can say that, "the good management sets up a central purchasing department for those items which can be best handled centrally leaving all other purchases to be locally handled. This usually means that large items as basic raw materials may be purchased centrally and shipped direct to the point of use and that most or many other items are purchased locally".

Purchasing Procedure

The different steps which are followed in purchasing the good are given below :

Requisition : This is the first step in the purchasing procedure because purchase starts on a purchase requisition. The various departments of the unit decide about the quality, quantity, time etc. for purchasing the materials and ask the purchasing department to do the same.

Obtaining Quotations : Once requisition from various departments is received the purchase manager finds on the sources of supply and makes enquiries for quotations. The main objective of asking for quotations to obtain the specific items at the best possible terms and conditions. The quotations contain all the information required by the purchasing department.

Selecting the Suppliers : On receipt of the quotations from various suppliers, a comparative statement of various quotations should be prepared. The suppliers who quotes the lowest price is generally selected. While selecting the supplier, the purchasing department should consider the reliability of the supplier, his financial condition, price quoted, terms of payment and delivery, specifications, etc.

Placing the Purchase Order : Once the supplier is selected, the purchase department prepares a purchase order for the supply of goods. It is the evidence of the contract between the buyer and the supplier that binds both the parties to the terms under which the order is placed. Usually three to five copies of the purchase order are prepared depending on the size of the organization. If five copies are prepared, then the original copy is sent to the supplier, another copy to the receiving department, one to the concerned department, one to the accounts department and the last copy is retained by the purchase department.

Follow-up and Inspection : There should be a regular follow-up of purchase orders placed so that the materials may be received in time. The department should enquire at regular intervals at the delivery dates agreed upon.

If the concern is big then the goods are received by the Receipt and Inspection department otherwise the storekeeper may receive the goods. Then the inspectors of the department check the quantity and the physical condition of materials received. This is done by comparing purchase order with delivery challan. Any shortage or breakage is intimated to the supplier.

Approval of Payment : If the inspection report is favourable the invoice of the supplier is approved by the purchasing department for payment to the accounts department.

26

Storekeeping

To strengthen the control over the materials there should be an effective stores control to avoid losses from misappropriation, damage, deterioration, evaporation and carelessness. Proper storekeeping helps in easy and quick receipt of storage and disbursement of materials. It is defined as the, " physical storage of materials carried into the store-room in a scientific and systematic manner with a view to saving them from all kinds of damages and losses and exercising over-all control over their movement ".

Objectives

The objectives of storekeeping are discussed below :

Reducing the Cost of Production : One of the objectives of storekeeping is to reduce the costs involved while at the same time providing efficient and effective storekeeping service.

Providing Efficient Service : The storekeeping should be able to provide efficient service by making available to the production department the required raw materials, equipments etc. within the shortest possible time and receiving the finished products from the production units and issuing them to the sales department.

Co-ordinating : The store keeping should develop co-ordination with other departments like finance, sales, inspection etc. for effective and smooth functioning.

Function

The following are some of the important functions of Storekeeping.

Receiving Materials into Store: The goods purchased and supplied from outside are delivered to the receiving section where they are inspected and then kept into proper storage area.

Storage : It refers to the custody of materials in a systematic way so that there can be a regular flow of materials from the storehouse for efficient and effective functioning of the entire organisation. The goods kept in the store should be preserved in such a way so that its value and quality can be maintained. Preservation helps in keeping the materials in perfect serviceable conditions.

Maintenance of Records : Maintenance of records of the goods received and supplied by the stores is a very important function. Proper record keeping helps the organisation in replenishing the stock at regular intervals. This also helps in planning the future course of production and purchasing.

Issue of Goods : The goods received, stored and preserved are issued to various departments on proper requisitions as and when demanded.

Location

The location of the stores department should be carefully planned and as far as possible it should be in the central place. This is because -

(i) it will help in receiving and issuing the materials in the shortest possible time;

(ii) the transportation charges will be minimum;

(iii) to avoid delays in production plans; and

(iv) to achieve strict control over the movement of stock.

To achieve the above aims a proper place has to be selected. Transportation facilities to and from the store building should also be taken in account. Besides this due consideration should be given to temperature, humidity, water and light facilities depending on the nature of materials to be kept in the building. Provision should be made for future expansion of the store department also.

Layout

It also has much influence on the success of the storage operations. The efficiency of storekeeping depends on how the internal arrangement is planned. The objectives of a good layout are as follows :

(a) Optimum utilisation of the place available;

(b) Better efficiency of the stores section;

(c) An easy access to all the materials;

(d) Maximum security of all the materials;

(e) Avoiding loss due to damage and pilferage; and

(f) Maintaining records efficiently.

Types of Stores

Following are the three types of stores :

- Centralised Stores
- Decentralised Stores
- Central Stores with sub-stores.

Most of the companies have a centralised stores. All the materials are received and issued from one stores department. The advantages of such stores are that (i) better control can be exercised; (ii) better stores layout is possible; (iii) investment in stock is minimised; (iv) inventory checks are easier; and (v) economy in cost. The disadvantages of such stores are; (i) it increases transportation costs because it is not necessary that all the departments of the company may be near the central store; (ii) departments away from the central store may have inconvenience in getting the materials; and (iii) greater loss in case of fire or theft.

The decentralised stores consists of independent stores situated in various departments. A departmental storekeeper handles the stores : Such types of stores are not very popular because of the heavy expenditure involved.

In large factories where the departments are situated at a distance and to keep the transportation and handling charges to a minimum the Central Store has a sub-store situated near the production department. A required quantity is kept in the sub-store and when the quantity is consumed the sub-shopkeeper will requisition from the central stores. It is also termed as Imprest System of Stores Control.

Inventory Valuation

To calculate the value of goods in store is a very important aspect of storekeeping. There are several methods and some are discussed below :

First In First Out Method (FIFO) : Under this method material is first issued from the first consignment and on the depletion of the first consignment, the goods are issued from the second consignment, third one and so on. Valuation is carried on the basis at the cost at which the earliest consignment was placed in the stores. But this method suffers from one defect that during rising prices the materials are under-valued and during falling prices they are over valued.

Last In First Out Method (LIFO) : It is also known as replacement cost method. Under this method materials are issued in a reverse order of purchase. In other words goods from the latest consignment is issued and price of the same in stock is used for calculating the value of issues. But this method suffers from the defect that during rising prices it over-values materials whereas at the time of falling prices it under-values them.

Average Cost Method : Under this method total value of goods in stock is divided by the total quantity in store and it gives the average cost per unit. On the basis of this cost materials are valued at the time of their issue. But whenever a new consignment is received, fresh calculation is necessary for a new price.

Inflated Price Method : There are some materials which are subjected to natural wastage like coal lost due to loading and unloading, timber lost due to seasoning, petrol lost due to evaporation. In such cases the materials are issued at an inflated price, i.e. a price higher than the actual price, so as to recover the cost of natural wastage of materials from the production.

Specific Price : When the materials are purchased for some specific job they are issued to that specific job at their actual cost. This method is used where job costing is there and the actual material issued can be identified.

Market Price Method : Under this method price is determined on the basis of the prevailing market price. This method does not recover cost price of the materials from production because materials are issued at the prevailing market price which may be more or less than the cost price. This is why it is not preferred by the department.

Materials Handling

It is the scientific study of handling materials from the source of raw materials to the place of production. It is very important that the materials may reach the production place with utmost efficiency and without any loss or theft. There are two types of materials handling equipments. They are either floor type or overhead type. The selection of specific material handling equipment depends on the nature of manufacturing process. A few advantage of materials handling are as follows :

(i) It reduces the labour cost of handling;
(ii) Cost of transportation is reduced;
(iii) Loss of goods are reduced because of scientific movement of materials; and
(iv) It helps in increasing productivity, reducing cost and thereby increasing profits.

Part 4

Human Resource Management

27

Human Resource Planning

Capital resources, material resources and human resources are the important factors of production which keep the wheels moving of an organisation. But manpower or human resources are regarded as the most important and dynamic factor of production which activities other resources in the organisation. Thus 'manpower' or 'human resources' should be used efficiently and effectively in order to achieve the objectives. It is defined as, " the total knowledge, skills, creative abilities, talents and aptitudes of an organisation's work force, as well as the values, attitudes and benefits of an individual involved. It is the sum total of inherent abilities, acquired knowledge and skills represented by the talents and aptitudes of the employed persons.[1] " Manpower planning" and "human resource planning" are synonymous. In the past, the term manpower planning was used but now the term human resource planning is used because it covers a wide range of activities. Human resource planning incorporates all human beings at different stages - organised and unorganised, employed, under-employed and unemployed; employees of the Government, public sector and private sector; managerial, technical, professional, skilled and unskilled; and persons who are engaged in any economic activity.

Concept of Human Resource Planning

All organisations may be in the public or private sector, have short-term and long-term plans, which are to be in the public private sector, have short-term and long-term plans, which are to be executed by proper personnel. Human resources or manpower planning may be defined in a narrow sense as the replacement planning which encompasses the analysis of labour turnover and recruitment policies and developing models for planning, recruitment and promotion of employees. Further, manpower may be considered as the quantitative and qualitative measurement of labour force required in an organisation to plan and develop human resources in line with broad objectives of the organisation. Vetter has defined manpower planning or human resource planning as "the process by which a management determines how an organisation should move from its current manpower position to its desired manpower position. Through planning a management strives to have the right number and the right kinds of people at the right places, at the right time, to do things which result in both the organisation and the individual receiving the maximum long-range benefit"[2]. In the words of Coleman, " Manpower planning is the process of determining manpower requirements and the means for meeting those requirements in order to carry out the integrated plan of the organisation".[3] Geisler has stated that, " Manpower planning is the process including forecasting, developing and controlling by which a firm ensures that it has the right number of people and the right kind of people at the right places, at the right time doing work for which they are economically most useful."[4]

According to Wickstrom, human resource planning consists of a series of activities, viz.,[5]

(a) *Forecasting* future manpower requirements, either in terms of mathematical projections of trends in the economic environment and development in industry, or in terms of judgemental estimates based upon the specific future plans of a company;

(b) *Making a inventory* of present manpower resources and assessing the extent to which these resources are optimally;

(c) *Anticipating* manpower problems by projecting present resources into the future and comparing with the forecast of requirements to determine their adequacy, both quantitatively and qualitatively; and

(d) *Planning* the necessary programmes of requirement, selection, training, development, utilization, transfer, promotion, motivation and compensation to ensure that future manpower requirements are properly met.

Need for Human Resources Planning

There are various reasons for human resources planning which can be categorised under three heads :

(a) External Environment
(b) Internal Environment
(c) Organisational Personnel.

These factors are basically responsible for the future plan of the organisation. Some are controllable factors and some are uncontrollable factors, but they are common to both short-term and long-term planning.

External Environment

Under this, the factors responsible for human resources planning are beyond the control of the company. They are :

(i) Ecological
(ii) Population
(iii) Economic
(iv) Socio-cultural
(v) Legal
(vi) Technological.

Internal Environment

The factors are within the control of the organisation. They are :

(i) Long-term and Short-term planning/objectives
(ii) Financial commitments
(iii) Production planning
(iv) Developing fresh units.

Organisational Personnel

The demand for human resource planning is modified on the actions of the people working the organisation. They are :

(a) Retirements
(b) Resignations
(c) Terminations
(d) Death
(e) Long leave

"Manpower is an important corporate asset and the economic performance of companies depends upon the extent to which is effectively utilised. So far prosperity of business enterprises has largely been due to technological progress and innovations in the different fields of management. It now appears that efficient utilisation of human assets may well become the crucial factor in determining the growth and prosperity of business enterprises in the years ahead. A formal manpower plan has become important because of the general increase in the size of business enterprise to meet the increasing needs of both domestic and export markets".

The basic objective of human resource planning is not only to maintain but also to enhance the capabilities of the organisation in order to achieve the pre-determined objectives set forth by the management. It should develop such strategies which may lead in optimum contribution of human resources. For this purpose, Stainer suggests the following nine strategies for manpower planners: [7]

(a) They should collect, maintain and interpret relevant information regarding human resources;

(b) They should report periodically manpower objectives, requirements and existing employment and allied features of manpower;

(c) They should develop procedures and techniques to determine the requirements of different types of manpower over a period of time from the standpoint of organisaiton's goals;

(d) They should develop measures of manpower utilisation as component of forecasts of manpower requirements along with independent validation;

(e) They should employ suitable techniques leading to effective allocation of work with a view to improving manpower utilisaiton;

(f) They should conduct research to determine factors hampering the contribution of the individuals and groups to the organisation with a view to modifying or removing these handicaps;

(g) They should develop and employ methods of economic assessment of human resources reflecting its features as income-generator and cost and accordingly improve the quality of decisions affecting the manpower;

(h) They should evaluate the procurement, promotion and retention of the effective human resources; and

(i) They should analyse the dynamic process of recruitment, promotion and loss to the organisaiotn and control these processess with a view to maximising individual and group performance without involving high cost.

Process of Human Resource Planning

With the expansion of business, adoption of complex technology and professional management techniques, the process of human resources planning has assumed proportionate dimensions and a never ending managerial function. It consists of the following stages :

1. Deciding Objectives
2. Analysing factors for Manpower Requirements
   (a) Demand Forecasting
   (b) Supply Forecasting
3. Developing Employment Plans
4. Designing Training and Development Programmes

I. Deciding Objectives :

Before undertaking the human resource planning of an organisation, the short-term and long-term objectives should be analysed. According to Sikula,[8] "the ultimate mission or purpose is to relate future human resources to future enterprise needs so as to maximise the future return on investment in human resource". Long term objective incorporate promoting a new product, creating fresh markets, adopting the technology, forming new company by mergers and amalgamations and so on. While framing long-term objectives the national, and individual goals should be borne in mind.

II. Analysing Factors for Manpower Requirements :

The factors for manpower requirements can be analysed by two ways -

(a) Demand Forecasting; and

(b) Supply Forecasting.

Demand forecasting is the process of estimating the future requirements of manpower, by function and by level of skills. It has been observed that demand assessment for operative personnel is not a problem but projections regarding supervisory and managerial levels is difficult. The future manpower demand forecasting depends upon employment trends in the organisation; resignations and deaths; changes in productivity due to technological changes and; the future expansion plans of various departments and operating units.

The demand forecasting for manpower requirements is categorised into two classes viz., *qualitative* and *quantitative*. The forecasts are based on the judgement of those managers or consultants who have intensive and extensive knowledge of future human resource requirements. A survey approach may be undertaken with the *Delphi technique*. The *Delphi Survey*, which is usually conducted by the personnel department, administers a questionnaire on experts or managers regarding future human resource requirements. The department makes a summary of the various responses and gives it back to the experts. The experts are again surveyed and feedback given to them. This exercise is repeated until the experts begin to agree on future human resource needs. Another forecasting technique is based on *Statistical Methods* - Extrapolation and Indexation, Ratio-trend analysis, Regression analysis and Econometric models. Another method is the *Work Study Technique*. Another method is *New Venture Analysis*.[9] It requires planner to estimate human resource needs by comparison with firms that already perform similar operations. The latest technique which is being used by multinationals and big companies is through computer models. *Computer models*[10] are a series of mathematical formulas that simultaneously use extrapolation, indexation, survey results and estimates of work-force changes to compute future human resource needs.

Supply forecasting is primarily concerned with manpower requirements from within and outside the organisation. The supply forecasting includes human resources audits; employee wastage; changes due to internal promotions; changes due to work environment and community attitudes. *Human resource audits* are analysis of each employee's skill and abilities. The audits of non-managers are called *skills inventories*; the audits of managers are called *management inventories*. This analysis facilitates the human resource planners an understanding of the skills and capabilities available in the organisation and identify manpower supply problems arising in the near future. These inventories should be updated periodically otherwise, it can lead to present employees being overlooked for job openings within the organisation.

After estimating the supply and demand of human resources the management starts adjustments when the internal supply of employees are more than the demand, *human resource surplus* exists and the external recruitment is stopped. Besides, the existing employees are encouraged to take voluntary retirement called *attrition.* It gradually reduces the surplus. If still it exists then employees are encourage to go on *deputation.* If *human resource deficit* exists then the planners have to rely on the external sources. They then proceed for scanning of the employment market for recruitment purposes.

Human resource planning requires considerable amount of financial resources besides time and staff. Small firms may not go for it but large organisations prefer human resources planning as a means of achieving greater effectiveness and long-term objectives.

Reference

1. Megginson, Leon C, Personnel and Human Resource Administration, 1977, p-4.
2. Vetter, Eric W., Manpower Planning for High Talent Personnel. 1967, p-15.
3. Coleman, Bruce P., An Integrated System of Manpower Planning, Business Horizon, Vol. 13, 1970, p-89.
4. Geisler, E., Manpower Planning : An Emerging Staff Function, AMA, New York, 1967.
5. Wickstrom, W.S., Manpower Planning : Evolving Systems, Conference Board, New York, 1971, p-2.
6. Tanneja, R.S., Planning Human Resources for Efficient Management in R.S. Dwivedi (Ed) Manpower Management, p-90.
7. Stainer, G., Manpower Planning, William Hineman Ltd., London 1971.
8. Sikula A.F., Personnel Administration and Human Resource Development, 1978, p-148.
9. Werther William B., and Davis Keith : Personnel Management and Human Resources, Mcgraw Hill Company, 2nd Edition p-97.
10. Ibid., p-97.

28

Personnel Management

Management means getting the work done through other people. It includes three major factors viz., objectives, resources (financial and material) and human. The objectives give direction to the staff to accomplish them. The financial and material resources like machines, raw materials, cash, credit, etc. which are scarce are to be allotted in a well planned manner. The human factor is by and large the most important factor in any organisation. It is very important that the persons employed in an organisation may be developed and utilised in an efficient manner so as to minimise wastage and increase productivity.

Definition

Personnel management is concerned with the human activities of an organisation. Flippo defines personnel management as "the planning, organising, directing and controlling of procurement, development, compensation, integration and maintenance of people for the purpose of contributing to organisational, individual and social goals". According to Brech, "personnel management is that part of the management process which is primarily concerned with the human constituents of an organisation. Its object is the maintenance of human relationships on a basis which, by consideration of the well being of the individual enables all those engaged in the undertaking to make their personal contribution to the effective working of that undertaking".

On analysing the above definitions we see that the scope of personnel management is very wide. It studies the policies and principles and other allied matters concerning the manpower of the organisation.

Functions

Personnel management involves two categories of functions :

Managerial Functions

Personal management performs four important managerial functions which are discussed below :

Planning : It means determining the personnel objectives, policies and programmes in advance. It is done to ensure that right person is rightly placed so that they can work efficiently and effectively and contribute towards the achievement of the objectives of the organisation.

Organising : Organisation means creating a structure of relationships among jobs, personnel and physical factors to achieve organisational objectives.

Directing : It is primarily concerned with the issuing of orders and motivating the people to work. Adequate guidance has to be provided so that the people work in proper direction.

Controlling : The basic idea of controlling to ensure that each worker is functioning according to the schedule and plans laid down, and if there are any deviations then corrective measures can be undertaken.

Operative Functions

Personnel management also performs five operative functions which are discussed below :

Procurement : The first operative function is to get proper type and number of personnel necessary to man the organisation. It includes jobs description.

Development : Next function is to give proper training to the employees and staff to increase their skill for job performance. It includes education and training and executive development.

Compensation : It is a very important function and is also termed as 'remuneration'. It includes job analysis, job evaluation, merit rating, job pricing, wage policies, incentive payments and other related activities and problems.

Integration : It involves developing an attitude among employees a sense of belongingness towards their organisation. It is actually integrating the individual's interest with the organisational objectives. It includes proper communication, keeping the morale of the workers high, removing their grievances, settling industrial disputes and other allied functions.

Maintenance : This function is concerned with the maintenance of physical conditions of the employees. It includes health, safety, welfare and good working conditions.

Basic Features of Personnel Policy

The main features of a personnel policy are given below :

(a) The policy statement issued by the management should be clear, positive and easily understood by everyone.

(b) It should be on legal sequence.

(c) It should be flexible.

(d) It should be in conformity with the social and human needs.

(e) It should be constantly adjusted to suit the changes in social, economic, legal and technological aspects.

(f) It should be uniform throughout the organisation.

(g) It should be acceptable to all members of the organisation.

(h) It should be properly communicated to all those for whom it is intended.

Procurement of Personnel

It is the first operative function of personnel management. The various activities necessary for procurement of personnel is discussed below :

Determination of Personnel Requirements : The first important step is to forecast the manpower requirements of the organisation. Forecasting or estimating has to be made both qualitatively and quantitatively. Qualitative requirements pertain to education, technical qualifications, experience, age, sex, language, etc. Qualitative standards require a careful job analysis, job description and job evaluation. Quantitative requirements pertain to the number of persons required for the entire organisation in view of present and future needs. To know the quantity the work-load and work-force analysis is conducted.

Recruitment : "Recruitment is the process of searching for prospective employees and stimulating and encouraging them to apply for jobs in an organisation". It is an activity followed by all organisations. It is a positive process as it encourages people to apply for jobs and increases the selection ratio. According to Roger H. Hawk, "the purposes of a recruitment function are patenly straight forward : to seek out, evaluate, obtain commitment from place and orient new employees to fill positions required for the successful conduct of the work of an organisation".

Sources

The sources of recruitment can be classified into two categories; (i) Internal sources or from within the organisation, and (ii) External or recruitment from outside.

Internal Sources

Under this the persons already working in the organisation are appointed to fill up the vacancies either by promotion or transfer. This policy is widely accepted by the organisations for filling up senior positions. The policy has many benefits. Firstly it increases the morale of the employees. Secondly the employer is in a better position to know his own employee rather than an outsider. Thirdly this simplifies selection and placement problem. Fourthly as they are already employees of the organisation, they are well versed with the organisational relationships and can be relied upon.

External Sources

Most of the organisation have to tap external sources to recruit the required personnel because the required persons may not be available within the organisation. The external sources for recruitment of personnel discussed below :

Advertisement : It is one of the most commonly used methods to recruit persons off all categories especially skilled and educated persons. Vacancies are advertised in newspapers and magazines which have wide circulation. Sometimes the organisation does not want to disclose the names and the applicants are asked to apply to a post number or to a consulting firm.

Employment Exchanges : They are an important source for the recruitment of all kinds of workers and employees. They register the names of job seekers and send them to the employees as and when required. It is compulsory for the government organisation to make use of these exchanges but no compulsion for the private organisations.

Unsolicited applicants : These are persons who gather at the factory gate to serve as casual workers. This source is very common but properly qualified and experienced persons never turn-up in such a way.

Recommendations : Some firms request their employees to recommend suitable names for the vacant posts. This policy has a favourable impact upon the employees. The only point against this method of recruitment is that it may promote favouritism and nepotism.

Educational Institutions : For the recruitment of technical and professional personnel many business organisations hold campus interviews in management and technical institutions and universities and directly recruit candidates who are suitable for the posts in their organisations.

Contractors and Jobbers : The jobbers and contractors who maintain contact with the labourers in the rural areas are also in close touch with the business concerns. Whenever, these concerns require causal labourers they contact these contractors who bring such workers at the place of work.

Selection

Selection of proper personnel is of great significance. If unqualified or less qualified persons are selected for the job, they will affect the functioning of the organisation in the long run. If a person who is selected and does not suit with the job he shall always feel dissatisfied and will tend to be inefficient for want of interest in the job. Proper selection has not only the economic aspect but also the social aspect because it effects the society as a whole. Therefore, the selections should be just and unbiased and based on merits.

There is a need of a proper procedure for the selection of candidates so that persons who are misfit for the job may not appointed. There are various steps involved in selection procedure, important among them are discussed below :

Scrutiny of Application : Once the applications of the candidates are received they are properly scrutinised and a list of candidates possessing requisite qualifications is prepared.

Application Blanks : Once the list of candidates having proper qualifications is prepared, application blanks are sent to them to seek factual information in a systematic and uniform pattern and which have direct and positive relationship with the job.

Testing : It is an important devise in the process of selection. The testing is aimed at measuring skills and abilities in the candidate. The testing is based on certain principles. Firstly it is based on job specifications. Secondly testing technique should be reliable. Thirdly tests should be regarded as additional selection devices rather than sole selection instruments. Fourthly tests should be controlled and standardised. Lastly they should have statistical validity.

There are several type of tests used in the selection procedure. Some of them are briefly discussed :

Intelligence Test : It is used to judge the mental capacity of an applicant. It measures the individual learning ability, ability to understand instructions, give reasoning and make judgements.

Aptitude Test : Aptitude is the potentiality which the individuals possess for learning the skill required to do a job quickly. Tests developed to measure such potentialities are termed as aptitude tests.

Achievement Test : This test measures the level of knowledge and proficiency of the candidate required for the job.

Trade Test : It is also known as proficiency test or occupational test. Such tests are designed to measure the skills already acquired by the individuals. For instance, for the recruitment of steno-typist a test can be given to find out his speed in dictation and typing. Trade test should be differentiated with aptitude test. Trade test measures skills already acquired through training and experience whereas aptitude test measures potentialities of the candidate in doing the job.

Personality Test : These tests are very important in the success of a job. They measure certain characteristics like self-confidence, emotional adjustments, creativity, sociability, dominance, submission etc.

Interview : Personal interview is the most widely used method for selecting. It helps in determining the candidate's physical appearance, general outlook and whether he possesses the qualities required for the job. The interview should be conducted in a congenial atmosphere and free from any sort of disturbance. But personal interviews has certain limitations. Firstly all the qualities of a candidate cannot be judged in a short span. Secondly the interviewer can be biased. Thirdly it is an expensive method. In spite of all these limitations it is used extensively.

Checking References : Usually the candidate is asked to give the names of certain persons as references. The prospective employer can get information about the accomplishments of the candidate.

Medical Examination : This is necessary so as to check the physical fitness of the candidate. If the health of the candidate is poor he will not be able to work regularly and his efficiency will be poor. He will be a burden in the organisation rather than an asset. Therefore medical examination of the candidates is very important.

Placement : Once the selection procedure is over and the candidate has cleared all the steps he is given an appointment letter. Placement is also an essential part of the selection procedure. The proper placement requires thorough orientation with the organisational objectives, policies, personnel and the job. This helps in adjusting with the work in the organisation.

Once the candidate joins the organisation he is tested for a specific period known as probation period. After successful completion of this period the candidate is given permanent employment in the organisation.

29

Job Analysis and Job Evaluation

Various problems relating to personnel management can be effectively solved if a detailed analysis and evaluation of each job is carried out. Also, if performance appraisal is carried out regarding each employee, it can be ensured that whatever amount he is paid, he deserves it because of his skills, abilities, experience etc.

Job

A job may be defined as a position or group of position that are similar as to kind and level of work. For a particular job there may be only one position in an organisation, as for instance, Secretary of a Company, whereas there may be many positions to perform the same job, as for instance, accounts, clerks, foremen etc.

Job Classification

It includes comparison of individual jobs, determination of similar duties and responsibilities, abilities and skills and qualifications for the purpose of grouping similar jobs into classes so that they can be commonly designated.

Job Analysis

It is also known as job study. It studies and determines the characteristics of each job like duties and responsibilities, working conditions, element of risk in performing each task, employment conditions, such as remuneration, working hours, opportunities for promotions and privileges.

Basically there are three aspects of job analysis. They are :

(a) identify each job regarding duties and responsibilities;
(b) determining the nature of work and working conditions; and
(c) determining the requirements for the successful performance of the job.

Process of Job Analysis

The process of job analysis is essentially that of data collection. This kind of information can be had through the following :

- Questionnaires completed by job holders;
- Record books or diaries maintained by the job holders;
- Personal observation; and
- Interviews with job holders.

Advantages of Job Analysis

The following are some of the advantages of job analysis :

Selection of Personnel : Job analysis facilitates in setting job specification. A job specification is the standard of personnel against which job applicant can be compared. The specification provides a basis for selection of personnel for various positions.

Training : Identification of duties and responsibilities and the usage of machines and equipment help in developing the content of the training programmes.

Job Evaluation : It facilitates job evaluation. The idea behind this is to determine the worth of each job in terms of money so that the wages can be fixed.

Performance Appraisal : It helps in evaluating the performance objectively. It makes it possible to know how far an employees has been successful in achieving the goals of the organisation.

Promotions, Transfers, etc. : It provides the basic for promotions, transfers and other related terms.

Guidance : Job information helps the candidates in ascertaining the jobs for which they have necessary qualifications.

Labour Relations : Job description sets the standard of performance which helps in resolving the disputes between unions and management.

Job Description : Job description gives the characteristics of each job so that it can be taken into consideration while recruiting or promoting or transfering any employee. The basic objective of job description is to provide information about the actual content of a job.

Usually job descriptions include indications of the purpose of the various tasks involved, the frequency with which these tasks have to be performed, the environment and conditions in which the work is done, the tools and equipment used, the nature and degree of supervision received or given, the degree of skill, knowledge, accuracy, judgement and attention required, and the responsibilities involved.

Job Evaluation

Job evaluation measures the worth of a job in terms of money. It ascertains the relative worth of each job through an objective evaluation so that relative remuneration may be fixed for different jobs. Job evaluation rates the job and not man. According to the United States Department of Labour, " Job evaluation is the evaluation or rating the jobs to determine their position in a job hierarchy. The evaluation may be achieved through the assignment of points or the use of some other systematic rating method for essential job requirements, such as skill experience and responsibility. Job evaluation is widely used in the establishment of wage rate structures and in the elimination of wage inequalities. It is always applied to jobs rather than the qualities of individuals in the jobs".

Purpose of Job Evaluation

(a) It helps the management in framing a rational and consistent wage structure.

(b) It facilitates in maintaining harmonious relationship between the union and management, because it tries to eliminate wage inequalities in the organisation.

(c) It takes into account many other factors like risks, hazards and other working conditions to determine the worth of jobs.

(d) It facilitates standardization of jobs and accurate job description which help in employee selection, training and promotion.

(e) It helps in determining the wage differentials for different jobs through job standardization.

Methods of Job Evaluation

There are various methods of job evaluation and they can be used either in their present form or in a modified manner. There are four major methods which are widely used. They are (i) Ranking or job comparison method, (ii) Grading or job classification method, (iii) Point method and (iv) Factor comparison method. Ranking and Grading represent non-quantitative methods where as Point and Factor Comparison represent quantitative methods.

Ranking Method : Under this method the various jobs in the organisation are arranged in order to their importance, starting from the most important to the least important. The jobs are taken as a whole and comparison is made of one whole job against another whole job. In ranking the jobs special attention is given to factors such as work-loan, difficulty of work responsibilities involved, working conditions, etc.

This method is suitable for organisations of smaller size. This method is very easy and can be understood both by the workers and the supervisors. But this method has certain limitations also. It does not indicate the degree of difference between and among the jobs and there are chances of subjectivity while ranking various jobs.

Grading Method : This method is a modification of ranking method. It consists of the following procedure : (i) Determination of the number of labour grades or salary groups, (ii) Setting the money value of each group; (iii) Preparing job specifications for each group of jobs or labour grades; (iv) Alloting jobs into appropriate salary groups. The jobs are usually grouped in terms of functions (e.g. clerical, engineering, etc.) instead of salary grades.

This method is very simple and it employes formal written, individual and class group job specifications. The ratings are more accurate and is not an expensive system to operate. This method also has certain limitations. The organisation may have some difficulty in preparing adequate group job or class specifications. There is a wide difference in the preparation of descriptions of office jobs and manufacturing jobs.

Point Method : It is a widely used method of job evaluation. This method consists of evaluating each job in respect of certain factors.

These factors are skill, efforts, responsibility and working conditions. There may be sub-divisions of each factor and for each sub-division there may be divisions into degrees, which may be assigned points. Total points for each job determine its relative position in the job structure. The following procedure is followed in designing 'Point Method'.

- Determining the type of jobs to be evaluated.
- Determining the factors to be used in this method.
- Determining the number of degrees to be allocated to each factor.
- Assigning points to each degree of each factor.
- Constructing points to each degree of each factor.
- Evaluating each job in terms of scales so framed.
- Selecting a certain number of key jobs and then evaluating each of them.

Let us take an example. If the factor of skill is assigned a maximum of 400 points, responsibility is given 300 points, effort is 160 points and working conditions 140 points. Each job is then assigned points on account of different factors subject to the maximum points fixed earlier. The total points for each job are then used for fixing the respective wage rate. If a job is worth 300 points and if its wage is fixed at Rs. 600/- p.m., another job worth 400 points will get Rs. 600 X 400/ 300 i.e. Rs. 800/- p.m. Thus the total points help in determining the worth of various jobs.

The basic advantages with this method is that if offers objectivity, simplicity and is less time consuming. However, it suffers from certain limitation also. It assumes that jobs are composed of certain case, some other factors are important they cannot be taken into account and the allotment of points is arbitrary.

Factor-Comparison Method : This method is an adaptation of the point method. It determines the relative rank of the jobs to be evaluated in relation to monetary scale. The job evaluation under this method consists of the following steps :

Selecting and Defining the Factors : Firstly all the fundamental job factors are defined. The factor comparison method requires five factors. They are mental requirements, responsibility, physical requirements and working conditions. These factors may differ from organisation to organisation.

Selecting the Key-Jobs : A key job is that whose contents have become stabilised over a specified period and whose wage rate has been accepted by the management and the workers. The second step is to select key jobs whose number should be 10 to 30.

Ranking Jobs by Factors : Under this, job descriptions of each should be analysed with respect to each job factor. It should then be ranked in order of importance taking into consideration one factor at a time.

Deciding the Rates of Key Jobs : Under this a rate of pay which is equitable both internally and externally is determined. The job comparison scale is developed and key jobs are inserted in them.

Ranking : Lastly the job is evaluated factor by factor in relation to key jobs on the job comparison, scale and the basic pay for each job is allotted to each factor.

30

Wage and Salary Administration

The most important problem which the management faces today is the problem of wage and salary administration. The relationship between the employers and employees depends mainly on wages. Wage and salary administration refers to the framing and implementation of policies and practices pertaining to employee compensation. It includes development of wage structure, wage surveys, wage incentives, profit sharing, wage adjustments and other related items concerning payment. Wages and salaries constitute a major part of the total cost in most of the organisations. The control of wages and salaries is of paramount importance because it effects numerous factors such as productivity, prices, capital formation, employment, standard of living and so on.

The objectives of wage and salary administration are as follows :

(a) To establish and maintain an equitable wage and salary structure;

(b) Cost control;

(c) Utilising wages and salaries as an incentive for higher productivity;

(d) Maintaining a satisfactory image within and outside the organisation.

There is a differences between wage and salary. Wage is compensation to the employees for services rendered to the organisation. If the services cannot be quantified then the payment is called salary. Payment made to labour is referred as wages. The wage period is shorter than the salary period.

Factors Affecting Wages

The following factors affect the wage rates :

Supply and Demand : The demand and supply position of labour affects the determination of wage rates. If there is shortage of labour in the market then the wage rates are high whereas if the labour supply is continuous then the wage rates are low.

Bargaining Capacity : If the labourers are organised into trade unions their capacity to bargain increases and can demand for higher wage rates.

High Cost of Living : If the cost of living increases the labourers demand higher wager to make their both end meet.

Government Policies : The government policies effect the wage rates. To protect the interest of the labourers especially in the unorganised sector, the government fixes minimum wages through legislative measures.

Methods of Wage Payment

The various methods of wage payment may be classified as given below :

Conventional Methods

Time Rate : It is also known as 'day rate system'. Under this system the worker is paid only on the basis of time he has worked on his job and no consideration is given to the quality and quantity of work completed by him. The longer the worker remains on his job, the higher is the payment. The formula for calculating wages under this system is :

Total Amount Earned = No. of hours, daus, etc. worked x Rate per hour day, etc.

There is no fixed rule for time rate. For instance when high level professionals are engaged on contract basis their duration is longer and their payment is on the higher side. Whereas unskilled workers are usually engaged for a short period and the rate at which they are paid is quite low.

Advantages

1. It is a simple method and the labourers can know how much

remuneration they will get.

2. Since the wages are fixed, the workers have not to rush to reach a particular level of output.
3. It is beneficial for the freshers as in the beginning they cannot give a higher output but they are assured of a fixed remuneration.
4. As the wages do not depend on output, the workers can produce quality goods.

Limitations

1. This system does not distinguish between efficient and inefficient workers and there is no incentive for the workers to increase their efficiency.
2. Since wages are not related to output it makes difficult to control labour cost.
3. As it gives security to the workers they are tempted to work slow which results in loss to the employer.
4. As it gives security to the workers they are tempted to work slow which results in loss to the employer.
4. It not only effects the quantity but also the quality of goods as there is no incentive for efficient workers.

Piece Rate : Under this system the worker is paid according to the work done or the number of pieces of work completed irrespective of the amount of time taken to do so. The rate per unit of output is fixed and the wages are paid on the basis of number of units completed. The formula for calculating wages under this system is :

Total Amount Earned = Units produced X Rate per unit.

But this system is applicable only in case of those jobs which can be measured in physical terms and can be standardised. Under this system the income of the workers depends on their efficiency to produce.

Advantages

1. Productivity increase as the earnings are directly linked with production.
2. This system induces to produce more regardless of quality.
3. It helps in estimating the cost per unit which helps in the fixation of prices of the goods produced.

4. As wages are paid according to the output is ensures a degree of fairness to everyone.

Limitations

1. No attention is paid to the production of quality goods.
2. In order to produce more there is improper handling of machines resulting in breakdown causing loss of employer.
3. There is no security to the workers and if the worker is unable to produce due to certain reasons his earnings are affected.
4. This system leads to unhealthy competition among the workers which causes jealousy and dissatisfaction among them.

Incentive Bonus Methods : An incentive method or plan is a system of wage payment which offers inducement to the workers in the form of bonus to maintain high levels of production. A well developed incentive plan should be beneficial to both management and the workers. From the management point of view it should result in reduced unit cost and increased output. There should be optimum utilisation of facilities, improvement on cost control leading to less variable production cost. From the workers point of view it should facilitate on their efforts to earn more and improve their efficiency.

If an incentive plan is to be successful it should meet certain requirements. Firstly there should be confidence among the management and workers regarding the fairness and efficiency of the plan. Secondly the plan should be simple so that the workers can understand easily. Thirdly it should have scientifically set standards regarding job standards and working conditions. Fourthly the workers should be assured a fixed income to develop a sense of security. Fifthly the plan should be followed for a specified period and should not be changed now and then. Lastly the management should try to cover all the workers engaged in different jobs.

There are different types of incentive plans. For instance personal incentive plans which are either time based or production based. Time based incentive plans are also called premium plans. Some of the incentive plans are discussed.

Personal or Individual Incentive Bonus Schemes : Under this system the individual worker is rewarded for his excellent performance or for making optimum use of the machines and equipment.

Halsey Plan : Under this plan bonus or premium is paid to the worker on the basis of the time saved. A standard time required for a job is determined before hand. If a worker takes standard time or even exceeds the standard time to complete a job he gets normal wages calculated at the time rate. If he completes the job in less than the standard time, he gets a bonus equal to 50% of the value of time saved. It is calculated by the following formula:

Bonus = 50% (Time saved X Time rate)

Total amount Earned = Time rate X Time taken +Bonus

For instance a job requiring 10 hours is done in 8 hours, the worker will be paid wages for 8 hours and also 50% of the time saved, i.e. 1 hr. He gets wages for 9 hours. If the wage rate is Rs. 5/- per hour, the worker gets Rs. 45/-.

Advantages

1. It is a simple method and can be understood by everyone.
2. The benefit resulting from time saving is equally divided between employer and worker.
3. There is a sense of security among workers because minimum wages are assured.
4. It encourages productivity.

Limitations

1. The worker is not given the full benefit of his efficiency.
2. This system does not ensure quality as the workers rush to produce more.

Rowan Plan : This plan is similar to Halsey Plan. The only difference is in the method of calculating bonus. The formula for calculating the total amount is given below:

$$\text{Bonus} = \frac{\text{Time saved}}{\text{Time allowed}} \times \text{Time taken} \times \text{Rate per Hr.}$$

Total amount Earned = Time rate × Time taken + Bonus

An example will make the distinction between the two clear :

Standard time for given job	=	10 Hours
Rate of Wage per hour	=	Rs. 5/-
Time actually taken to complete the job	=	8 Hours
Time saved	=	2 Hours

Under the Halsey Plan system the worker will get

8 Hrs × Rs. 5/- = + 50% of 2 hrs., i.e. Rs. 5/- = Rs. 45/-

Under the Rowan Plan the bonus is calculated by different method and the worker will get :

$$\text{Bonus} = \frac{2}{10} \times 8 \times 5 = \text{Rs. } 8/-$$

Wage due for 8 Hrs. = Rs. 40/- = Total Rs. 48/-.

Advantages

1. It provides a minimum wage to the worker.
2. It is favoured by the management as the bonus can never reach 100% of the time wage as likely under Halsey Plan.

Limitations

1. It is difficult to understand by the workers.
2. The workers are not likely to exert themselves not beyond 50% saving in time, for as the percentage of the standard time saved increased the wages of time used to which the percentage is applied in calculating the bonus decreased.
3. It does not offer sufficient incentive to the more efficient workers.

Taylor's Differential Piece Wage Plan : This system of wage payment was devised by F.W. Taylor, the Father of Scientific Management. Under this system standard task is fixed for all workers. This task is developed after careful time and motion study. There are two piece rates. The higher rate is meant for those who can complete the standard task within the allotted time and the lower rate is for those who cannot complete the standard task within the allotted time.

For example the standard may be fixed at 40 units per day per worker and the piece rates may be 50 paise and 40 paise per unit. Those who complete 40 units per day get the wages at the rate 50 paise; i.e. Rs. 20/- per day. And those who complete 39 units would get at the rate of 40 paise per unit, i.e. Rs. 15.60 per day. This clearly shows that the worker who has completed the task within the allotted time will be getting

Rs. 3.40 more than the worker who could not reach the standard.

Advantages

1. It is simple and can be easily understood.
2. It gives sufficient incentive to workers to achieve standard level of efficiency.
3. This scheme favoured both the management and the workers.

Limitations

1. The penalty for lesser efficiency is too severe and workers resent it.
2. It does not offer minimum wages which develops a sense of insecurity among the workers.
3. Because of two piece rates it becomes difficult to calculate the labour costs accurately.
4. This scheme did not find favour with many concerns and today it is almost out of use.

Merrick's Multiple Piece Rate Plan : This is an improved version of Taylor's plan. While Taylor prescribes two rates one for slow workers and other for efficient workers. Merrick's plan lays down three rates : One for the beginners, second for the developing workers and third for the highly skilled and efficient workers. Like Taylor's plan it lays down standard task to be achieved. Those who achieve less than 83 percent of the standard task are entitled to the first and low piece rate. Those who achieve more than 83 percent but less than the standard task are entitled for the second and a high piece rate and those attaining or exceeding the standard task are entitled for the third and the highest piece rate.

Advantages

1. It is simple and easy to operate.
2. It reduces the severity of the Taylor's plan.

Limitations

1. The demarcation lines between inefficient, average and efficient workers is arbitrarily fixed.
2. Multiplicity of wage rates makes it difficult to ascertain the labour costs accurately.

Gantt's Task and Bonus Plan : This plan was developed by Gantt one of the associates of Taylor. The main features of this system are (a) it includes time rate, differential piece rate and bonus (b) it guarantees minimum daily wage (c) if the standard task is completed within the allotted time there is bonus which is at very high rate (d) if the worker completes the standard task within the allotted time he is given a bonus of 20% to 30% of the standard time allowed.

Let us study with the help of an example :

Standard task	30 units per day
Guaranteed day wage	Rs. 50.00 for 10 hrs. day at the rate of Rs. 5/- per hr.

Bonus rate 30% of the time allowed.

Job No. A

No. of units produced	27 in 10 Hrs.
He will get day wage	Rs. 50.00 (10 Hrs. x Rs. 5/-)

Job No. B

No. of Units produced	30 in 10 Hrs.

He will get

(a) Day wage of Rs. 50.00
(b) Bonus at Rs. 5.00 per Hr. Rs. 65.00

for 3 Hrs. Rs. 15.00 (30% of 10 Hrs.)

Job No. C

No. of units produced	36 in 10 Hrs.

He will get

(a) Basic wage for 12 Hrs. (Time for 36 units on the basis of 30 units for 10 Hrs.)	Rs. 60.00
(b) Bonus at Rs. 5.00 for 3.36 Hrs. (30% of 12 Hrs.)	Rs. 18.00
Total	Rs. 78.00

This plan is also known as 'Progressive Rate System'.

Advantages

1. It is simple and easy to operate.
2. It provides a strong incentive to efficient workers.
3. It provides a sense of security for the freshers and substandard workers.
4. It encourages better supervision because when workers qualify for bonus, so does their foreman.

Limitations

1. The management fixes the standard task at a high level so as to make it impossible for the workers to achieve it and earn bonus.
2. It divides workers into two categories one who earn bonus and others who are not able to do so.

Emerson's Efficiency Plan : This system was developed by Emerson and his aim was to encourage workers who were efficient. The main features of this plan are (a) Minimum day wage is guaranteed to every worker (b) any worker who completes the standard task is regarded an 100% efficient (c) a worker becomes eligible for bonus only when his output exceeds 66.7%. If it is lower than this then he is entitled for day wage only. (d) it provides graded bonus.

Let us take an example. The standard output is 1500 units. If the worker produces 900 units, efficiency will be 60 percent. Since it is less than 66.7% of the standard, the worker will get the day wage rate only (say Rs. 30/- per day). If production is 1.350 units then efficiency will be 90 percent and the worker will get day wage rate plus 10 percent, i.e. Rs. 30/- + Rs. 3/ = Rs. 33/-. If production is 1500 units total earnings will be day wage rate plus 20 percent i.e. Rs. 30/- + Rs. 6/- = Rs. 36/-.

Advantages

1. It is simple and easy to operate.
2. It provides encouragement to freshers and incentive to efficient workers.
3. It guarantees a minimum daily wages.

Limitations

1. The standard output may be fixed too high.
2. Once the worker reaches the standard efficiency he may not

make much effort to increase his efficiency.

Bedeaux Plan : The distinctive feature of this plan is that the value of time saved is divided between the workers and the foreman, three-fourths to workers and one-fourth to foreman. It is done because the worker cannot save time without the help of the foreman and therefore foreman is also entitled for an incentive. Under this plan the standard time for each job is determined in terms of minutes which are called 'Bs'. Supposing the standard time for a job is five hours, it is expressed as 300 'Bs'. The standard 'Bs' of various jobs done by a worker are calculated and compared with the actual time taken by the worker. If the time taken by the worker is more than the standard time, then the worker gets the wages for the actual time worked. Whereas, if the actual time is less than the standard 'Bs' then three fourths of wages of the time saved is given to the worker as bonus and one-fourth to the foreman.

Let us take an example. Supposing a worker performs 5 operations for which the time is 30 Hrs. (1800 'Bs'). If the worker takes 36 Hrs. (2160 'Bs') to do the job then he will be paid wages for 36 Hrs. i.e. wages on time basis are assured. If he completes the task in 25 Hrs. (1500 'Bs') then the time saved is 5 Hrs. (300 'Bs'). If the worker is paid Rs. 5/- per hr. the total value of time saved is Rs. 25/- Out of this the worker will get Rs. 18.75 as bonus in addition to Rs. 125/- on time basis and the foreman will get one-fourth share which comes to Rs. 6.25.

Advantages

1. It assures minimum wage to everyone.
2. It is useful where workers are shifted from one job to another.

Limitations

1. The standard task may be too difficult to perform on the allotted time.
2. In this scheme the workers resent dividing bonus with the foreman.

Group Incentive Bonus Schemes

There are various types of group incentive schemes. Some of them are discussed below :

Priestman Bonus Plan : This plan takes the productivity of all workers, as a whole into ccnsideration. According to this system, if the productivity of all the workers rises above the standard output or output of the previous year, the wages of the workers are increased in the same ratio. For instance if in 1986 the output per worker was 20 units and in 1987 it rises to 22 units per worker, the wages in 1987 would be 10% higher than in 1986. The basic limitation with this system is that as the individual's efficiency is not taken into account it cannot have much effect on individual's initiative.

Scanloan Plan

Under this system with every 1% increase in productivity the workers are paid 1% participating bonus. Thus benefit is given to all the employees except the top management. Further, the workers are not paid the entire bonus earned by them in any month. One-half of the first 15% of such bonus is set aside as a reserve fund. This fund is used to neutralise the effects of any fluctuation in labour costs. Any unused part of this reserve is distributed among workers in the last month of the year and a new reserve fund is created for the new year.

Profit Sharing

The basic idea of profit sharing is to give employees an incentive to increase their output and to develop a healthy relationship between the management and the workers. According to Kimball, "under profit sharing scheme a certain percentage of the profit is distributed at fixed intervals usually annually or bi-annually, in some definite ratio to all employees who have been in employ of the firm for a stated term". According to International Labour Organisation, "profit sharing is a method of industrial remuneration under which an employer undertakes to pay his employees a share in the net profit of the enterprise, in addition to their regular wages.

Features of Profit Sharing : The basic features of profit sharing are as follows : (a) profits of the enterprise are shared between the employers and employees on a predetermined basis; (b) the payment arising from profit sharing is in addition to the normal wages paid to workers; (c) the payment is made after net profits have been ascertained and is not a part of the cost of production; (d) the share of profits is usually fixed in advance so as to create an incentive to work.

Basis of Profit Sharing : Profit sharing can be introduced in the organisation on any of the following basis :

a) *Individual Basis* : Under this the individual worker is paid the share of the profit which the enterprise has earned due to his effort.

(b) *Departmental Basis* : Different departments are allotted the share of the profit on the basis of their contribution to the total profit. The department will distribute the share among workers of that department.

(c) *Unit Basis* : Under this the Workers working in each particular industrial unit share the profits.

(d) *Industry Basis* : Under this the profits earned by all the units on a particular industry are added together and then it is distributed to all the workers of that industry.

Method of Distributing Share in Profits : The share of the profits earmarked for the workers can be distributed to them on any of the following methods :

(a) Each worker can be given the amount in cash.

(b) The share in profit may be credited in the savings account of the individual worker.

(c) It can be credited in the provident fund account of the individual worker.

(d) It can be paid to the worker partly in cash and partly by issue of bonus shares.

Labour's share : To determine what portion of the profit should be given to the workers, either the management can take its own decision or consult the trade unions. To decide this either return on capital investments of ratio of capital investment and the total wage bill is taken into consideration.

Individual Labour's share : After fixing the labour's share it is necessary to ascertain the basis of distribution of profits among individual workers. The various methods which form the basis are : (a) Length of service of each worker; (b) number of hours worked during the years; and (c) wages earned by each worker. Of these three methods the wages earned by each worker provides the basis for the distribution of profits among workers.

Advantages

The following are the advantages of profit sharing : (a) It helps in promoting good industrial relations between the management and the workers. (b) The workers are induced to work hard to increase productivity and reduce cost of production. (c) It is an additional earning for the workers as it is in addition to their normal wages. (d) It encourages the worker to remain on his job resulting in reduced labour turnover. (e) Workers develop a sense of responsibility and supervision costs are reduced. (f) It helps in achieving social justice.

Limitations

The following are the limitations of profit sharing : (a) It does not distinguish between efficient and inefficient workers. (b) During the period of depression, the workers may not get the share in profits and during this period their morale will be very low. (c) Many times industrial disputes arise over the profit sharing issues. (d) If the management is not efficient the workers will be deprived of the share. (d) Trade unions oppose this move as their movement is weakened by such methods.

Co-partnership

It is a system of profit-sharing. Under this system the workers are given share of profits partly in cash and partly by way of allotment of shares in the organisation. By becoming shareholders they acquire ownership rights. Thus it implies control sharing and profit sharing. As share-holder he can attend general meetings of the company and participate in various activities.

But co-partnership is opposed on many grounds. It is very dangerous for a worker to invest all his savings in one company because if the company fails the worker will loose everything. Secondly the worker cannot be effective because he will have very little voting rights.

31

Employee Training and Development

Training is an organised and systematic activity for increasing the knowledge and skill of an employee for a definite purpose. The basic aim of training is to achieve a change in the behaviour of trained personnel so that they can do their jobs in a much better way. Any training programme lays down the ways and means through which people attain knowledge and acquire better skills so that they can perform their tasks more efficiently and effectively.

Need for Training

There are numerous reasons for the need for training. Some of them are given below :

(i) An increased use of modern and high technology in production.

(ii) To increase the productivity level of the workers.

(iii) Special training is needed so that it can be consistent with the peculiar job requirements in the organisation.

(iv) To enable employees to work more efficiently and effectively.

(v) The training programme becomes essential if an organisation plans to diversify its activities.

Importance of Training

From Employees Point of View

(i) Training helps them in acquiring greater skills.

(ii) It provides safety and security.

(iii) It helps in getting more remuneration.

(iv) It minimise accidents, reduces damage to machines and facilitates the usage of materials in a more optimum manner.

From Management Point of View

(i) It increases productivity, qualitatively and quantitatively both.

(ii) It reduces damages to machines and equipments and teaches proper way of operations.

(iii) It relieves the supervisory staff and allows more freedom to the operating employees.

(iv) It brings stability and continuity in the organisation.

(v) It facilitates skill building and increase in knowledge which heightens the morale of the employees thereby effecting the entire functioning of the organisation.

Training is an integral part of any organisation. It bridges the gap between the existing performance ability and the performance desired. It is a continuous process and entails lot of expenditure. Therefore an organisation should have a well defined training policy.

Methods of Training

Following are the methods of training to the personnel of an organisation.

On the Job Training

It is considered to be the most effective method of training. Under this method, the employees are given training while he is performing any job. He is placed under the supervision who trains the employee about performing the various tasks at his workplace. The main advantage is that the trainee learns on the actual machines and environment of his job. It is very economical and shortens the training period.

Vestibule Training

It is the adaptation of the on the job training in the organisation classroom. This is done to train fresh recruits in specific skills so as to prepare them to handle jobs on the shop floor. The difference between on-the-job training and vestibule training is that the former is given by the supervisor on the shop floor. The difference between on-the-job training and vestibule training is that the former is given by the supervisor on the shop floor where as the latter is given by the instructors away from the floor i.e., in a classroom. Vestibule training is useful where large number of employees are to be trained and the supervisor cannot deal with all of them. It is generally used to train clerks, typists, inspectors banking people and so on.

The main advantages of this system are, firstly distractions of the workers/learners are minimised. Secondly production is not hampered, thirdly the trained instructor gives full attention towards the trainees.

The main disadvantages of this system are, firstly the training atmosphere is artificial and the trainees are unaware about the real problems of working situations, secondly, splitting of responsibilities leads to certain organisation problems and thirdly it requires huge investment in machines and equipments which is a mere duplication.

Apprenticeship Training

It involves imparting knowledge and skill in performing a craft or a series of related functions and jobs. Apprenticeship training is combination of on-the-job training and classroom instructions in particular subjects. Such type of training is very elaborate and systematic. It is offered in the field of draughtsman, printing press, building machinists, electricians, welders, etc.

The advantages of such training programme are that it helps in maintaining a skilled work force and immediate returns can be had from training.

Refresher Training

Rapid changes in the scientific and technological areas make even the highly qualified persons obsolete in due course of time. Due to this the highly trained persons have to undergo training or new methods and techniques. These training programmes are usually short-term in nature ranging from 3 months to 12 months.

Training for Promotion

In many organisation some of the vacancies are filled through promotions from the existing staff. It is an internal source of recruitment. Before the workers are promoted to senior positions they are given some training so that they can discharge their new responsibilities efficiently and effectively.

Job-Rotation

The basic idea behind job-rotation is to broaden the background of the personnel in various positions. On-the-job experience, coaching and understudy are narrow because they give skill and knowledge in a particular job only. If the trainee is rotated in different jobs for a specified period in a systematic and planned manner he acquires wider experience, knowledge and skill.

Off the Job Training

It means that training is not a part of regular job-activity. It is also termed as class-room training and is more associated with knowledge than with skill. Such training is imparted through a number of methods. Some of them are discussed :

Lectures : A lecture is a formal organised talk by the instructor on a particular topic. It is useful when there is a large group of persons and they have to be given the concepts, ideas and theories.

Committees : This is an effective method of training. The personnel of different departments discuss mutual problems and proposals for the benefit of the organisation by forming a committee in different areas common to all. It helps in learning the various activities of the organisation.

Case Study Method : A case is a written form of an actual situation in a summarized manner. It seeks to describe the problems faced by managers. The learners are given such cases and asked to give their own views. It is an effective method of developing analytical abilities among the learners.

Role-Playing : It is an effective method for increasing the skills of trainee in the field of human relations and leadership training. Under this method two or more trainees are assigned different roles to play. The trainees who play the role are given the description of the situation and the role they are to perform. They are given sufficient time to plan their actions and then asked to perform before the audience. Though the scope of role playing is narrow but it is practical way of training.

Group Discussion : It is also termed as 'Sensitivity Training'. Its basic aim is to influence the behaviour of a trainee through group discussion. Usually it is based on a paper prepared by one of the trainees or a topic given by the supervisor. The trainees are brought together at a common place and asked to discuss in a group. They express their views freely. The group is headed by a senior official who does not express his own views. Such type of training helps the trainees in introspecting themselves as well as developing understanding of others' views and behaviour. It also helps in resolving differences and developing tolerance.

Management Development

Success of any organisation depends on the quality of leadership provided by the managers. The assumption that by serving for a number of years as a manager a person can acquire management skills and abilities has become obsolete. Every personnel having a long experience in the organisation cannot be a good manager. A manager should be able to provide leadership and motivate people so as to achieve the predetermined goals.

It is now being realised that the management job is highly complex in nature. The problem of human relations, trade union activities, technological development, rules and regulations of the government and so on, have made it imperative that only trained managers can run the modern organisation successfully. Therefore, management development and training is of utmost importance for the success of any modern business organisation.

Management development can be defined as a systematic training and planned personnel development so that the skills, knowledge and attitude acquired can be applied in manning the organisation efficiently and effectively. According to George R. Terry, " Management development should produce change in behaviour which is more in keeping with the organisation's goal than the previous behaviour. This change frequently consists of a number of small steps resulting from the training but the cumulative effect is considerable and at the end result sought. It is also basic that a terminal behaviour is identified before the development efforts start".

There is a difference of opinion regarding the terms "executive development" and "management development". Some regard "executive development" as the programme only for top managerial personnel whereas others who do not distinguish between the various levels of management call this programme as "management development".

Management development depends more on individual efforts rather than the organisational efforts. There is no substitute for self-development and initiative. The organisation should create such an environment so that the personnel who are willing can develop themselves.

Promotion

The word promotion is referred to the advancement of an employee to a better and higher job with more pay and perks, higher status and more responsibilities. Promotion is a method of filling up vacancies which occur in any organisation from time to time. Instead of recruiting fresh people in these vacancies, some persons already working at the lower level may be moved upwards. Promotion is classified as horizontal and vertical. Horizontal promotion is a minor promotion within the same classification on job. Whereas Vertical promotion crosses the boundary of job classification. When the promotion is within the department it is termed as departmental promotion and when from one department to another it is inter-departmental promotion.

There are many advantages of promotion to the personnel as well as to the organisation. Firstly it develops loyalty towards the organisation. Secondly it is an incentive for the employees who are meritorious and performance is excellent. Thirdly it reduces frustration and discontent among the employees. Fourthly it facilitates recruitment and is a good source of internal recruitment.

Promotion Policy

Promotions can only take place systematically when certain policies are framed and implemented honestly. Firstly the selection policy should be clear, whether the candidates will be selected from within, by promotion or selected from outside. Secondly the basis of promotions should be clearly stated–seniority, merit, or seniority-cum-merit, training courses completed, education previous record, etc. Thirdly job requirements should be developed on the basis of job analysis, so that the employees will be able to know how a job will lead to a higher job. Fourthly the performance of the workers should be evaluated on scientific basis to consider their claims for promotion. Fifthly promotion should be made for trial periods. Sixthly training courses should be conducted for those employees who fall within the promotion zone.

Basis of Promotion

When an employee is to be promoted within the organisation, it is done on the basis of seniority or merit. Seniority refers to the relative length of service of employees. The length of service is calculated on the basis of continuous employment. Occupational seniority may be within a department, within a section or in the entire organisation.

There is a great controversy on the question of whether promotion should be given on the basis of the seniority or merit. The management usually favours merit whereas the trade unions lay more stress on seniority as the sole criterial for promotion.

Promotions based on seniority have following advantages : (a) It is the most objective basis of promotion. (b) It is a fact and cannot be misused by the management. (c) It reduces conflicts and rivalries among employees. (d) It generates confidence among the employees. (e) Employees try to work hard and efficiently. (f) The assessment of employees becomes simple and economical.

Promotion based on seniority have the following limitations : (a) It is not necessary that the senior employees may be competent and efficient and if they are given higher positions, the organisation has to severely suffer. (b) It adversely affects the morale and productivity of the efficient employees. (c) As the employees are assured of promotion they become indifferent and inefficient. (d) There will be no difference between inefficient and efficient employees.

Promotion based on merit have the following advantages : (a) Efficiency and merit are rewarded. (b) The efficient worker will try to improve more and more. (c) The morale and productivity of efficient workers will increase.

Promotion based on merit have certain limitations : (a) It places a high responsibility on the management for the measurement of merit which is a tough task. (b) The management may misuse the power and merits may be wrongly assessed. (c) It has an element of subjectivity and employees can be promoted on the basis of caste, creed, religion, personal favour and so on. (d) The trade union leaders have no confidence on promotion based on merit. (e) Employees who are senior in service and have been bypassed by junior employees in the name of merit may be dissatisfied and frustrated which may lead to conflicts and indiscipline in the organisation.

From the above discussion we can conclude that neither seniority nor merit should be considered as the sole criteria for promoting employees. The best way should be based on seniority-cum-merit. Promotion should be based on the merit of the employee but due weightage should be given to the seniority of the employee. The best policy would be to ensure that whenever there are two persons at equal seniority then merit should be the deciding factor whereas if there are two employees of equal merit and ability then seniority should be the criteria for promotion.

Demotion

It is the lowering of rank and pay and is the opposite of promotion. The demotion may take place under the following conditions : (a) When there is wrong promotion. (b) When business activities are diverted then certain departments are eliminated and some new ones created, employees may be asked to work at lower positions until everything normalises. (c) Due to technological advancement old hands are unable to cope with the changing conditions and at the same time the management does not want to discharge them. Demotion should not be used as disciplinary measure because it creates managerial and human relation problems.

Transfers

Transfer is the lateral movement of an employee from one position to another without involving any significant change in duties, responsibilities, pay and status. Transfers are made within an organisation for a variety of reasons. There are many types of transfer. When a transfer is done so as to fulfil the requirements of the organisation it is termed as productive transfer. In other words when an employee is transferred from one department to another department to complete the work, it comes under this category. A replacement transfer is the transfer of a senior employee to replace a junior employee when the latter is laid off versatility or training transfers have a basic idea of giving varied experience in all different departments. Personal transfers are done on the initiative of the management or on the request of the employee himself.

Layoff and Discharge

Layoff refers to the temporary separation whereas discharge refers to the permanent separation of an employee from employment. The lay off and discharge become necessary when the following conditions develop : (a) When there are production cutbacks; (b) When an employee becomes incompetent due to permanent disability; lack of skill and on the other hand alternative job is not available; (c) When disciplinary action is taken against any employee due to gross negligence or misconduct; (d) When the employment is on the contract basis and the contract period is over.

32

Performance Appraisal

In the present socio-economic system human resources have been recognized as the most valuable and potential resources which can create great many things in an organisation. The success and failure of any organisation depend on its ability to use the manpower adequately.

In a group, people make an opinion about one another. But informal evaluation is insufficient as it seldom leaves any documentation of either good or poor performance. Thus in order to generate confidence, performance appraisal should be systematic and objective.

Performance appraisal in the process by which the organisations evaluate the job performance of their employees. These human resources are capable of attaining a high level of performance if properly motivated and under a suitable environment. The performance appraisal system is not only concerned with the analysis of individual performance but it also provides a comprehensive feedback to the workers about their performance and their potentiality. It facilitates the identification of specific training and development needs of the employees of an organisation. The performance appraisal programme helps the management and the employees in the following manner:[1]

Performance Improvement

Performance feedback allows the employee, the manager and personnel specialist to intervene with appropriate actions to improve upon the performance.

Compensation Adjustment

Performance evaluation help decision makers determine who

should receive pay raises. Many firms grant part or all of the pay increases and other fringe benefits based upon merit which is determined mostly through performance appraisals.

Placement Decisions

Promotions, transfers and demotions are usually based on past or anticipated performance. Often promotions are a reward for the past performance.

Training and Development Needs

Poor performance may indicate the need for retaining. Likewise, good performance may indicate untapped potential that should be developed.

Career Planning and Development

Performance feedback guides career decisions about specific career paths one should pursue.

Staffing process Deficiencies

Good or bad performance implies strengths or weakness in the personnel department's staffing procedures.

Informational Deficiencies

Poor performance may indicate errors in job analysis information, human resource plans, or other parts of the personnel management information system. Reliance on inaccurate information may lead to inappropriate hiring, training or counselling decisions.

Job Design Errors

Poor performance may be a symptom of ill conceived job designs. Appraisals help diagnose these errors.

Equal Employment Opportunity

Accurate performance appraisals that actually measure job related performance ensure that internal placement decisions are not discriminatory.

External Challenges

Sometimes performance is influenced by factors outside the work environment, such as family, health financial or other personal matters. If revealed through appraisals, the personnel department may be able to provide assistance.

Methods of Performance Appraisal

The performance appraisal system is used in the formal system of organisation. The appraisal system should be effective and accepted by the employees of the organisation. It must identify performance-related criteria, measure those criteria and then give feedback to the employees and the management. The appraisal system should be job-related, which means that the appraisal system should evaluate various behaviours that constitute the success of the job. The system should be practical so that it could be understood by the employees and the management. The system also requires dependable performance measures. They are the ratings used to evaluate performance. These can be objective or subjective. Objective performance measures are those indications of job performance that can be verified by other evaluators, whereas subjective performance measures are those ratings that cannot be verified by others, as they are the rater's personal opinion.

These are various methods of evaluating the performance of the personnel in the organisation. Some methods lay emphasis on the rating of the individual's personality traits like initiative, drive, dependability, intelligence etc.; some methods emphasize the evaluation of work results; some methods give importance to future performance by evaluating the potentiality in the employee and by setting future performance goals.

The various methods of performance appraisal are discussed below :

Straight Ranking Method

This is the oldest and the simplest method of performance appraisal. The rater places each worker in simple rank order from the best to the worst in accordance with his/her job performance. This method is easy in a small group but difficult in a large one. Secondly, the management knows that this person is better than the other one, but it does not show the degree of his superiority over the other.

Paired Comparison Method

Under this method, each person is compared with every other person, one at a time. The results of these comparisons are tabulated and a rank created from the number of times each person is considered to be superior. This is slightly better than the previous method, but it requires a large number of comparisons.

Man-To-Man Comparison Method

Under this method, certain personality factors, such as leadership, initiative, dependability etc., are selected for the purpose of analysis. A scale is created for each selected actor. The person to be rated is compared with the key man, one factor at a time. Thus, a scale of men is created for each selected factor. Instead of comparing one man with another, personnel are compared with key man taking one factor at a time. This system is used for job evaluation and it is also termed as 'factor comparison' method.

Grading Method

Under this method, the rather establishes certain features and marks them on the scale. Certain categories of worth are identified and carefully defined. The selected features may be dependability, self-expression, job-knowledge, leadership and so on. The grades may be : Outstanding; Excellent; Very Good; Good; Fair; Poor.

The actual performance of the worker is then compared with these grade definitions and he is assigned the grade which best describes the performance.

Graphic or Linear Rating Scale

Under this method, the rating of an individual's performance is based on the pre-determined rating scale. The number of factors included in the scale may vary according to the category and the job. The factors include dependability, initiative, attitude, coöperation, loyalty, leadership, analytical ability and so on. Each factor is broke down into points scale like 5, 10, 15, 20, 25.

This method is easy to use and to understand. The rater can easily tabulate and the comparison of scores among the employees is easily possible. If this is done objectively, it provides a useful feedback for both the employees and the management.

Forced Choice Description Method

Under this method, the rating elements are several sets of pair phrases (usually one pair phrase is positive and the other one negative) relating to the employee's job proficiency or personal qualities. The rater has to identify among the four statements one which is the most characteristic and the other which is the least characteristic of the employee he is rating. An example is given below :

1. He is hard working and cooperative.
2. He possesses cool temperament.

The rater is forced to choose either of these. Though he can say that both the statements are applicable or not applicable, yet he has to choose the nearest one in rating the person. Similarly, the rater is also forced to select between the statements that are unfavourable such as :

1. He is not dependable.
2. He does not motivate the workers.

This method has the advantage of removing rater bias, is easy to administer and can fit in for a wide variety of jobs.

Checklists

Under this method, a series of questions concerning an employee's behaviour are presented. The rater has to check and indicate in positive or negative terms about the behaviour of the employees. Sometimes the personnel department may assign relative weight to different items on the checklist according to the importance of each item. It is then called weighted checklist. The weights permit the ratings to be quantified so that the source can be determined.

The limitations of this method are : Firstly, it suffers from the rater's bias; Secondly, a separate checklist must be used for different classes of jobs; and thirdly, the weights assigned are improper.

Critical Incident Method

Under this method, the rater measures the performance of an individual in terms of certain events. There events are known as critical incidents. The immediate supervisor keeps a written record of the events (may be good or bad) which are used for the evaluation of the subordinate. Various behaviours are recorded under such categories as the type of job, ability to learn, responsibility of work, initiative, tackling of the situation and so on. The collected incidents are then ranked in order of frequency and importance. This method helps the employees in providing them job-related feed-back.

Behaviourally Anchored Rating Scale (BARS)

Under this method, the behaviour of the employee in different situations is evaluated by the rater. The procedure of BARS is covered in five stages :

Recording critical incidents : The persons to be evaluated are asked to describe critical incidents of effective and ineffective performance.

Clustering the Events : These incidents are then clustered into small sets of 5 to 7 of performance dimensions. Each cluster is then defined.

Reallocating Incidents : These critical incidents are again reallocated into different clusters, if required, by another group of people. If the group desires it can redesign the incidents also.

Scale of Incidents : This group then rates the behaviour on the rating scale known as behavioural expectation scales. It can then determine the effectiveness of the appropriate dimension.

Developing Anchors : These scales are anchored by specific behaviours within each category. This facilitates feedback to each employee.

Self Appraisals

Under this method of performance appraisal, the management is able to know how an individual perceives himself. It enables an individual to improve himself and facilitates the management to design the necessary programmes for developing the effectiveness. One of the important dimensions of self-appraisal is the employee's involvement and commitment to the improvement process.

Management By Objectives (MBO)

It is a management philosophy and a powerful tool of the

evaluation process. Under this approach, both the employee and his superior jointly set objectives for the future and use them as standards for evaluating the employee's performance. The objectives should be measurable. If both these conditions are met, the employees are motivated to achieve the objectives since they were involved in framing them. Secondly, since the employees can measure their progress, they have to change their behaviour to ensure attainment of objectives.

This method lays emphasis on the present and the future instead of the past. It focuses attention on the results that are achieved rather than on the individual's traits. The main advantages of this approach are as follows : (a) Everyone gets an opportunity to contribute to the enhancement of the overall organisation objectives; (b) There is greater employee involvement in the objective-setting process; (c) The commitment and involvement of the employees leads to better and more realistic objectives; (d) By framing measurable objectives, it helps the employees in performing their tasks in a much better way.

Assessment Centres

Under this method, the future potential of an employee is evaluated by a group of evaluators. Assessment Centres are a standardized form of employee appraisal that depends on multiple types of evaluation and multiple rates. The basic feature of the assessment centre is job related simulation. These simulations include those characteristics which are considered to be important for job success. The rates observe the participants when they perform various activities. Some of the characteristics of this system are :

(a) It is applied to middle level managers who have the potentiality to perform more responsible jobs in the organisation;

(b) The employees are evaluated individually and collectively;

(c) In the process of evaluation, the individuals are subjected to indepth interviews, psychological tests, personal background histories, peer ratings by other attendees, leaderless group discussions, rating by managers and psychologists and simulated work exercises (such as an in-basket exercise, business game, a role-playing incident and leaderless group discussion) to evaluate their future potential.

(d) These activities are carried out for a few days and during this period the raters evaluate the strengths, weakness and potential of each manager at the centre.

(e) A report is prepared by the raters for each individual.

The basic advantage of this method is that it helps the management in human resource planning and management development.

Problems in Performance Appraisal

The fundamental idea behind performance appraisal is that it should be effective, free and fair and should not be influenced by the rater's biases. But in actual practice, various personal factors affect the appraisal. Some of the factors affecting performance appraisal are given below :

The Halo Effect : The halo effect takes place when the personal opinion of the rater regarding the employee affects his performance appraisal. In other words, the halo effect permits one characteristic, either good or bad, to influence the rating of all the performance factors. If the rater likes or dislikes an employee, his opinion may affect the rater's appraisal of the employee's performance. The halo effect, at times creates a situation in which a capable employee is superseded by a less capable employee.

The Leniency and Strictness Effects : The leniency effect results when the rater's tend to be liberal in their ratings. Such raters view the performance of all the employees as good and rate it favourably. The strictness effect is just the opposite, i.e., the raters are too tough in their evaluation of performance.

The Central Tendency Problem : Under this, the rater does not rate the employee as effective or ineffective but assigns average ratings to everyone in order to avoid any commitment. Such a tendency of evaluation distorts the entire rating of the employee.

Personal Prejudice : A rater's dislike for the employees on grounds of sex, race, religion, caste or position distorts the ratings those people receive. Such a prejudice prevents effective appraisal and violates the antidiscrimination laws. The halo effect influences the ratings of an individual, prejudice affects those of the entire group.

The Recency Effect : Under this, the ratings are often influenced by the employee's most recent actions. The recent actions, either good or bad, are more likely to be remembered by the rater and this may affect the appraisal of the employee.

Performance appraisal is one of the most important activities of the personnel Management Department. Its basic objective is not only to review the past performance but also to provide feedback to the employees. It facilitates employee performance in the future. There are many appraisal methods but the management selects those methods that effectively measure the past performance of the employee and anticipates performance in the future.

Reference

1. William B. Werther Jr. and Keith Davis : Personnel Management and Human Resources, International Student Edition, Mcgraw Hill Company 1985, p. 284.

Part 5

Industrial Labour

33

Industrial Relations

The economists have identified five factors of production - Land, Labour, Capital, Entrepreneurship and Organisation. During the period of Industrial Revolution *'Capital'* was the most important factor of production but with the passage of time *'Labour'* became a more important factor of production because on the one hand, capitalists required skilled labour as the technology used became more sophisticated and, on the other, labour started organising themselves to enhance their collective bargaining power. Labour, which plays an important role in the prosperity of industry, comes in direct contact with the employer, demands a requisite share, and, if denied, may resort to strike. This leads to industrial unrest and measures are taken to resolve the crisis so as to keep the wheels of the industry moving. Sometimes the Government intervenes to resolve the dispute either through negotiation or through legislation.

'Industrial Relations' usually refers to the relationship between the parties concerned within and outside the industry. It constitutes a highly complex problem of the modern industrial society. According to *Dale Yoder* "It is the relationship between managements and employees, or among employees and their organisations, that characterize or grow out of employment." According to *ILO* "Industrial relations deal with either the relationships between the State and employers and workers' organisation or the relation between the occupational organisations themselves." The *Encyclopaedia Britannica* has given a comprehensive definition of the term "Industrial relations", as "relations of all those associated in productivity work including industry, agriculture, mining, commerce, finance, transport and other services. The main aspects are the establishment of the conditions under which the proceeds of the work are divided as dividends, salaries and wages between shareholders, employers, management and work people of various grades - manual, clerical and technical. The concept of industrial relations has been extended to denote the relations and joint consultation between employers and work people at their work place; collective relations between employers and their organisations and trade unions and the part played by the state in regulating these relations."

On analysing these definitions the following points emerge.

(a) "Industrial relations" emerge due to the "employment relationship" in an industry. It requires the employer and the workers for the existence of such relationship.

(b) This relationship requires adjustment and co-operation with each other; and

(c) The Government influences and shapes the industrial relations.

Industrial relations are a complex form relation depending upon a number of variables like social, economic, historical, psychological, legal, political and so on, and its study requires are integrated approach. Industrial Relations are multi-dimensional in nature and are determined by *Institutional, Economic* and *Technological factors*. Besides, *External factors* influence the industrial relation in a country. According to an author, "A country's system of industrial relations is not the result of caprice or prejudice. It rests on society which produces it. It is a product not only of the industrial changes out of which industrial society is built (and industrial organisation emerges). It develops and moulds itself according to the institutions that prevail in the given society (both the pre-industrial and the modern). It grows and flourishes or stagnates and decays, alongwith these institutions. The process of industrial relations is intimately related to the institutional forces which gave shape and content to the socio-economic policies at a given time".

Objective of Industrial Relations

The objectives of industrial relations are given below :

(i) To protect the interest of labour as well as the management by developing mutual understanding between all sections in industry which participate in the process of production;

(ii) To avoid industrial unrest;

(iii) To raise the productivity level;

(iv) To reduce the high labour turnover and absenteeism;

(v) To increase workers' participation in management;

(vi) To provide reasonable wages, better working conditions and other frings benefits to the workers; and

(vii) To bring sick units under Government Control.

Industrial dispute or conflict is a general concept. According to the *Industrial Dispute Act 1947*, Industrial dispute means any dispute or difference between employers and employers or between employers and workmen or between workmen and workmen, which is connected with the employment or non-employment or terms of employment or with the conditions of labour of any person". Industrial disputes means disputes relating to existing industry. It must be real dispute and the person regarding whom the dispute is raised and the parties to a dispute must have direct or substantial interest.

Industrial disputes are usually classified into four categories : (i) Interest disputes; (ii) Grievance disputes; (iii) Unfair labour practices; and (iv) Recognition disputes.

Interest disputes, also termed as *conflicts of interests or economic disputes* usually relate to the creation of fresh terms and conditions of employment for the general body or workers concerned. Generally, the disputes originate when the trade unions demand an increase in wages, fringe benefits and some other terms and conditions of employment and they are unable to reach an agreement with the management.

Grievance disputes, also termed as *conflicts of rights or legal disputes* involve individual workers only or a group of workers in the same group. They generally arise from day-to-day working relations in the organisation, usually as a protest by the worker or workers concerned against an act of the management that is considered to violate workers' rights. Grievances typically arise on such questions as discipline and dismissal, the payment of wages and other fringe benefits, working time, overtime, time-off entitlements, promotion, demotion, transfer, rights deriving from seniority, rights of supervisors and union officers, job classification problems, etc.

Unfair labour practices, also termed as *Trade Union Victimisation* is an attempt by the management of an organisation to discriminate against workers who actively participate in trade union activities. Unfair labour practices are generally concerned with interference, restraint or coercion of employees from exercising their right to organise, join or assist a union, failure to implement an award, settlement or agreement, etc.

Recognition disputes arise when the management of an organisation refuse to recognise a trade union for purposes of collective bargaining.

Consequences of Industrial (Disputes)

The consequences of industrial disputes have a far reaching effect on the socio-economic and political life of a country. Industrial disputes result in heavy wastage of production and mandays. Besides, it disturbs the entire public life, throws the economy out of control and the consumers have to face untold hardships. Industrial disputes in basic industries affect the user industries, their short supply pushes up the prices, besides their non-availability in the open market. The workers are also at a severe loss. They lose their wages for the strike period, and become indebted, tension develops and their family life is disrupted. The employers also suffer heavy losses due to stoppage in production, reduction on sale and in protecting the plant and machinery. Prof. A.C. Pigou has observed, "When labour and equipment in the whole or any part of the industry are rendered idle by strike or lock-out, national dividend must suffer in a way that injures economic welfare..... It may happen in two ways. On the one hand, by impoverishing the people actually involved in the stoppage, it lessons the demand for the goods the other industries make; on the other hand, if the industry in which the stoppage has occurred is one that furnishes a commodity or service largely used in the conduct of other industries, it lessons the supply of them of raw material or equipment of their work. This results in a loss of output, ultimately reducing the national income."

34

Trade Unionism

It is rather a complex task to define the trade union because there are wide differences in the use of the term in different countries. Trade unions have many facets - economic, social, political, psychological etc. In a developing country like India have their impact on the economic development and the community as a whole.

Trade unions are basically associations of workers and are formed with the intention of protecting the workers against exploitation by their employers and also improving their living conditions. With the advent of the industrial Revolution in Great Britain and other European countries and the exploitation of workers by their employers led to the formation of Trade Unions. It was felt that workers who were unorganised were exploited by their employers whereas organised workers could resist exploitation. Thus the trade union movement arose for the purpose of defending their rights and interests and improving their living and working conditions.

Definitions of Trade Union

Various definitions have been given by different authors some of which are given below :

According to Dale Yoder, "A union is a continuing long-term association of employees, formed and maintained for the specific purpose of advancing and protecting the interest of members in their working relationships."

According to G.D.H. Cole, "A trade union means an association of workers in one or more professions- an association carried on mainly for the purpose of protecting and advancing the members' economic interest in connecting with their daily work."

According to the British Trade Union Act 1953 "Trade union is a combination with the main objective of the regulation of the relation between workmen and masters or between workmen and workmen or between masters and masters for imposing of restrictive conditions on the conduct of any trade or business and also provision of benefits to members."

According to the Indian Trade Union Act 1926 "A trade union is any combination whether temporary or permanent, formed primarily for the purpose of regulating the relations between workmen and employers, or between workmen and workmen, between employers and employers, or for imposing restrictive conditions on the conduct of any trade or business, and include any federation of two or more trade unions."

On analysing the above definitions we can conclude that trade unions are associations of workers who are engaged in securing economic well-being for their members.

According to the Indian Trade Union Act 1926, "The unions must work to protect and promote the interest of the workers and the conditions of their employment." This is their basic objective. Trade unions can also have some other objectives which are not inconsistent with the basis objective or opposed to any law.

The National Commission on Labour has pointed out the following basic functions on which the trade unions have to put considerable emphasis:

(i) to secure for workers fair wages;

(ii) to safeguard security of tenure and improve conditions of service;

(iii) to enlarge opportunities for promotion and training;

(iv) to improve working and living conditions.

(v) to provide for educational, cultural and recreational facilities;

(vi) to co-operate in and facilitate technological advance by broadening the understanding of workers on its underlying issues;

(vii) to promote identity of interests of the workers with their industry;

(viii) to offer responsive co-operation in improving levels of production and productivity, discipline and high standard of quality; and generally;

(ix) to promote individual and collective welfare.

Besides these basic functions of trade unions, the commission also entrusted the following responsibilities to the trade unions:

(i) promotion of national integration;

(ii) generally influencing the socio-economic policies of the community through active participation in their formulation at various levels and

(iii) instilling in their members a sense of responsibility towards industry and the community.

The First Five Year Plan, while spelling out the role of the trade unions desired that they should (a) present plans to workers so as to create enthusiasm among them for the plans, (b) exercise utmost restraint with regard to work stoppage, (c) formulate wage demands which are attuned to the requirements of economic development in keeping with the considerations of social justice, and (d) assume greater responsibility for the success of the productive effort.

Trade Unionism in India

Trade unionism in India which is essentially an outcome of the factory system of production, came very late. The reasons for its late coming can generally be given as the slow progress of the industralisation of the country, illiteracy among the workers, their migratory habits and the heterogenous composition of the labour force at the industrial centres. "The development of industries led to large-scale production on the one hand and social evils like exploitation of women and child labour and the deplorable working conditions, the Government's attitude of complete indifference in respect of protection of labour from such evils on the other". In 1875 Shri Sorabjee Shapurji Bengalee started an agitation to focus the attention of the Government on the deplorable conditions of the workers and demanded an early legislation to protect their interests. Accordingly, the Indian Factories Act 1881 was passed but its provisions were miserable, inadequate and dissappointing. The founder of the organised labour movement may be said to be Shri N.M. Lokhande, who was a factory worker himself and who organised a conference of workers in Bombay to make representations to the Second Factory Commission in 1894. When no heed was paid to this, he called a mass meeting at

Bombay in 1890 and prepared a memorandum containing demands for limitation of hour of work, weekly rest days, mid-day recess and compensation for injuries. A new Factories Act was passed in 1891 which introduced several amendments. Mr. N.M. Lokhande formed the first labour association in India known as the Bombay Mill-hands Association. This was followed by the formation of a large number of associations, such as the Amalgamated Society of Railway Servants of India and Burma (for European and Anglo-Indian Employees); The Printers Union of Calcutta, 1905, the Bombay Postal Union, 1907; the Kamgar Hitwardhah Sabha, 1909, and the Social Service League, 1910.

The aftermath of the First World War in 1918 gave fillup to the trade union movement in India. The main reasons were the worsening economic conditions, the Swaraj movement and the Non-co-operation movement launched by Gandhiji, the formation of International Labour Organisation and the success of the Russian revolution. Those reasons helped in the organisation of trade unions in the country. In 1920 the All Indian Trade Union Congress was formed under the chairmanship of Lala Lajpat Rai in Bombay. A number of upheavals took place in the Trade Union movement. In 1947 the Indian National Trade Union Congress was formed. Later many other unions were formed.

Present Position

The Indian trade unions have come to stay now as a permanent feature of the industrial society. They have achieved in attaining a legal status and represent the workers. They have been able to influence the public policy and labour and industrial legislation. Besides the Central Trade Unions, there are various registered federations of unions in various industries and occupations. One peculiar feature of the trade unions in India is that they are affiliated to different political parties and are dominated by their ideologies.

The Indian National Trade Union Congress (INTUC)

The INTUC came into existence in May 1948 and is an affiliate of the National Congress Party. Its basic objectives were inspired by the Sarvodaya Philosophy. The constitution of the INTUC emphasises the adoption of peaceful means, consistent with the Gandhian Philosophy. Of co-trusteeship, Ahimisa and Truth. It has been associated with ILO since 1949.

All-India Trade Union Congress (AITUC)

It was established on 1920 as a result of the resolution passed by the organised workers in Bombay and its first President was Lala Lajpat Rai. It is today controlled by the Communist Party and radicals. The AITUC is affiliated to the World Federation of Trade Unions.

Hind Mazdoor Sabha and Hind Mazdoor Panchayat

When the Socialists separated from the Congress, they where dissatisfied with the pro-communist policies of the AITUC and the pro-congress policies of the INTUC. They formed a new organisation, the *Hind Mazdoor Panchayat*, which was merged with the Indian Federation of labour in 1948 under the name of the *Hind Mazdoor Sabha.* Its basic aim is to keep the trade union free from the domination of various political parties.

Bhartiya Mazdoor Sangh (BMS)

The BMS is the outcome of a decision taken by the Jana Sangh in its convention at Bhopal on 23rd July 1954. The BMS is a productivity-oriented trade union and stands firmly for the principle of public accountability for each industry and the consequent enunciation of public discipline.

Centre of Indian Trade Union (CITU)

The Union was formed in 1970 when as a result of the rift in the AITUC, some members of the communist party seceded. The CITU stands for the complete emancipation of the society from all exploitation.

Problems of Trade Unions

Although trade unions have made considerable headway, they have not grown on sound lines due to many weaknesses and problems which are discussed below:

(a) **Uneven Growth**

Trade union activities are mostly 'concentrated in the large scale industrial centres, in big industrial centres and only in a few States. Trade union activity among the white collar workers and in the lower management cadre is negligible. There is practically no trade union activity in small-scale enterprises, domestic servants and agricultural workers. Dr. G.K. Sharma in his book '*Labour Movement in India*' has observed, "The history of Indian labour movement is, to a great extent, the story of labour in the organised industry and there has been no movement amongst the vast mass of labour in the primary sector and the small establishment."

(b) **Small Size of Trade Unions**

Though trade unions are of various sizes, the majority of them in our country are characterized by their small size and low membership. There are various reasons for the small size of the unions. Firstly, under the Trade Union Act of 1926, any seven members can form a union and get it registered; secondly, the plant or unit is spread over different places and so wherever the employees in a particular plant or unit organise themselves, they form a union; thirdly, rivalry among the leaders of the national level organisations has resulted in multiplicity of unions, thereby reducing their average membership. Because of the small size and low membership of the unions they suffer from the lack of funds; their collective bargaining power is reduced and thus they have to depend on people outside the union who command political influence on the employers and the Government machinery.

(c) **Inadequate Finances**

Because of low membership, the unions suffer due to lack of funds. There are certain other reasons also for incomes of the unions. Firstly, it has been observed that workers are apathetic towards the unions and they do not contribute their shares regularly. Secondly, the workers make adhoc payments if a dispute arises. This shows a lack of commitment towards the union. Thirdly, because of multiplicity of union, the unions are interested in increasing their membership and therefore they keep a low union fee. The poor financial position adversely affects the functioning of the trade unions. They cannot undertake any social welfare programmes of publish any periodicals.

(d) Trade Union Rivalry

Multiplicity of trade unions and inter-trade union rivalry are two of the greatest weaknesses of the trade union movement in India. These reduce the power of collective bargaining and the effectiveness of workers in securing their legitimate rights.

(e) Absence of Craft Unions

Usually in our country all the workers working in an organisation regardless of the respective crafts, become members of the same union. The interests of workers having different crafts are not uniform and therefore their problems are not easily solved.

(f) Domination of Unions by Political Parties.

Indian trade unions are affiliated to different political parties and are dominated by their leaders. Though political parties have helped the trade union movement in our country, at times the political parties incite the workers to go on strike in order to solve their selfish political motives rather than to help the workers.

(g) Hostile Attitude of the Employers

One of the biggest hinderances to the growth of trade union movement is the opposition of the employers. They try to disrupt the unity among the workers by victimising the trade union leaders and by following unfair labour practices.

35

Workers' Participation in Management

The concept of workers' participation in management is a debatable issue in the field of industrial relations and has therefore acquired different meanings for different people. According to Keith Davis "Participation is a mental and emotional involvement of a person in a group situation which encourages him to contribute to group situation which encourages him to contribute to group goals and share responsibility in them." In the words of Douglas McGregor, "It provides an opportunity for very member of the organisation to contribute his ingenuity as well as his physical efforts for the improvement of organisational effectiveness and for enhancing his own economic welfare". According to G.D.H. Cole, "Better participation and greater responsibility in the decision-making-process on the part of workers trends to develop in them organisational loyalty, confidence, trust, a favourable attitude towards supervision and a sense of involvement in the organisation".

Workers' participation in management forges ties of understanding among individuals and leads to an all-round development. It helps *firstly* in increasing productivity for the greater benefit of the enterprise, employees and the community, *secondly* the employees are in a better position-to understand their role in the working of the industry and of the process of production, and *thirdly* the workers are able to express themselves thus leading to industrial peace, better relations and increased co-operation.

In the last few decades it has been increasingly felt that the workers should participate in the decision making process at various levels because of the following factors :

(a) the increased application of technology to industry which has necessitated the growing co-operation of workers because of the complex operations of production;

(b) the changed view that employees are no longer servants but are equal partners with their employers for the attainment of the goal of the enterprise;

(c) the growth of the trade unions which safeguard the interests of worker and protect them from possible exploitation by their employers;

(d) the growing interest of the government in the development of industries and the welfare of the workers; and

(e) the need for increased and uninterrupted production which can be achieved only when there is a contented labour class.

Workers' participation in management is necessary from the economic, the psychological and the sociological points of view.

(f) From the *Economic* point of view employees can contribute substantially to the progress and prosperity of the organisation and therefore have a legitimate right to share equally the gains of higher productivity of the organisation in which they are employed. Higher productivity is obtained through fullest co-operation between labour and management.

(g) *Psychologically* speaking recognition of the employees' non-economic needs. Effective participation helps in raising the levels of motivation. "Participation gives the worker a sense of importance, pride and accomplishment, it gives him freedom and opportunity for expression, a feeling of belonging to the place of work and sense of workmanship and creativity. It provides for the integration of his making the worker a joint partner in the enterprise."

Sociologically, in the modern world, industry is considered to be a social organisation in which the interests of the shareholders, the workers and the community are equally vested. "Participation forges ties of understanding between individuals leading to better efforts allround; and its absence leads to stagnation of minds and allows the abilities of producers to remain dormant, introduces a sullenness in between which ultimately may flare up into breaches of discipline and a consequent loss in production."

Generally it is observed that workers' participation in management is confronted with many problems due to which it is not successful. Sometimes the management creates such a situation on the organisation as may not be conducive for the effective participation of workers in the management. Sometimes the employees are to be blamed for their indifferent attitude. Keith Davis in his book *Human Relations in Business* has stated some prerequisites which are necessary in order to make the workers' participation in management effective. They are :

(a) There must be time to participate before action is expected. In emergences, participation is hardly appropriate.

(b) The financial cost that is involved in participation should not exceed values, economic and otherwise, that come from it.

(c) Participation should take place only in such subject as is relevant to the organisation or a subject in which the participant has interest.

(d) The participant should have the ability to participate. He should be qualified, trained and experienced.

(e) The participants should be in a position to exchange ideas with each other.

(f) The participants should not feel that their position is threatened by participation.

(g) A sincere interest on the part of the management to consult the workers' delegates before and not after decisions have been arrived at.

(h) The management must provide the particulars necessary for taking decisions.

(i) There should be a trade union which is recognised by the management.

(j) The initiative should come from both the sides.

Workers' participation in management is nothing new in India. Long back in 1920 Mahatma Gandhi had suggested this, on the basis that workers contributed labour and brains, while shareholder contributed money to an enterprise and that both should therefore share in its prosperity. Capital and labour should be a great family, living in unity and harmony.

The Industrial Disputes Act 1947 made a provision for the establishment of *Works Committees* in all the undertaking employing 100 or more workers for the purpose of maintaining good relations between the employers and the workers. *The Industrial Policy Resolution 1948* expressed its intention to associate labour in all matters concerning industrial production. *The First Five Year Plan* also called for the constitution of *Joint Committees* for consultation at all levels and reiterated the governments faith in Works Committees.

The Second Five Year Plan pointed out that the greater association of workers in the management is necessary for the successful implementation of the five-year plans. The Second Plan recommended the provision of management councils in large establishments of organised industries consisting of management, technicians and workers. As per this recommendation, the government set-up a *Study Group* consisting of the representatives of workers, management and Government which after studying the various schemes of the workers participation in a number of European countries recommended to the Government the setting up of *Joint Management Councils* (JMC).

The sub-committee of the 15th Indian Labour Conference which selected 48 units in the public and private sector for the introduction of the scheme of the joint management council had laid down the following criteria for selecting the units :

(i) The undertaking should have a well-established, strong trade union functioning.

(ii) There should be a readiness in the parties between the employers and the workers' union to try out the experiment in a spirit of willing co-operation.

(iii) The size of the undertaking should be at least 500 workers.

(iv) The employer in a private undertaking should be a member of one of the leading employers' organisations; and similarly the trade union be related to one of the Central Federations.

(v) The undertaking should have a fair record of industrial relations.

In 1960 a seminar on workers' participation management was held and the general consensus was that the MCs had not been successful. *The National Commission on Labour*, which was appointed in Dec. 1966 under the chairmanship of Shri P.B. Gajendragadkar, the former Chief Justice of the Supreme Court to undertake a fresh and comprehensive review of the labour policy and working, also observed that the scheme for the establishment of the JMCs had not been successful. The Commission observed that even where the Councils existed they were ineffective and their functioning was unsatisfactory. It was felt that both the employers and the workers do not have interest in the JMC scheme. *The Fourth Five Year Plan (1969)* urged the extension of workers' participation to the public sector undertakings and emphasized its importance as an essential functional link in the structure of industrial relations.

Under the *20-point Economic Programme (1975)* of the Congress Government (Point No. 15) a new *"package programme for labour"* in the form of "*workers' Participation in Industry* at the shop floor and the plant level was announced. The scheme embraced a two-tier participation model, i.e., it envisaged establishment of *Shop Councils* at the shop level (or department level) and *Joint Councils* at the plant (or interprise) level. The scheme provided for setting up of Shop Councils and Joint Councils in the undertakings employing 500 or more workmen, in manufacturing and mining industries whether in the public, private or co-operate sectors. The scheme contemplated participation of workers in the decision making process in the matters relating to production productivity, absenteeism, safety measures, general discipline, working conditions and welfare, and the over-all efficiency of the shop department.

In June 1977, a high powered *Expert Committee on Companies and MRTP Acts* was setup by the Government under the Chairmanship of Shri Rajendra Sachar. The terms of reference for the Committee were "(i) to consider the provisions of the Companies Act and the MRTP Act, and (ii) to suggest measures by which workers' participation in the share capital and management of companies can be brought about." The Report was submitted in August 1978. Regarding the representation of the Workers on the Board of Directors, the Committee suggested that the Worker Director should be from amongst the workers of the company and should be elected by all the workers at the company's premises by secret ballot. At the initial stages the participation should be limited to companies which employ 1000 or more employees excluding casual and badli workers. Regarding Workers' Participation in Share Capital the Committee failed to evolved any formula acceptable to both the workers and the employers. It did not therefore recommend any "mandatory participation in equity by the workers."

In September 1977 a Committee was set-up under the Chairmanship of Ravindra Varma, the then Union Minister for Labour, to give a practical shape to the *Workers' Participation in Industry.* The committee submitted its report in 1979. The recommendations of the Committee were considered at the 31st Session of the Labour Ministers' Conference in July 1980. Most of the recommendations were generally endorsed.

The Sixth Five Year Plan (1980-85) suggested that workers' participation in management should become an integral part of the industrial relations system to serve as an effective instrument of management.

Forms of Workers' Participation in India

Workers' Participation has been introduced in the following forms in Indian Industries :

(i) *The Works Committees* (set-up under the Industrial Disputes Act 1947);

(ii) *The Joint Management Councils* (set-up as a result of the labour-management co-operation Seminar, 1958);

(iii) *The Scheme of Worker Representative on the Board of Management* (under the Management and Micellaneous Scheme, 1970);

(iv) *The Shop Council* at the shop level;

(v) *The Joint Council* (scheme of workers' participation in management in commercial and service organisations in the public sector undertakings).

Works Committee

According to the Industrial disputes Act, 1947, provision has been made for setting up of a Works Committee, consisting of the representatives of management and employees in every undertaking employing 100 and more workmen. These committees have been regarded as the most powerful social institutions of industrial democracy. They are statutory bodies established within the units with representatives of employers and workers engaged in the establishment. They are purely consultative bodies and by the joint meeting of the management and workers they try (i) to remove the causes of friction on the day to day work situation by providing a grievance solving machinery; (ii) to promote measures of securing amity and good relationship between the employers and the workers; (iii) to serve as a useful adjunet in establishing continuous bargaining relationship; and (iv) to strengthen the spirit of voluntary settlement.

The usefulness of the work committees as a channel for joint consultation and the need for strengthening and promoting these committees were stressed in the Labour Policy Statement in the successive five year plans. The encouragement given by the Government led to the setting up of works committees on a number of organisations in the country.

Joint Management Councils

The Indian Labour Conference, at its 15th session in July, 1957, after considering the ' Report of a Study Group on Workers' Participation in Management in European countries' adopted in principle the idea of setting up Joint Management Councils (JMCs) in India. The essential features of the JMCs are :

1. The Joint Management Council should be consulted by the management on matters such as the administration of the standing orders and their amendments when needed, retrenchment, rationalisation and closure, reduction in or cessation of operations;
2. The Council should receive information to discuss and give suggestions on the general economic situation of the concern, the state of the market the production and sales programmes, the methods of manufacture and work, the annual balance sheets and profit and loss statements, and the long-term plan for expansion;
3. The Council would be entrusted with the administrative responsibilities for the administration and the supervision of welfare measures, safety measures, vocational training and the apprenticeship schemes, provisions of schedules for working hours, breaks and holidays.

All matters, e.g., wages, bonus etc. which are : subjects for collective bargaining are excluded from the scope of the JMC Industrial grievance are also excluded from the scope of the council.

The Scheme of Worker Representatives on the Board of Management

On the recommendations at the Administrative Reforms Commission, in its report on public sector undertakings of workers should be included in the Boards of Directors of the public sector enterprises. It also suggested that the representative of workers on a Board should be one actually working in that enterprise. Such representation will apply only in the case of industrial units and not in the case of financial and commercial undertakings.

The Shop Council

Each shop council, which is set up for each department or shop, consists of an equal number of representatives of employers and workers. Workers' representatives have to be selected from amongst workers actually engaged in the department or shop. The employer has to decide the number of councils and also the strength of each council, not exceeding 12 in any case, in consultation with the recognised trade unions. The council should meet once in a month. All the decisions of a shop council should be on the basis of consensus. Every decision of the shop council has been implemented by the parties concerned within a period of one month unless otherwise stated in the decision itself.

The main function of the shop council is to assist the management in increasing production, productivity and the overall efficiency of the shop or department through the elimination of wastages, optimum utilization of the machine capacity and the manpower, reducing absenteeism, introducing safety measures, maintaining discipline, improving physical conditions of work, welfare and health measures etc.

The Unit Council

A scheme of the workers' participation in management in commercial and service organisations in the public sector having large-scale dealings was initiated in January 1977 which envisaged setting up of Unit Councils in units employing at least 100 persons. These councils are to eliminate factors which hamper operations and the methods of operation.

The matters which a unit council handle include creation of conditions for achieving optimum efficiency, better customer service in areas where there is direct and immediate contact between the workers at the operational level and the consumer and higher productivity and the elimination of pilferage and all forms of corruption.

But the fact is that in actual practice the scheme of workers' participation in management at various levels has not functioned well. "The workers" representatives are more concerned with the enlargement of their amenities and facilities and with the redressal of grievances, higher wages, better conditions of work and the security of service than with such larger problems as reducing the rate of absenteeism, increasing productivity affecting economy in the operations of the enterprise and suggesting better methods for a more efficient utilisation of plant and equipment. In a majority of cases the joint management councils are not functioning satisfactorily."

Employers, employees, Government authorities and social researchers have attributed various reasons for the unsatisfactory progress of workers' participation in management in our country. Some of the causes are given below :

(a) Lack of appreciation of the scheme by the employers and the employees.

(b) The existence of the large number of joint bodies - works committees, joint management councils, production committees and other host of committees causes confusion and duplication of effort as well as the waste of time and energy.

(c) The absence of a strong trade union, the multiplicity of trade unions and inter-union rivalry have made the working of the scheme somewhat difficult.

(d) Lack of knowledge and proper training in human relations, co-operation, finances etc., makes the workers apathetic towards this scheme.

(e) Many a time there is delay in implementing the suggestions and recommendations of these bodies which leads to the warning of the workers' interest in such bodies.

(f) Absence of congenial and constructive climate of industrial relations in the country.

The scheme can be a success only when there is a change in the attitude of the employer and the employee. It has not made much progress in the past. Since we are moving towards massive industrialisation there is a need to create a conducive atmosphere for the economic development of the country. Joint consultation should form a part of the labour management decisions in important issues pertaining not only to production but also the living conditions of the workers. The scheme seems to have a bright future. Both the employers and workers should work in better and spirit to make the scheme successful.

36

Unemployment

Today all the countries of the world are eager to develop economically and industrially at a faster rate. The underdeveloped countries, which have been poor for centuries, have virtually waged a war against poverty and economic hardships. They are busy in strengthening their economic and industrial base for initiating a higher rate of economic growth.

Economic growth depends on various factors, the prime being the management and development of human resources. Economic growth is characterised by capital formation which helps in furthering the investment thereby generating more employment opportunities. In the under developed countries unemployment exists due to poor production capacity the scarcity of capital and so on. But before studying the nature of employment we should discuss the problems of economic development of an underdeveloped economy.

According to the *United Nations* experts "the term Underdeveloped Countries is used to mean countries in which per capita real income is low when compared with the per capita real incomes of the United States of America, Canada, Australia and Western Europe." M. Eugene Stanley in his book, *The future of Underdeveloped Countries* (1954) defines an underdeveloped country as, "a country characterised by mass poverty which is chronic and not the result of some temporary misfortune and by obsolete methods of production and social organisation which means that the poverty is not entirely due to poor natural resources and hence could presumably be lessened by methods already proved in other countries".

Broadly speaking, the underdeveloped countries can be divided into two categories. In the first category are those countries which are overpopulated and have a considerable amount of surplus labour. In the Second category are those countries which do not experience acute pressure of population on land. The problems of the two groups of countries are different. Here we are chiefly concerned with the first category of countries to which India belongs.

Problems of Economic Development – A Vicious Circle of Poverty

It is usually observed that underdeveloped countries suffer from the vicious circle of poverty. The vicious circle operates on both the supply and the demand sides. First, low incomes lead to low levels of savings and investment. The low rate of investment in turn leads to the perpetuation of low incomes and the circle is completed. This is the vicious circle on the supply side. Second, the low rate of investment keeps the productivity and incomes low. Therefore the purchasing power of the people in real terms is low. This leads to a relatively low private marginal productivity of investment. Inducement to investment being low, low incomes are perpetuated. This is the vicious circle on the demand side.

2. Scarcity of Capital

The major constraint on the developmental effort of the developing countries is the scarcity of domestic resources for investment. Capital is one of the major determinants of economic development. The savings rate on the underdeveloped countries is very low resulting in a low rate of capital formation and a low level of investment. Every country does not channelise its entire savings into investment. A certain part of savings has to be held for various purposes. But the higher the saving are the higher will be the rate of investment in a productive system.

The causes of low savings in the underdeveloped countries are as follows :-

(a) The UDCs are basically agricultural countries. The major part of the population lives under chronic poverty. Whatever income is earned is consumed leaving no scope for savings.

(b) Agriculturists avoid rise in consumption levels and transform a part of their real incomes into hoarded wealth like gold, silver ornaments which does not contribute to further production.

(c) The infrastructure facilities are inadequate which impedes the economic development. Therefore, the saving and in turn overhead capital expenditure are very low in the underdeveloped countries.

(d) The manufacturers and producers of the underdeveloped countries prefer to invest in light labour intensive consumer goods industries rather than in heavier capital-intensive capital goods industries which does not yield higher income and saving.

In the underdeveloped countries the major impediment to economic growth on the one hand is inadequate productive capacity and on the other hand a limited supply of internal resources to expand the productive capacity. Further, the situation is much worsened as the capacity to import is also limited.

3. Under-Investment

In the underdeveloped countries the people are hesistant to invest because of low incomes and the small size of the market. Private investment is usually of an unproductive nature and entrepreneurs are attracted towards quick returns and speculative gains. Real estate, urban construction and luxury buildings are preferred resulting in the starving of capital in agriculture and the manufacturing industries. In India, where planning operation takes place, investments are taken up in the manufacturing sector like steel, power, cement etc. but the project over runs and this escalates the costs leaving other sectors to be neglected.

According to Harrod and Domar, investment plays a crucial role in the process of economic growth. They emphasise that investment has a dual character. On the one hand, investment creates income; on the other, it augments the economy productive capacity by enlarging its capital stock. In a country like India, investment is not upto the mark and this results in less income and less productivity and at the same time less employment.

The people of the underdeveloped countries even after substantial savings at their disposal do not want to invest in the economy and keep them with themselves, the reason being the lack of suitable atmosphere and of proper facilities of investment in the economy.

Besides, technology has a direct bearing on investment and vice versa. Low technology results in low per capita productivity which in turn leads to low real income and capital deficiency.

Population Pressure

The biggest bane of the underdeveloped countries like India is the enormous growth in population. Any rate of growth of population that is accompanied by inadequate expansion of investment and national income to maintain the existing level of income and standard of living may be defined as excessive rate of the growth of population.

The underdeveloped countries are invariably over-populated and every increase in population brings more economic difficulties. The standard of living cannot be raised unless the aggregate output increases more rapidly than the total population. Child population in the underdeveloped countries is very high as compared to that in the developed ones which not only reduces the labour supply but also increase the dependency load on the economy. Subsequently social investment gets priority over economic investment. Thus the increase in population turns to be the surplus manpower aggravating under-employment instead of generating more income to the economy.

Urbanisation increase with population growth bringing more problems both social and economic. The quality of population is poor because of inadequate health, education and food. Motivation to work hard, which is the most important factor in economic development, is lacking among the masses because of the corrupt management, the defective tax system, the caste system, inflation, the feudal system and several other factors associated with poverty.

Low Productivity

One of the basic features of the underdeveloped economy is low productivity in the field of agriculture. Agriculture is the mainstay of the underdeveloped countries, especially for a country like India. It provides major share of the national income, livelihood to the majority of population and employment to a major extent. In India, the importance of agriculture arises from the fact that it provides raw materials to a number of industries like cotton, jute, sugar, vanaspati, plantation and so on. There are many other industries which depend on agricultural goods play a pivotal, role in foreign trade by earning foreign exchange. Tea, coffee, jute and jute goods, tobacco, spices etc. are some of the items which are exported from India. Agricultural development is of utmost importance for the economic development of the country. But unfortunately the productivity of agriculture is very low in the under-developed countries including India on both the fronts-productivity per acre and productivity per labourer. The main cause for this low productivity are, *firstly*, the pressure of population on land which has led to the sub-division and fragmentation of holdings, decline in per capita availability of land, disguised unemployment in agriculture, inadequate finance and marketing facilities, and, *secondly*, the outmoded technology being used by majority of the Indian farmers.

Our manufacturing and mining industries are also suffering from the dreaded diseases of low productivity. The underdeveloped tertiary sector also contributes to the low productivity in an underdeveloped economy.

Predominant Agricultural Sector

Rural domination is the basic feature of an underdeveloped country. The distribution of population in towns and villages deeply affects the socio-economic structure of the country. The pattern of the economic activity of villagers is totally different from that of the urban people. More than 70% of the total population in India lives in villages and earns its livelihood either directly from agriculture or from its allied activities. Despite massive industrialisation in the last thirty years the percentage of the workers engaged in agriculture has been steadily increasing.

Agriculture has occupied a predominant role in the Indian economy as it provides most of the raw materials for the industries. It also has a signifant say in the foreign trade of India. Agriculture plays an important role in the other sectors as well. Most of the agricultural commodities are transported by road and by railway from the production areas to the consumption areas. Finances of the state governments largely depend on the prosperity of agriculture. Good crops give to the farmers a better demands of consumer goods. Failure of crops leads to depression in business.

It is amply clear from all this that agriculture is thc backbone of the Indian economy and agricultural development can bring about prosperity of the Indian economy. But there are two major implications for the growing unemployment is our country. Firstly, the entire working force working in agriculture and allied activities cannot be gainfully employed under the prevailing circumstances and this contributes to the problem of disguised unemployment. Secondly, the problem of seasonal unemployment occurs as mostly the agricultural occupations are mainly seasonal in nature.

The Term 'Unemployment'

Every human being wants to live in peace and pass a satisfactory life. To maintain that life he requires remuneration for a specified period of time. For this purpose employment opportunities should be made available on the basis of the prevailing conditions. But unfortunately unemployment has become an acute problem for all the countries of the world today may be developed or underdeveloped. The percentage of the human resources engaged in different activities is the barometer of the economic development of a country.

The term 'unemployment' emerged at the fag end of 19th century. Later various economists profounded certain theories on unemployment.

According to Prof. Rajhidehna there are only four major conditions under which a person may be called unemployed or underemployed. He is unemployed or underemployed if :

(i) he is gainfully occupied during the year for a number of hours (or days) less than some normal or optimal hours (or days) defined as full employment hours or days; or

(ii) he earns an income per year less than some desirable minimum; or

(iii) he is willing to do more work than he is doing at present; he may either be actively searching for more work or be available for more work if it is offered on terms to which he is accustomed; or

(iv) he is removable from his present employment in the sense that his contribution to output is less than normal productivity and therefore, his removal would not reduce output, if the productivity of the remaining workers is normalised with minor changes in technique and/or organisation.

The first one is the time criterion the second one the income criterion, the third one the willingness criterion and fourth one is called the productivity criterion.

The Meaning of Various Terms

Most underdeveloped countries are suffering from

unemployment and underemployment. The Ninth International Conference of Labour Statisticians, (1957) suggested the following definition. "Underemployment exists when persons in employment who are not working full time would be able and willing to do more work than they are actually performing, or when the income or productivity of persons in employment would be raised if they worked under improved conditions of production or transferred to another occupation, account being taken of their occupational skills. Underemployment appears in various forms, some of which can be measured with reasonable accuracy by means of statistical enquiries. The following major categories of underemployment may be distinguished:

(a) Visible underemployment which involves shorter than normal periods of work and which is characteristic of persons involuntarily working part-time;

(b) Invisible underemployment, which is characteristic of persons whose working time is not abnormally reduced by those earnings which are abnormally reduced by those earnings which are abnormally low or whose jobs do not permit full use of their capacities or skills (sometimes called 'disguised underemployment) or who are employed in establishments of economic units whose productivity is abnormally low (sometimes called potential underemployment).

According to NSS from the 14th round (1972) onwards the following definitions were used:

Labour Force : All persons classified as "Working" and seeking or not seeking work but available for it together constitute the labour force, that is all the employed and the unemployed ones constitute the labour force.

Unemployed : The class comprises those persons who are reporting as not working during the reference week and who are either seeking work or working or are not seeking work but are available for it. All persons reported and not seeking work but available for it constitute what is familiarly known as unemployed.

Moderately Underemployed : Those who worked for 29-42 hours per week and reported available for additional work might be treated as moderately underemployed.

Severely Underemployed : Those who worked for 28 hours or less per week, or on an average four hours or less per day and reported available for additional work are treated as severely unemployed.

An underdeveloped country suffers from the problem of secular unemployment because of the lack of employment opportunities, the lack of capital and modern production techniques. Cyclical unemployment considered by Keynes is applicable only in the developed countries, where the problem is to control economic instability. Frictional unemployment takes place because of industrial disputes in which stagnation in labour mobility, ignorance about employment opportunities, lack of raw materials etc. are included A.P. Lerner says that sometimes unemployment takes place because of the wrong ability of labourers and sometimes because of the wrong placing of labourers in service. This is frictional unemployment. The seasonal unemployment is very much in existance in India because of the agricultural character of the economy. Agriculture and its allied activities are influenced by seasons. Where there is a single crop system in a year seasonal unemployment is very much in existence. But where there is double and triple cropping, seasonal unemployment does not exist as people remain engaged for the whole year.

Five Year Plans

Employment generation for the social, economic and industrial development emphasises the determination of approaches and techniques designed to assure the full quantitative and qualitative participation of the working population in the production of goods and service. But the problem of unemployment was given a secondary importance during the Five Year Plans. Our planners, thinkers and economists presumed that the accelerated rate of growth would itself take care of unemployment and this made them give secondary importance to the unemployment problem. The First Plan simply stated that employment opportunities would be increased and the standard of living would be improved. The Second Plan accepted full employment as its objective but no firm steps were undertaken. During the Third Plan employment expansion was expressly stated as an objective, yet the treatment given to it was mixed. A number of heavy industries were established during this period. In addition to the employment opportunities expected to flow directly from these industries, it was anticipated that many more job opportunities would be provided through the downstream industries and a complex of ancillary industries developed by these heavy industries.

By the time the Third Plan was nearing completion the economic condition of the country as a whole had gone from bad to worse and so virtually a plan holiday was to be declared. With only some marginal adjustments, the development strategy of the Fourth Plan and also of the Fifth Plan remained the same. During the Fifth Plan efforts were made to augment the industrial production pattern in the light of the agricultural requirements. With the coming in of the Janata Government (1977) the development strategy under went a sea change. The Draft Five Year Plan (1978-83) gave the highest priority to the removal of unemployment and poverty with Agriculture as the focal point.

But the Janata Government was toppled and the Congress returned to power. The Congress Government Scrapped the Sixth Plan initiated by the Janata Government and developed a new Sixth Plan (1980-85) in which new schemes regarding employment opportunities were started. The Integrated Rural Development Programme (IRDP) was extended to all the blocks in the country, the NREP, RLEGP, TRYSEM, Food for Work scheme etc. were started to create more employment opportunities. In spite of several programmes of rural development initiated during the Sixth Plan, the backlog of unemployment could not be reduced.

The Seventh Plan (1985-90) asserted that the major objective of the Plan was to ensure that the growth of employment opportunities was faster than the growth of the labour force. The Seventh Plan intends to follow broadly the employment strategy of the Sixty Plan with added emphasis on technological upgradation and modernisation of the productive process.

During 1989-90, the final year of the Seventh Plan, a new scheme known as Jawahar Rozgar Yojana (JR) was initiated for creating employment opportunities to at least one adult member of every family living below the poverty line in the rural areas. The NREP and RLEGP were merged with the JRY.

Causes of Unemployment in India

The menace of unemployment in India has been due to a number of causes which are given below:

1. *Poverty*

   Poverty and unemployment go together. A person is poor because he is unemployed and vice-versa. He does not possess sufficient resources to be gainfully self-employed. Since he is illiterate he has to go for those jobs which are unskilled in nature.

2. *Increase in Population*

   There has been a tremendous increase in the population of the country. This has led to an increase in the labour force and it has not been possible to generate so many employment opportunities. Therefore unemployment and under employment have tended to increase.

3. *Slow Growth*

   There is a direct relationship between the employment opportunities and the growth of the economy. Despite more than four decades of planning, the growth of Indian economy has not been upto the required level. The natural resources more or less remain underutilized. The growth of agriculture and the development of industrial sector have been sluggish. As a result, employment opportunities have failed to keep pace with the increase of labour force.

4. *Under-Utilisation of Capacity in Industries*

   The majority of industries are not able to utilize their capacity to the fullest possible extent due to many reasons, such as power shortage, transport bottlenecks, shortage of raw materials industrial unrest etc. Because of these reasons the capacity is under-utilized and hence industries are not able to absorb enough labour.

5. *The Use of Capital Intensive Techniques*

   In the recent years the Government has been emphasising rationalisation, modernisation and upgradation of technology and the use of computers in the industrialisation of the country. These techniques of production have failed to generate sufficient employment opportunities.

Government Measures

Since the planning era started, sizeable employment opportunities have been created in the different sectors of the economy. But the rural areas is underemployed with inadequate work and low incomes. A number of schemes have been launched to alleviate poverty and remove unemployment in the rural areas during the last 10 years. These are discussed below.

(a) The National Rural Employment Programme (NREP) envisages generation of employment opportunities during the lean agricultural period through productive activities in rural areas. Similarly, the Rural Landless Employment Guarantee Programme (RLEGP) was introduced in 1983 to provide jobs to the rural landless labourers.

In 1989-90 a new scheme known as Jawahar Rozgar Yojana (JRY) was initiated by merging NREP and RLEGP. The basic objective of the JRY is to provide employment opportunities to at least one adult member of every family living below the poverty line in the rural areas. The funds of the JRY are to be raised through the contributions of the centre and the states in the ratio of 80:20. The main work to be undertaken is the creation of durable assets for strengthening the rural infrastructure which will lead to a rapid growth of the rural economy.

(b) The integrated Rural Development Programme (IRDP) aims at raising the levels of people living below the poverty line by providing productive assets and employment financed by the Government and the banks.

(c) The scheme of Training Rural Youth for Self-Employment (TRYSEM) was started in 1979 with the basic objective of removing unemployment among the rural youth. It aims at providing the rural youth with skills to enable them to become self-employed.

(d) The Food for Work Programme (FWP) aims at the creation of additional employment in rural areas on work of durable utility by giving to the workers foodgrains as wages.

(e) The Operation Flood, Dairy Development Project and some other dairy development schemes are there to benefit the rural families producing and other dairy products.

(f) Fish Farmers Development Agencies (FFDA) have been created to help fishermen's families in adopting modern techniques and training in fisheries culture.

(g) There are various schemes to assist in the development of khadi, village and small industries including handloom, handicrafts, sericulture etc. There provide employment both in the rural and urban areas.

(h) The Minimum Needs Programme (MNP) introduced during 1974-75 comprises two sets of activities: (i) activities pertaining to human resources development which include elementary and adult education, health, supply of drinking water, nutrition and rural housing, and (ii) activities regarding area development like rural roads and village electrification. The various elements of MNP increase the productive capacity of the community as well as the economic condition of the individual.

(i) The Maharashtra Government launched the Employment Guarantee Scheme (EGS) in the rural areas for unskilled labour. Under this scheme productive employment to rural unskilled labour provided and this scheme guarantees right to work at a specified wage per day.

(j) Flood control, irrigation schemes and C.A.D. programmes provide enormous employment opportunities in rural aries, especially for the weaker sections of the society.

(k) For the urban educated unemployed a scheme for Self-Employment of Educated Unemployed Youth has been started through the District Industries Centres under which a composite loan of Rs. 25,000 is provided through banks to set-up a small industry or business.

Thus, we can see that the Government has initiated a number of measures to generate employment opportunities. If they are sincerely followed we can reduce the level of unemployment to a large extent.